WALLAÇONIA

BOOKS BY DAVID PRATT

Bob the Book (novel)

My Movie (stories)

Looking After Joey (novel)

WALLAÇONIA

a novel

DAVID PRATT

Beautiful Dreamer Press

Wallaçonia
Copyright 2017 by David Pratt

Beautiful Dreamer Press
309 Cross St.
Nevada City, CA 95959
U.S.A.
www.BeautifulDreamerPress.com

Paperback Edition
Printed in the United States of America

ISBN: 978-0-9981262-0-3

Library of Congress Control Number: 2016959297

Cover design by Ann McMan
Front and back photography by Dot
Author photo by Eva Mueller

For Michael,
with my greatest appreciation

CONTENTS

AUTHOR'S NOTES

Most of this novel takes place on Cape Cod, the peninsula extending from southeastern Massachusetts into the Atlantic Ocean in the shape of a human arm making a muscle. The arm analogy makes the southern portion the "Upper Cape," as it would be the upper arm. The "Lower Cape" is the eastern portion, analogous to the lower arm.

Also, regarding the name of this book: it is pronounced with a soft *c*, a long *o*, and emphasis on the third syllable—"woll-uh-SO-nee-uh."

—DP

WALLAÇONIA

CHAPTER 1

THE HALLOWEEN QUESTION

OUR KITCHEN WAS dim and cold. Mom's keys and gloves lay on the table. She and Dad were going out! I could invite my girlfriend, Liz, over. We had been talking about sex. Well, I had. She said she wanted to, though. Maybe tonight. Then everything would finally be normal.

I was hopeful because I'd seen a raccoon out on the marsh. Raccoons are my "spirit animal." They don't hibernate in winter; they sleep all day but come out at dusk. If I were an animal, that's what I'd do—come out of my den only when *I* wanted.

I thought of Liz's sweet-smelling hair and the warm wetness of her mouth, and I started to get aroused. We were totally great together. We hadn't done it yet, though. I first mentioned it at Halloween; she said she wanted to, "sometime soon." Every few weeks I said, "Have you thought about the Halloween Question?" And she'd say, "Boo!" or go all wide-eyed and say, "It's . . . the Halloween Question!!!" like it was a slasher pic. She'd say that she seriously wanted to; it just wasn't time yet.

I heard footsteps upstairs and my mom fretting: ". . . *never* get there . . ."

I wanted to respect Liz. I was just so afraid it would never happen to me. Other kids I knew had sex all the time, no big deal. Why did I have to do so much thinking, doubting, trying to respect, and trying to be normal? Maybe I didn't "do it" for her. Maybe I didn't give off what a real guy was supposed to give off. I had a missing piece, and it was too late, and I just couldn't.

Mom marched downstairs. A gust rose outside; the kitchen window shuddered.

Lately, Liz and I were on a plateau, like this cute couple that couldn't quite grow up. I loved her, she said she loved me, and she never lied. Realizing that made me feel bad, because there was stuff I sort of left out when we talked. Maybe that's why we were on a plateau, not climbing the mountain, like other couples. I heard Dad following Mom down, slower.

I was afraid to ask the Halloween Question again. What if she felt the plateau, too? I'd never find another girlfriend. It was amazing that I'd found her. I felt powerful with her. Having her helped me settle my insecurities. I was afraid I was the one stopping us from climbing. But having sex would be like getting a diploma, or when they stamp your passport (I guess; I've never been to another country except Wallaçonia, which I'll tell you about in a bit). My worries would be over. But what if, when I said, "Let's make love," she stopped and gave me this sad smile, and said, "We're on a plateau, Jim, and I think I know why"? Then I'd have nothing at all.

Mom came into the kitchen, adjusting an earring. She was "put together," as she would say—wearing her car coat, her shortish blonde hair brushed the same as in her high school pic, and fresh, red lipstick, a bit of it on her front teeth, which were prominent, like mine.

"Jim, good, you're here." She didn't look at me. She wasn't happy to see me. Something big had come up, and I happened to cooperate by coming back from my walk at the right moment. Mom was always saying, "If you people would just *cooperate!*" but she wasn't happy when we did. She pulled on her gloves. I hoped there wouldn't be tons of Instructions.

Dad kind of loped in. He wasn't put together. He was just Dad, frowning and silent. The houses and the people here are both weathered—lines on people's faces and shingles on the houses gone gray.

It turned out Dad's Aunt Lillian, up in Falmouth, had gone to the emergency room. When I was little, we visited Aunt Lillian in her house on Skunk's Tail Road. Now she was in a nursing home, and I was a senior, so they didn't make me visit her anymore. Her being in the ER didn't worry me that much. It happens with old people, right?

Mom was saying she and Dad would be gone overnight. Excellent! Liz and I could get together, then after she left, I could be all alone in Wallaçonia! Like I said, I'll explain Wallaçonia in a bit.

Mom dictated the motel phone number, "just in case." I pretended to put it in my cell, but I was really texting Liz. My finger shook, so it took me a while to get it right.

Mom opened the fridge and pointed to what I should have for dinner. I rolled my eyes. She stopped and looked at my phone and said, "Can you put that away for a second?" Then she started in about which blankets to use if I got cold. "I won't get cold!" I sighed.

"Forgive me!" she said. "But one never stops being a mother. You'll be gone next year"—meaning to college—"and I won't have anyone to take care of."

5

Right then, Dad came in. I thought, *What about him?* but didn't say it.

"I called Pat Baxter," she said, "and told him you'd be by yourself. You should give him a call and say you're okay." She went off to check that all the windows were locked.

Pat Baxter lived next door and ran a secondhand bookstore in his barn. I would *not* be calling him. I wasn't a child. Of course, I wasn't a man, either, until I straightened out my insecurities and loved Liz the right way. But I might take care of that this very night. They'd come home to a different son, more like what they'd always wanted, and then Mom would be happy.

Dad grinned. "Oh, *yesssss. Do* call Mr. *BAXSSSTER!*" He chortled. He did that because Mr. Baxter was single and, like, *natty*, I guess. *Gay,* I guess. Not that we ever *saw* anything. He was just single and into books (but, hey, until recently, I was both of those things) and when he got a little dramatic his fingers got very busy. Dad sometimes chatted with him about the weather and how much certain houses sold for—the only two grown-up topics allowed on Cape Cod. But if Mom brought out a dessert at dinner and said Pat Baxter made it, which he did for us now and then, Dad leaned over to me and tried to make it his and my little joke.

I wouldn't tell Dad, but it hurt me because I was afraid that I myself wasn't too manly. Like I said, I had insecurities, I liked books, and there were guy things I didn't like, even though I had Liz, and I wouldn't want anyone calling me "Jim Walla*SSSS!*" It was a mess in my head, and it got worse when the subject of Mr. Baxter came up and Dad joked. Maybe I thought Mom and Dad should have understood how insecure I was and helped me sort it out. But I didn't need help, because it was temporary. After I had sex, I wouldn't need help.

"Stop it!" Mom called from the dining room. "Pat is perfectly nice." Manners were big with her, and Mr. Baxter had good ones. "And good-looking," she added. That was also *mucho importante* to her, and I guess she was right—he was handsome and kind of distinguished. He talked in this thoughtful, like, *expressive* way. He had pale blue eyes and this optimistic smile. He was definitely better-looking than I was, though Mom sometimes said I was good-looking, and Liz said so. I had to lose a little weight, though, and figure out my hair. I combed it forward in a little sticky-out shelf, like you're supposed to, but it didn't work. Or it worked the best it could for me.

Mom was back, checking the kitchen window. She'd fixed the lipstick on her teeth. I knew she would. Dad said, "Yesssss, perfectly nicccce," and waggled his eyebrows, like I was eight instead of eighteen. I wanted to tell him right there how I had my own insecurities. I felt it coming up my esophagus or whatever. But tell him . . . what? I had just invited my girlfriend over to maybe have sex. If I mentioned insecurities, then what? Plus, I needed them to pay for college, and I needed this place to come back to, obviously. And maybe there wasn't anything so much to talk about anyway. *And* Aunt Lillian was sick. I'd heard you weren't supposed to bring up stuff when there was other stuff going on in the family. And why should I even be thinking all this?

Maybe I would call Mr. Baxter, just to take a stand against Dad's prejudice or whatever. Like those guys holding up rifles in *Les Misérables*, like, in every number. (I shouldn't be mean. Liz loved *Les Misérables*. I took her to see it in Boston, and she put up with me singing my own lyrics in the car: "I dreamed this song would never end/I dreamed this stage would not stop turning!") I'd be Mr. Baxter's "ally." That was cool, right?

Except I didn't really want to *talk* to him so much. I didn't know him that well. I just hated Dad's "us guys" routine.

A text came back: "Sure. I'll bring Uno!!!" Liz liked board games and card games. Sometimes choosing the game seemed like the most important part of our get-togethers for her.

I followed Mom and Dad to the front hall. As Dad opened the door, I looked right at him and said, "I'll definitely call *Mr. Baxter!*" I even put in a little "*sss.*" Maybe he didn't hear. I didn't put it together till later that, duh!, his aunt was dying. Even though one of my grandparents had died, it didn't seem like a big deal. Just a thing that happened. I also didn't realize till later that maybe Dad knew he'd said something wrong and didn't know what to do about it. I was more interested in hurting *him* for how put-upon I felt, and how I could never say anything serious to him about that stuff. But if everything went okay with Liz, I'd never have to say anything to anyone.

I was *not* going to call Mr. Baxter. I didn't need him. I didn't need anyone but Liz. I loved her. I loved my parents. But whatever was going to happen, I'd have to figure out for myself.

CHAPTER 2

A KNOCK AT THE DOOR

THE CAR BACKED out the driveway. The head-lights swept the dining room, dark except for the plastic candles Mom put in the windows for Christmas. I went to the fridge. I was scarfing down Christmas cookies when a knock came on the back door. It was so loud and unexpected I literally jumped. I slammed the fridge shut. I spit a cookie out in my hand and had to rush to the sink.

It couldn't be Liz; our house was twenty minutes from her place in Brewster. It had to be Mom; she forgot something and didn't want to fish for her key. I wiped my hands. "Coming!" I said and went for the door.

Cold came in, clean and quiet. Nothing out there, just darkness and my breath, and wind swaying the pine trees behind Mr. Baxter's barn.

I saw something beyond the light from the porch.

"Oh, Jim! *There* you are!" Mr. Baxter walked toward me. He seemed pleased to see me.

He took careful steps on the ice and held his hands out a little delicately. That was the kind of thing that used to embarrass me, little gestures that weren't

9

quite right, that I tried never to do myself. I would have tensed my legs and planted my feet hard. To avoid seeing Mr. Baxter's balancing act, I looked down.

There on the back step was a foil-covered pan. He must have left it when I didn't answer. Now he scooped it up like an orphan and held it out to me. He was close to me, his face lit by the porch light. He had perfectly combed hair—what I think they call salt-and-pepper—receding a little. I checked out other guys' hair because I could never get my own right. Other guys got theirs right, like there was no other way it could be, but I couldn't figure out how Jim was supposed to look.

What made him nice-looking, more than his features, was how his eyes sparkled, how his smile was gentle and hopeful as he held the pan out. He spoke in a formal way—thoughtful, like I said—but friendly. I was too busy wondering what they said about *him* when *he* was in high school to catch what he said. Plus, I was trying to think if he was really "handsome," like Mom said. His smile was kind, and that reassured me. I didn't know what it reassured me *about.* I did notice handsome guys sometimes. I even could get a little hung up, because I envied them. I knew that if I could be as good-looking or talented as those guys, I wouldn't notice them.

"I heard you were going to be by yourself," he said, "so I thought you might enjoy a little something!"

I cringed a little and felt awful, because it was so nice of him. I took whatever-it-was from him. I knew Dad would make fun of the whole thing, even though Mr. Baxter was technically being nice. Still, I didn't exactly want anything from him right then. I thought it would mean I depended on him or was like him. Somehow I thought he wanted people to be like him. Or maybe he wanted just one person to be like him.

Part of me wanted whatever he had made; I just wished I didn't. I wondered if I could ever make anything that another person would want as much as I wanted whatever this was he'd made.

"Well, I am *freezing*," he said. "I'm going to let you close the door, and I'm going back where it's warm." His fingers were busy, like he was massaging something between them. His hands were big. I noticed guys' hands, too. I wished he'd hold his hands still, so I could really see them. "Enjoy!" he said. "And do give a call if you need anything." He walked backward, then sideways, like a little dance, watching me but being careful on the ice. "Not that you will, but—"

"Okay!" I said. I couldn't help smiling. He seemed so—I don't know if "caring" is the word. Something I liked but that made me uncomfortable. I shut the door and pulled the foil off the pan. Date bars! He'd made these before. They were insanely good, like there should have been a town ordinance against them. (Town ordinances is the other thing they always talk about here.) I took out a knife and cut a big piece.

It sounds like I was being mean to Mr. Baxter, but I have to be honest about how I thought back then. This isn't just my story; it's other people's, too, and I'm responsible to those people, almost like they were my kids—which I do want to have someday. If I left out bad things I thought about Mr. Baxter, you wouldn't understand what—well, what we *both* went through. You wouldn't see how we were surrounded by polite people thinking bad stuff and not saying it. And some of us who felt surrounded also went around thinking bad stuff about other people. And each other.

I finished my date bar and cut one more small piece.

If Mom said about something, "Pat made it," Dad would say, "Just a small piece." I'd say, "Me, too" but sneak back for more when the kitchen was dark.

11

That's how I got a little pudgy. I wasn't *fat*, and I have these striking green eyes and a nice smile, though my eyeteeth are a little prominent (thanks, Mom). Plus the hair. I didn't think I was "handsome," like Liz said. It was more like, with Liz, it didn't matter. That's one way I knew the relationship was right.

My phone went off. My heart thudded. Liz's text said, "Almost ready had to help Mom w dishes."

Liz always helped people. Her dad had died recently, and there was just Liz and her mom and her kid brother, Randy. There was always something she had to do for them.

I stared at Liz's text and thought, *Can't it finally happen to me? Can't it happen to* us?

I tucked the last piece of date bar in my mouth and went to the bathroom to check my hair. Another text: "almost done."

I got this uh-oh feeling. I didn't thank Mr. Baxter. He took me by surprise, but I should have said, "Thank you." Mom would have invited him in. Was I expected to, or was that an adult thing? I wanted to "be a man" with Liz, so didn't I have to be grown-up in other ways? Was my first manly act actually supposed to be inviting Mr. Baxter in? Should I call him? Liz was practically in her car. I hoped I wouldn't be able to find the number. I scanned the kitchen bulletin board. There it was: "Pat B," with a 978 number. (He used to live near Fitchburg.)

I'd tell him to drop by tomorrow, and he wouldn't because with Christmas he'd be busy at the bookstore. The first two times I dialed wrong. Then I got his voicemail ("Greetings, friend! You have reached . . .") Was he still on his way back home? Maybe he fell on the ice?

This always happened. I'd be about to do something great, and then I'd imagine some disaster. But if Mr.

Baxter *had* fallen and hurt himself, who would know? He'd get hypothermia, and it would be my fault!

I texted Liz: "Hang on. Trouble with neighbor." She texted back: "Can I help?" Other kids made fun of Liz and her helping. That hurt me so bad. You lose your dad, you try to make the world nice so someone *else* won't die, and then some (pardon my French) bitch like Mimsy Barrows is like, "Liz, can I *help*?? Are you sure I can't *help*, Liz?" I gave Mimsy a rude suggestion how she could help. Then I hugged Liz hard and said, "I'm sorry." She giggled and said, "People are looking." I said, "I know," and kissed her.

I texted back that this would be quick. She texted back a question mark and a smiley emoji, which I didn't understand and which kind of annoyed me, so I texted, "Just a sec," pulled on my coat and went out.

On the porch I stopped. Up at Mr. Baxter's house the lights were on bright, but I didn't see him in any of the windows. Of course not; he was cozily sitting down where I couldn't see him. No other kid I knew—no boy—would get all worried and actually go look. I was being a "nervous nellie," as Dad would say.

I patted my hair, pulled one last time to make a better little shelf in front, and marched down the steps, like a raccoon coming out of his den. My phone lit up. Another question mark, then emojis of a clock face and a car.

My hands were freezing, and emojis aren't my thing. So I didn't respond.

CHAPTER 3

WALLAÇONIA

MY NAME IS James Howard Wallace, and I have a one-sentence biography: I always wanted to be normal. I was sure I *would* be normal. I had to be. In West Sicassett, Mass., in the crook of the arm of Cape Cod, there is nothing but normal. "We-Sick," as Liz called it, has about 3,000 people, and the guys, other than me, spend the summer racing boats, talking about boats and boasting about boats, and spend the winter getting their Cape Cod Community College buddies to buy them beer and their girlfriends to have sex with them in the Nauset Beach parking lot.

We lived on the Cape year-round. When the tourists leave, they don't roll up the Cape and put it in the garage. It's actually better in fall, *I* think, when the glasswort turns the salt marsh bright red, or winter when twinkle lights decorate the widows' walks of old sea captains' houses. It's remote. The only ways off are the bridges in Bourne, plus these mosquito-planes that fly out of Hyannis (#Kennedys), and the Provincetown ferry. Everyone cheers for the Red Sox and eats scallops and ice cream, and everyone owns a boat. Ours is a Herreshoff 12½ that my dad learned to sail on, and me, too, except I don't race like everyone else;

I just zigzag around our little cove. They might let me go out on the bay, but I don't. It's too open. I'm afraid I'd never get back, though I know perfectly well how to.

Everyone complains that the Cape's not what it used to be—more expensive, more overdeveloped. Even my dad and Mr. Baxter have this conversation. I think it never changes. Sometimes it's too much Paradise. You get afraid you'll never leave. You'll want one more summer night, watching fireworks from your friend's boat, or one more winter with churches glowing in the snow and lights on the whale jawbones out front of the Captain Penniman House. One more fall when the bay is brilliant blue and the glasswort brilliant red. One more spring when the alewives (they're an endangered type of herring) run in the brooks.

We faced the bay side of the Cape, not the ocean. That night, as I made my way up to the road past Mr. Baxter's to the barn, Namoquog Creek was on my left, dark with clumps of spartina, aka cordgrass; Cape stuff has all kinds of names—Indian name, white name, scientific name. The best is compass grass. It doesn't point where to go; when the wind blows it bends and draws circles in the sand. Beyond, in the moonlight, lay Wrestling Cove, named for one of the Pilgrims, Wrestling Brewster, who died when he was about my age. In summer I sailed there. Beyond was Cape Cod Bay, where I didn't go.

As I looked down at the creek, something moved. I tried to see. Maybe the raccoon was still out. I stared into the dark but couldn't tell. I began to get nervous about Mr. Baxter again, so I bounded up to the road. He wasn't there. I was afraid to call out.

Normally that night I would have been upstairs reading. I'd turn all my lights off, look down and follow the dark twists of the creek and hug myself. Beyond the bay was the rest of Massachusetts, parts of the

15

U.S. I'd never been to, and eventually Asia, which existed only on stamps and in storybooks. But I wasn't sure I wanted to go anywhere. Yet. I had applied to college, like everyone, but part of me wanted to stay in my bedroom with my books and shells and maps. As a kid I loved to line my books up alphabetically by author with the spines even, and write labels for the shells with common and scientific names. *Ensis directus*, the razor clam. Books and shells were the things I could depend on, and I liked old maps, where the Cape looked like a lobster claw, better than new, accurate ones. But life, sex, finding someone . . . I couldn't believe I could. At the same time, I didn't want to have a life like Mom or Dad, him silent in his chair in the living room, her fretting over unlocked windows. I dreamed I would change how weak I was. I'd stop envying handsome guys and become the young man I was supposed to be, the one my parents wanted, the one even Liz probably secretly wanted, and the world and the future would be safe and secure.

Now, as I stood freezing my ass off, fretting over Mr. Baxter and craning to see over the snow banks, I had just turned eighteen, and nothing had changed. Except, incredibly, I had Liz. Being eighteen hadn't changed anything. I felt older and more left out than ever. To top it off, Liz was already eighteen in June, when we started going out officially (she was repeating senior year because of all the crap when her dad was sick). Her being six months older made me feel even more pressure to get on the ball and *do it*. Make her want me. Make her want me *more*, for the *right* reasons. Not because I was Nice Jim. I had to be, like, stronger or more in charge or animalistic or something else that wasn't me.

Maybe having Liz was an illusion. Life could be mean. A dream would look like it was coming true, and then fall totally apart. And there'd be this voice in my head, "Eighteen and still a virgin." Like this judgment. A label. A sentence. A diagnosis. Worse, though, was imagining a year from now: "Nineteen and still a virgin." I couldn't move. I had worried about Mr. Baxter being out here unable to move, and instead it was me. Shuddering crazily I checked again to see if Liz had texted. Nope. I tried to pull my jacket tighter around me. I looked up at the moon between the black tree branches, the moon watching over Wallaçonia. I stumbled to the foot of Mr. Baxter's front walk.

While I walk up to the house, I'll tell you about Wallaçonia.

When I was six, Mom gave me her stamp album from when she was a kid. I began to collect, but soon I wanted to make up my own stamps. I needed a country. Our name was Wallace, so I called my country Wallasonia. It bugged me because there's no *s* in "Wallace," but "Wallaconia" has a hard *c* you can't get away from. There was no way to express this one simple thing.

Then I saw "Curaçao" in Mom's album. Dad pronounced it for me and explained about cedillas. Dad was great for explaining eclipses and hurricanes and cedillas. He put me on his lap and showed me a French newspaper online. I realized I could call my country "Wallaçonia." There'd be a grown-up symbol in its name, like Curaçao, whose stamps, according to the pictures in the album, showed maps and tropical fish and a man named Jacob Binckes, dressed in armor but with long hair and lips like a girl. My stamps for Wallaçonia showed maps of our marsh and drawings of the barn next door, which I named "Wallaçonia Palace."

My stamps did not show people because I couldn't draw people. I tried to draw Jacob Binckes, but I ripped it into little pieces and threw it in the garbage.

That night I lay in bed and thought what it was like to be Jacob: femmy but a soldier. I imagined him naked under the armor. That was my first sexy thought. I didn't envy Jacob, but I wished I could be naked with armor on.

I divided our yard into the states of Wallaçonia. I gave our marsh and woods frontierish names— "Southwest Territories" and "Midlands." I was bad at sports, so bushwhacking in the "Southwest Territories" was my way to feel boyish. I went out to our marsh and woods Sunday afternoons and pretended I was brave and strong, a real boy, until the sun went down, and I had to come in and have hot chocolate and listen to my mom go on and realize there was no Wallaçonia, just a week of math and sports and put-downs ahead before I could go back to the Territories. Even when the next weekend came, all I could think was how it would end. While math and sports and put-downs would go on forever.

Meanwhile, in real life, I had to leave John Sturbridge Elementary and go to Sicassett Middle School, then Lower Cape High. I had to be made fun of in gym. I had to be ignored by girls and picked on by cooler, better-looking guys. That's when I founded "New Wallaçonia." I went for long walks on the marsh, but I didn't pretend I was an explorer now. New Wallaçonia was more made up of fantasies of how I'd change and get a girlfriend. I'd have sex with her and walk the school corridors with my arm around her and be a hero.

But each year it looked less likely. "Sixteen and still a virgin. Seventeen and still a virgin." Meanwhile, I had to think about college and a job and becoming like my parents.

I loved my parents, and I guessed they loved me. They had to. But *proud* of me? I got okay grades and stayed out of trouble. But "proud of" is when your son is a football hero. And/or has a girlfriend and has sex with her.

Those guys—jocks and student council guys—were the ones who put me down. They were also the ones parents and teachers and girls liked. My mom was real enthusiastic about this one guy, Eric Cantler. She was in the historical society with his mom, and one summer Eric painted their building. With his shirt off. And when he crouched to pour paint, you could see he didn't have underwear on. Mom called him "sterling." I thought it was because somehow she knew he had a big dick. (I knew from gym class.) She also called him "upright." I got "sterling" out of her maybe once a year, like, for wearing a tie, but she never called me "upright."

Because I was *not* upright. I was a virgin and I did other bad stuff. I talk about how I was put down at school, but I did some picking of my own. Not a lot of guys were weaker than me, but I found one:

Nate Flederbaum.

Nate came from what Mom called the "well-to-do" part of South Sicassett. He was a pudgy know-it-all with a fat butt, and kind of femmy. He trotted up to me—"Hey, Jim, I got a question for ya!"—asking stupid stuff. I insulted and even threatened him. When I thought about it, I was still ashamed. The poor kid wanted a friend. But he wasn't the friend *I* wanted. People couldn't think I was *like* him. And I have to admit, once in a while I liked being the one to pick on someone else and think, *At least I'm not like him. Maybe I'll be okay.*

I came up the hollow to Mr. Baxter's house, a tidy Cape Cod. Icicles hung from the eaves and light blazed from the windows. Down to my left was the barn, windows liquidy-black, books asleep. Why did I have to choose anything? Couldn't I just stay with the pines and the wind and the deep, black starry sky?

Thinking of how I'd treated Nate had brought me down. I hugged myself, but I couldn't stop shivering. I was mean to Nate Flederbaum, so I couldn't be sterling, plus I had perverted feelings waiting for me around the corner every day—worse bullies than any guys I knew. Not that guys bullied directly. Eric Cantler mostly ignored me. But I was bullied by his existence. So bullying Nate helped me feel like I was holding my own. I thought putting Nate down would make me a *real guy*, but it never did.

Then there were my dad and my uncles joking about what "young Jim" must be doing with girls, which I *wasn't* doing, and yeah, I felt stuff about girls sometimes, but other times I envied the Eric types and had thoughts about them that my family probably couldn't imagine.

And then, amazingly, Liz came along.

We'd been friends, like I said, and then we started dating. I thought she was pretty and sexy with her long, blonde hair, and the way her smile teased me. I thought I'd satisfy my dad and uncles and everyone. When I passed some Eric Cantler type, especially if I was with Liz, I tried not to look, but I'd think, *That's who she really wants.* I'd be crazy inside with these thoughts, and I'd get quiet on the outside. Liz would say, "Is anything wrong?" I'd feel so lonely, but I'd kiss her and say no. And it would pass.

When I was alone in my room I pictured Eric Cantler and those guys stripping for girls, guyishly unbuttoning their shirts and climbing out of their pants, beautiful like I could never be.

I came to the turn in Mr. Baxter's front walk. Of course he wasn't there. What if he saw me? Still, I had to look around the side of the house, just to be sure he wasn't there.

I did love Liz. She turned me on, and we were best friends. We were the only ones who got certain stuff, who loved foreign films and obscure music. We watched this movie, *The Seventh Continent*, and were excited not just about the movie (super creepy and artsy), but how no one could *possibly* get it like we did. She gave me Bon Iver's *For Emma, Forever Ago*, and I took her to see Low Anthem in Providence when they had fires on the canal. We gave each other looks in class or sent snarky texts when people said stuff. Liz came out with wicked droll stuff. I loved that she was fun like that but had a good view of people. If I got angry at someone, she'd have a reason why I should be understanding. It made me feel like a better person. I was, like, redeemable. That's the best thing to find in another person. It aroused me more than her body did. So, I'd found the Great Thing in Life. How could it not be? I wanted to be a good person for her, sterling and upright, with no weird thoughts about Eric Cantler.

But I still had them. I imagined Liz, if she ever found out about my thoughts, saying, "Jim, how could you?"

I heard a sound I loved: the wind in the pines behind the barn and the trunks creaking, and I felt better. Here the wind and the waves just go on, and eventually you feel like everything's going to be okay. Birds go and come back. Fish hatch. They don't know what you think and don't care. I kept shells because I was in love with the waves and the dawn and the snow. I wanted to hold them; I wanted them to keep me company. More than I wanted any person, sometimes.

A gust came through the pines. They roared, and underneath was the creaking, like a kindly old man in a rocking chair saying it was okay.

Around the corner of the house: No Mr. Baxter. The wind died. The old man's rocking slowed.

Once, after I was mean to Nate, he looked so hurt as he walked away that I called after him. He wouldn't stop. So I walked off, too. But what I'd said echoed in my ears, and I asked myself, "How could you?"

We went to different high schools—me to Lower Cape High, him to a private school near Boston. I imagined how, if I saw him again, I might apologize. But I never did see him again. But I remembered what I said. And what I thought and felt about myself. I turned on him to feel powerful, then came home to Wallaçonia and curled up with my books and shells.

Mr. Baxter's house shone before me.

But what had Nate done when I picked on him? He didn't go pick on someone else. He wasn't mean. Maybe he went home to a place called Flederbaumia. Maybe he jerked off. Maybe he curled up with a copy of *Charles Bissell, First Mate* (my only Christmas present ever "from Dad" instead of "Mom and Dad"), and wondered why he could never be like virtuous, upright Charles.

Or did he sometimes lie down in the middle of another country with all the lights off and cry?

Text from Liz: "leaving now."

I didn't answer. And I heard the voice in my head saying, "Jim, how could you?"

CHAPTER 4

MY JOB

STANDING IN FRONT of Mr. Baxter's door, I felt useless. I had kind of wanted to find him fallen down and hurt a little, so my fear would be justified, and I could be the strong, normal guy saving him. But he wasn't anywhere. This whole thing was silly. I took out my phone to text Liz.

Wait. I still had to say thanks and apologize for not inviting him in. No, I could visit him at Bay View tomorrow. I didn't want to knock now and have him be all perplexed and me look stupid.

What does a *real grown-up guy* do? Invite the nice, considerate gay guy over, or give him the brush-off because girlfriend, because sex, etc.?

I took a deep breath, climbed up, and rang the bell. I didn't have to wait long.

He swung the door open, started back, and said, very jovially, "Well, hello *again!*" He wore little furry slippers and a rugby shirt and chinos, and he looked as happy to see me as before, like this wasn't weird at all. Like he knew I had some kind of good news even I didn't know I had. Like he was making me better, like Liz did. I felt awkward because I was panting, like the walk had tired me out. But I was just anxious, facing

23

him again and seeing how distinguished and handsome he was, *plus* waiting for Liz's text back. After
Orleans she usually texted, "Almost there! ☺☺☺." I
took deep breaths but could say only a few words at a
time. I thanked him for the date bars, reminded him
they were my favorite, and said how I should have invited him in, and he said not at all, but I was still
unsure so I repeated it, and he said, "Why don't *I* invite *you* in?" He held the storm door open and stood
aside.

"No, that's okay!" I said. I did look in, though. His
living room was bright and orderly and full of brass
clocks and dark portraits and stuff, like a museum.
"Are you sure?" he said, like he really wanted me to
come in. When my parents said, "Are you sure?" they
wanted me to do the thing so they'd win. Mr. Baxter
seemed to be inviting me in so *I* could get something.

I hooked my thumb back at our house and said,
"My girlfriend's coming over." I figured he'd back
down. When you say "girlfriend" people are supposed
to know you're okay and you don't need anything
fixed.

"Oh," he said. This look passed across his face, like,
amused, but doubtful. Did I sound like a jerk? Was he
surprised? Well, it was the truth! "Maybe," he said,
"you could come in just a second and save us both
from the cold, because I actually have a business
proposition for you."

Well, yeah, I was freezing him, too, so I stepped in.
But I stayed on the mat. He closed the door with that
vacuum-seal *whoompf.* He stood a little too close to
me, like he did sometimes in the bookstore, and I
couldn't step back because I couldn't drip on the rug.

It was hot, and I felt even more out of breath. The
living room, like I said, was perfect—all brass and silver and framed maps and leather-bound books lined
up and classical music playing. I had ideas about that

type of guy: they loved paintings and antiques but couldn't love people. I'm sorry; I'm just describing one of the Eight Billion Stages of Growing Up Confused. I worried, because I saw myself fussing over shells and books, but I hadn't had sex. I envied guys who had. I loved Liz. Maybe I didn't love her enough, and that's why we hadn't had sex. And I wasn't completely sure I loved my parents. I was always mad at them for assuming I needed blankets and assuming I thought "Mr. Baxssster" was funny, and assuming other stuff.

But what was your purpose on earth if you couldn't love other people? Did you go through life collecting books and baking date bars?

"Can I get you anything?" he asked. "Tea? Coffee?"

"No. Thank you." Again I gestured back toward our house. "My girl—"

"Your girlfriend, yes," he said, and gave me a look that I'd say was "understanding." I don't know why that bugged me. I wondered if Liz had exited Route 6 yet. As soon as she texted, I'd have my excuse to go.

It's not like I thought every guy who was that way couldn't love. Will loved that cop on *Will and Grace* (I saw it at friends' houses and pretended not to like it). But there were some who couldn't. Maybe God, if He existed, was showing me Mr. Baxter in order to make me accept how I might end up. Well, I'd show Him!

Meanwhile, Mr. Baxter was telling me his business proposition: He wanted me to work at Bay View Books—for twelve dollars an hour!

Wow! Way more than I made scooping ice cream in the summer. And it was Christmas, so I could definitely use it. That's what I could tell Liz and anyone at school who made fun. And Mom and Dad. Plus, suddenly I think I sort of wanted to get back at Dad. If he was going to say nasty stuff about "Mr. Baxssster," I'd go work for Mr. Baxssster, and then what would he say? Plus, it was obvious Mr. Baxter was lonely with his books and maps, and it was Christmas, after all, so I would do a nice thing and accept his offer, and it would prove I was not a totally cold, unloving mistake. *And* I'd prove it with Liz, too! I decided that starting that night I'd really love her the way I should, and it felt good. She was going to be here any minute. *Yeah*, I told myself, *my* girlfriend *is coming over.*

I told him yes, I'd do it, but I really had to go now.

He said, "Of course," and opened the front door with a sucking sound, like something sealed a long time was being opened. "Come at nine forty-five," he said. "We'll do your W-4, and I'll set you up at the computer. There'll be a flood of telephone calls and emails. I will put you in charge of mail order."

"Sure," I said. What else would I say? And why wasn't Liz texting?

"Excellent!" he declared. It looked like I'd totally made his day. Why, I don't know.

I turned to leave. On a bookshelf I noticed a framed picture of a girl about my age. I guessed maybe Mr. Baxter had a kid sister. I didn't know him well enough to ask. Meanwhile, he was telling me to be careful on the way down because of the ice. He hadn't slipped, but now I would! All his fussing made me slow up, which made me self-conscious, and I almost did slip. I couldn't wait to be gone. I didn't even think too much about working for him the next day. It was just to make money, right? And be nice. Be an ally. That was a cool thing to be.

I stopped and looked down at our house, our porch light on, the little radon pipe and our recycle bin, and it felt like I was looking back at the past, at this cozy, innocent place called Wallaçonia. Liz would be there soon. Expecting so much.

As I walked back down, my phone rang. It was Mom. They'd arrived in Falmouth. Aunt Lillian was stable. "Where are *you?*" she suddenly said. "No place," I said. For some reason I was thinking about Mr. Baxter's hands again. I hadn't seen much of them at his house because his arms had been folded most of the time. I guessed he was cold. I made up something about taking a walk. "Oh," Mom said. "Look," I said, I'm fine." I looked over at our back porch and there was Liz. She had her arms around herself, shivering as she waited. But she hadn't texted! I jogged toward her. Mom said she'd call again in the morning. "Right, right," I said. I hung up before I realized I had not asked how Aunt Lillian or Dad were. I came toward Liz feeling like I'd done something wrong but pissed that she hadn't texted. She smiled and held up the Uno box in her pale hand. (Mr. Baxter's hands. Like I said, they were bigger and broader than you'd expect on a short guy like that. I'd seen in the showers at school that—how do I put this?—smallish guys sometimes aren't so small. Mr. Baxter's hands seemed like they'd grasp something and take charge.)

I was close enough now to see the look on Liz's face, scared and hopeful. "Are you all right, friend?" she said. Her voice trembled. Liz had been through so much, and yet she was soft, like a scallop without its shell. When she was being affectionate, she called me "friend" or "Mr. Wallace." She called me "Jim" only if she was upset, or in front of other people. We called each other "Cubby" or "Cubs" a lot, too, after this mix-up with cubbyhole assignments freshman year. So the "friend" thing was true. We'd been friends that long, really since the winter choral concert that year. In rehearsal breaks we played Yahtzee and she told me about her dad dying. The next year I dropped chorus, but we were in some classes and a study group together, and she got me a summer job at this ice cream place where she worked, the Big Dipper, in Wellfleet. The best times were when just the two of us were on together. We did routines to entertain the customers, and when there were no customers we debated movies and complained about our parents. Mostly I did; Liz was very understanding about her mom.

Because, last spring, just before we started up again at the Big Dipper, that's when Liz's dad died. He had this awful thing called an "aortic dissection," and he died in, like, a day. I was amazed: at the funeral, the only kids from school were me and Liz's best friend Amelia. And I was the only one who sent flowers. Not that I'm so special. Mom insisted I do both those things before I could think of them myself.

Liz was hurt no one else came from school, though she tried to make it sound trivial. I thought it was lousy, so just to break the sad mood, I said, "Yeah, Mimsy's not here." With this total poker face Liz looked up at me and mouthed two words that I definitely *cannot* share with you. But it made me pass some punch through my nose. So I mouthed back another word, and she passed punch through her nose, and we went back and forth, silently mouthing every horrible thing we could think of and cracking up.

Suddenly she put down her punch glass and hugged me hard and said, "Oh, Cubs, you always make me feel better!" I hugged back. We hung on a long time. My face was right in her hair, and it smelled soft and nice, and I was aroused. We knew right there, we were now boyfriend and girlfriend.

I was kind of shocked. I'd never thought it would happen so suddenly and emotionally. I was still uncertain if this was even really happening to me. I'd hoped to get a girlfriend, but now it made me anxious. I kept asking myself, was this how it was supposed to be? It was a lot easier to look forward to being one of the chosen ones than it was to actually do, with all you were supposed to feel and all the obligations that I didn't understand till I'd failed at them.

Like, right now she had a tear in her eye. She blinked and it ran down. I had been a bad friend, making plans on my own and not telling her. I came up the steps in one stride and put my arms around her. (I couldn't believe my arms got to do that.) I said, "Hey, Cubs," low and gruff but gently, too. We kissed, and a wave of relief swept over me. Everything was okay now. This was the center of my world. And *because* everything was okay, because Liz and I were okay, I could work in Mr. Baxter's store tomorrow, as a nice thing to do. Plus the money. It felt strange to think of Mr. Baxter when I was in Liz's arms. It didn't seem real that I had just been in his house. None of those thoughts from before seemed real. I could barely remember his face. Liz and I kissed a few times. She lay her head on my shoulder and said, a bit tensely, "Where were you?" She gave a little shiver as she said it. She raised her head and we looked at each other. She frowned, and her forehead made a concerned little tent.

"No place," I said.

"Is your neighbor all right?" she asked. I fumbled for the key.

"Yeah. Fine. Everything's fine." I checked my hair in the back-door window.

"What was the problem?"

"There was no problem."

"But, originally?" We came into the kitchen, and I locked the door behind us. "Originally what was the problem? What did you *think* it was?"

Jeez! Liz could be so specific. She always said it "just made sense" to ask these questions. "Nothing. There was no problem."

"But you said—"

"How about some cocoa?" I said. "Then some Uno?"

There was a silence. She looked down and said softly, "I'm sorry."

I had this really squirmy feeling like she knew something that even I didn't about what I'd been doing and thinking. "No no," I said. "*I'm* sorry." I kissed her again. That made the feeling go away, mostly. Or at least the kissing gave me something much better and more real. Liz was *mine*. She felt *right*. All the other stuff was imaginary. Just insecurities bedeviling me. They'd go away, soon.

CHAPTER 5

CAN'T

AS WE MADE cocoa, I explained the Aunt Lillian situation. I knew Liz would relate to it because of her dad. I asked more about that, even though I already knew most of it, so we wouldn't get back on the subject of Mr. Baxter. I wasn't avoiding any one specific thing. I had no idea what to say at all. Where would I begin? I'd gone looking because some part of me was afraid he'd fallen, but my whole walk outside seemed like much more—impossible to put into words and too much even to think about with Liz there.

We played Uno for a while and then Bananagrams, saying "Peel!" in funny voices, and then when she said, "How about another game?" I said, "I'd definitely like to play another game," and we made out for a while. I put my hand inside her sweater—slowly, so she could say no if she wanted to. I'd done this a couple of times before, and it felt right and also exciting, like a little violation. I was definitely aroused. I was relieved and excited to be doing what upright boys did. I thought I might be okay and now life would be easy and really real. But I also wondered, what if I did this but kept having those envious thoughts about other guys? Of course, Liz had no idea what I was thinking and no idea why I was doing what I was doing. I mean, I was into her, into finally taking a girl's breast like other guys. I pulled back and looked into her eyes and asked myself, *Do I love her?* I had a hard time asking, but the answer was instantaneous: *Yes!*

I put her hand on my thigh, right at the top, toward the inside, but not right on my hard-on. My heart was thumping like crazy. I couldn't ask the Halloween Question, though. A couple of times I thought I might but my heart just shot up into my throat and practically choked me. She kept her hand on my thigh, maybe once brushing the bulge with her fingertip, and then she took it away, a little at a time. Suddenly she reached for a pillow, like, to make sure I got that that was why she took her hand away.

We played another round of Bananagrams; then I took our dirty dishes to the kitchen and went to pee, which at that point wasn't easy. And check my hair. When I got back she said she was sorry, but her mom was expecting her. Her eyebrows made that concerned little tent again, like she was afraid I'd be mad, so of course I told her five times that it was okay.

"You wanted to do it tonight?" she asked, with a little understanding smile.

"Well," I said, "I thought maybe . . . you know . . ."

"We will, okay?" She took my hand. "Soon."

"Soon," I repeated. I took her hand in both of mine. "'Sokay, Cubs," I said, gruff again, but cool and confident, like I totally believed we would. I didn't want her to be worried about anything. Her dad had died, and I'd told her I didn't want her ever to have to worry about anything ever again. That was love, wasn't it? Making people feel like they don't have to worry.

But now, I was the worried one. All along I'd had trouble believing I had an actual girlfriend. Now, maybe, faced with *It*, with *the Biggie*, she was rethinking this. Yeah, she wanted me *around*, but she didn't want me *inside* her. I had that awful thought again: if Cubs didn't want me inside, who would? If I were a girl, would *I* even want me inside?

I walked behind her to her car, without my coat. I watched her hips move. She wore her jeans low, though I couldn't actually see her butt right then, under her coat. I had believed she was the one. We hadn't been *together* together all that long, but this is what people did. Unless they weren't really together. Unless it was all an illusion.

At the car she asked if we could go shopping for presents that weekend. I said I was busy the next day, but instead of saying anything about Mr. Baxter, I said I might have to drive to Falmouth because of Aunt Lillian. Of course, Liz asked if she could help. I thanked her and said I'd be sure to let her know. We kissed again. By then I was freezing, so I said I had to go back. I stayed just long enough to wave and call "'Night, Cubs!" and then I ran back. I turned once on the porch to wave again and watch her taillights disappear. Then I disappeared, too, back into the warmth.

I slumped in a kitchen chair. *Let's see—frustrated, alone, can't be like other guys, must be Jim Wallace!* Yet it felt comfortable at the same time. I was used to it. I wasn't cool, I wasn't a big winner, I could come home to Wallaçonia—more date bars, some late-night TV, reading in bed, the forecast in the morning—and not have to face all the great expectations yet. But I was asking myself the same question Liz had asked me last fall, after we'd been going out, like, four weeks and I still hadn't kissed her. Her voice shook then. We were walking on the marsh, and she looked down at this cloudy little pool and said, "Is something . . . *wrong* with me?" I said, "No! No!" and I kept saying it. I put my arms around her and brought her inside, and we made out in the den like crazy. Maybe we were making up for lost time. It was like some outside force took us over.

It seemed to me we never quite made out like that again. If I told Liz that, would she agree? A sterling guy wouldn't have to ask something like that. A sterling guy would have had sex already.

I got up and cut myself more date bars. (I'd told Liz that Mom had made them.) I had an idea. I immediately felt a rush. I felt elated and guilty. Still chewing, I ran around the house, locking up, laying these crocheted dachshund things we have on the thresholds to keep out drafts. I turned out the lights. When the downstairs was secure I took the stairs two at a time to my room. I'd been thinking of this in the back of my mind all evening. Now I was alone with no duties, not to my parents, not to Liz. What happened now wouldn't count. It was just my thing that I wanted to do, and it wouldn't mean anything. It wouldn't get weighed or figured in. I would not have to answer, "How could you?"

I closed the door to my room, undressed, and turned on my laptop. I turned it away from the window.

I clicked open a folder called "Miscellaneous." Inside was a bunch of other folders, including one called "Exercise." Inside that was another folder, "Examples." I clicked it open. It was pictures of guys I envied. Not muscle-bound, just normal guys I might look like if I exercised. But they were more than that. They were guys who seemed good. Sterling. Guys who made their parents proud, who would be better to Liz than I was. I just wanted to be absorbed by them and be one of them for a while. I wanted to be an invisible god, luxuriating in the good, beautiful guys in his world.

They all had shorts on, and some were actually exercising, so if I was ever caught I could say, "Like it says, they're *examples*. Like, I could show a trainer and say I want arms like him or abs like him." I don't think it was conscious then, but my final criterion was that they all looked a little shy about being photographed. And they were always alone. I didn't like looking at guys exercising together.

I clicked through, wanting to stay on each one and at the same time wanting to hurry up. In some pictures you could see a little something through their shorts. They weren't showing off; it was natural. I knew those guys were with their girlfriends tonight, succeeding. Their mothers knew and smiled. I stared at the pictures those guys had left behind for me.

I clicked through again and again. Sometimes I'd click back. I had to see a little more of one guy, really get something about him, but I couldn't quite.

Finally, I had to see just a little more.

I never downloaded anything explicit. But I had memorized three URLs. I'd visit them one by one and then delete them from my history, telling myself that this was the last time.

One guy with mussed hair and dimples seemed so nice. Looking at him I felt like a live animal was pawing at the inside of my chest, trying to get out. The guy was lying on a bed, propped on his elbow, naked and smiling and not afraid, like someone I might know, like the bed was *his*, like someone who loved him had given it to him and he was proud of it and belonged in it. He smiled goofily, like the guy taking the picture was his buddy. Two guys who were friends taking pictures of each other naked for fun. Somewhere out there was the picture of the guy who took this picture, taken by the guy *in* this picture. It killed me that I'd never know if I found it and I probably wouldn't anyway.

Two things about the picture made it so I couldn't bear to look and yet couldn't stop looking. The guy was totally naked, by which I specifically mean he had bare feet. Some pictures of naked guys, they had those little low, no-show socks on, like they refused to really be naked. Somehow a regular guy letting everything show was sweeter to me than any muscle guy showing everything but wearing socks or cleats or boots. Then the other thing that made me crazy: this guy was soft, as in, not aroused. He wasn't showing off or proving or anything, other than that it was fun to be alive and naked and with his friend, and letting his dick show was part of that. It wasn't that big, but he didn't care. He liked it the way it was. His friend didn't care, either. "Hey, man, five bucks says you won't take off your underpants." "'Kay, dude, you lose!" "Whoa! Look at you, man!" "Hey, take a picture!" "Cool. Stretch out on the bed." "Hey, I took mine off, you gotta take yours off . . ."

My throat constricted. I wasn't supposed to be doing any of this; I wasn't even supposed to be thinking it. I felt tears in my eyes as I looked at the guy and thought, *He's so beautiful. This can't be wrong. It just can't. I'm eighteen. Why don't I get to say?* I thought, *Poor Liz, no dad and having to help everyone. I* can't *let her down. I'm the only son my parents have. I* can't *be like this! How could it be? Who can I appeal to? Because it just can't be!*

I closed my browser and closed the "Exercise" folder and put the computer to sleep. I sat in the dark, feeling better, feeling comforted. Out the window, moonlight made a path on the water. A path away.

There was time. I would change. This had to happen, and I even found myself thinking, *Liz has to get it. She must see she has to do this.*

I imagined being twenty and being with Liz. We'd go back and forth between our colleges. My first-choice college was in the Berkshires in western Mass., an hour from her first choice, near Albany. We'd sort of planned it, without any real discussion. Mom loved the place in the Berkshires. She kept saying, "I'm so happy we found it!" or, "I'm so happy you found it," or, "Aren't you happy you found it?" I guessed I was. I'd visited the fall before, and it was beautiful and peaceful—hillsides of yellow and red and wood smoke and owls calling at night. It had a great English department. I pictured it now. I pictured Liz and me there. I pictured us tangled in this tiny bed at dawn. I pictured friends I'd have there, impressed with my girlfriend. I imagined one guy friend who'd be kind of like a brother to me. Maybe on some weekend Liz couldn't make it we'd go off and do stuff, go for a hike or a movie, stay up late talking, maybe stay and spoon, jerk off together, just like a joke. But something gnawed at the back of my mind—something I couldn't control. I couldn't stop it. I didn't want to stop it. I had to relieve myself, if you know what I mean.

Once I decided that, everything else went away. It was just me and my need. How could I? How could I not? I tried to think of Liz as much as possible. Of touching her breast. But sometimes the exercise guys got mixed up in it, too. And then one of them was having sex with her.

And suddenly I was done.

I felt small. I was kind of cringing. I cleaned up and got dressed as fast as I could. Just to feel normal—or to feel nothing—I sat at my desk and flipped through Facebook. Of course, I had to "like" everything Liz had posted. I stopped and stared at her profile pic. It was the two of us at the Big Dipper last summer, grinning and wearing little paper hats like the hulls of boats. Who were those two? Who was that guy? Behind, her cover pic was from *Les Miz*: flags and smoke and guys raising rifles. Was that what she wanted? To tell the truth, I didn't like *Les Miz* because I knew I could never be those guys—so serious and good and strong. I remember sitting next to Liz in the theater and feeling so inadequate, and then I had to do it all over again for the movie.

Sitting in that movie theater I wondered the same thing I wondered sitting at my desk that night, staring at myself in a paper hat and at a bunch of guys with guns:

How much more of this do I have to take?

And then I felt guilty because, after all, I was thinking about my Cubs, the girl I loved.

CHAPTER 6

BLACK HOLE

I USED TO love the rare occasions when I woke up alone in our house, snuggling under the covers and looking out over the marsh as the first light came and gulls made circles; hearing 'QRC-FM give the forecast, then getting up, pretending I had real business to attend to, turning on the heat, making breakfast, and the smells—warm air in the vents, coffee and toast, and at this time of year, pine from the Christmas tree and bay from the wreaths on the doors. I checked the window periodically, the way we do on the Cape, because we always say we don't trust forecasts; we have to see for ourselves how the sky is and how the day will be.

I didn't really know what I was looking for. I'd heard Mom say this or that meant snow or rain or whatever. The day looked fine to me. I kept checking, though. It made me feel grown-up.

In Wallaçonia, adults always left early for work, so kids got the house going and made breakfast on their own. I dabbed jelly on toast and thought, *This is how I will be someday—when I have my own house and can do what I want.* I wasn't sure if Liz was there or not, though. I hoped Mom wouldn't call, though I did want to make up for not asking how Dad and Aunt Lillian were. I didn't know how to ask Dad directly, and even Mom kept quiet about certain stuff, I guess to protect me. She dealt with the bills and the guy who inspected the basement and with Aunt Lillian, and I ran free. She kept saying she didn't need help. I wished I could talk to my dad more, but he didn't want to hear lots about feelings or worries. When I was in grade school, he said I was a "worrywart." Mom and Dad wanted today to be just like yesterday. I shouldn't stir things up. But I kept worrying. Worrying that I wasn't good, that I wasn't sterling. I couldn't begin to tell them, especially if I wanted them to support me for four more years!

I had to be down at Bay View at nine forty-five. I checked the sky again—blue, with purplish clouds broken up—and I checked the clock. Still, I was almost late because of trying to fix my hair just so.

Out the bathroom window I saw, beyond a drift, the back of Mr. Baxter's head as he went down to the store. The low clouds moved quickly. I guessed the raccoon was back asleep. A flight of Canada geese landed out on the marsh. Today would be bright and cold. Breath puffed from his mouth as he stuck the key in, gripped the door handle, and turned it. I grabbed my coat and ran out. The ice in the driveway crackled under my feet. He looked back. "A-ha! I thought that might be you!" he said, and smiled. He braced himself and gave the door a good yank. His coat pulled smooth across his shoulders. For a second I thought something like: everyone has stuff they have to do, no matter how much the world is against them. They do what they have to, and the world doesn't care much or even know. The only one who really knows is the person doing it.

Bells jingled against the inside of the door. I came up panting, and Mr. Baxter motioned me in ahead of him. Inside was cold and dark and smelled of wood and old paper, the most reassuring smell in the world. It meant that here was a place where there was all the time and quiet in the world, and everything was worn and natural, and words mattered and I did not have to be or do anything. A place I could vanish into.

Mr. Baxter followed me in. Just before he closed the door I looked back for half a second at our house, and I had that feeling again—of Wallaçonia, of the past going away.

Mr. Baxter flicked on the lights and wrestled his coat off. "First, a fire," he said. He rubbed his hands together. He unwound his scarf. He had on a bright checked flannel shirt and chinos and a braided leather belt. Tidy and normal, so much a part of him it looked like he never took them off. He removed his L.L. Bean boots, set them on newspaper by the door, and put on worn loafers. For a second I saw his sock-feet. It was strange to think of his feet ever being *bare*. He crouched by the stove and swept it out, as I had seen my dad do to our fireplace.

We twisted up old copies of the *Boston Globe* and the *Cape Codder* and stuffed them in with sticks of kindling. Mr. Baxter palmed a log, fit it in on top of everything, then struck a match and held it to the newspaper. A piece of a headline about Fourth of July fireworks curled black and went up in flames. He shut the door. The hinge made a cry and everything inside was suddenly consumed. I shucked my coat. I gazed around the big, shadowy interior, heard the crackles from the stove, and looked at the rows and rows of books rising. I dreamed they'd never be sold, never go anywhere, just stay quiet, smelling of the old houses they came from and the lives they were part of. I even imagined they smelled of the dens and studies where they were written.

There were polished wood chests with shallow drawers for maps and prints. Some were framed on the walls—an old map of Portugal and Spain, all misshapen; a chart of the Bering Sea; a Coast Guard training map of Martha's Vineyard and Naushon Island; diagrams of a lobster and a horseshoe crab and huge, detailed, kind of creepy drawings of beetles and flowers. Above the bookcases were posters with sayings like, "The man who doesn't read has no advantage over the man who can't read," which is by Mark Twain. Some old, leather-bound volumes stood in locked cabinets with glass fronts, there were huge volumes on sailing and photography wrapped in plastic and set on special stands, and, like in every old bookstore, there were boxes of unsorted books and CDs—*The Sun Also Rises* and Tchaikovsky jumbled together. They probably just kept coming, and he put off organizing them. Maybe I could do that. Mr. Baxter was plugging in strands of twinkle lights he'd put around the windows.

I hadn't been in Bay View that much before. I liked old bookstores. I pulled over for every one I found. Sometimes Liz stayed in the car, which was okay. I liked being alone there, everything quiet except a clock ticking, and that old-paper smell. How at home and taken care of I felt. I'd find something just for me that no one else would understand, like a hardcover of *My Family and Other Animals*, which I used to read at Aunt Lillian's while the adults talked. When I came back to the car, Liz would ask, "Is everything okay?" I'd show her what I bought and she'd say, "It's not online?"

I wasn't comfortable at Bay View, though. The thing about old bookstores is you can be completely alone, in your own private world. You turn corners, finding one back room after another. It's like it's your house, with extra rooms that surprise you, and all the books are yours. But at Bay View, no matter how far I went, Mr. Baxter followed and asked if he could help me find something. I didn't want help. The fun was just looking, and suddenly something would speak to me that I never thought of. But he'd stop and ask me what subjects I was taking in school and what books I had read lately. I wanted people to ask about my reading (no one did, except Liz sometimes), but I didn't like *him* asking. He was too enthusiastic. "Oh, that's an *excellent* one!" "I'm not at *all* familiar with that; *tell* me about it!" It was, like, *too much* of what I wanted. Putting him off made me feel more like what I *did* want— to be upright and masculine, but still interested in books, of course.

But so far, sterling and masculine hadn't worked out too well. What would Mr. Baxter say if he knew how mean I was to Nate? Not that he ever would, but if he did, I thought he wouldn't want to know what I was reading. He wouldn't even want me in the store.

He went behind the counter, dug in a desk drawer, and produced a pen. He waved me over, and I filled out a W-4 while he chose some music on his phone and stuck it in a dock on a shelf. Mozart started playing softly around the barn. Next he taught me how to download orders. Mr. Baxter leaned over my right shoulder, his hand gripping the edge of the table, the knuckles prominent. This was the closest we had ever been, but he didn't seem to be thinking about that. He was looking around; he wanted the day to get started. We printed all the new orders; then I went to pull the books from the shelves and maps and prints from the map cases. If he had set a book aside specially for a customer, he would get it himself from the "Employees Only" room in back. He never told me not to go there. I just felt I shouldn't. But I was an employee, wasn't I? Maybe, in spite of the W-4, I somehow wasn't a *real* employee.

The bells jingled and the first actual person came in. It felt like an intrusion. Mr. Baxter called me to the front and showed me how to ring up the order. The guy was a professor type, with a corduroy vest and long gray hair, who sniffed and sighed and looked around a lot and tried to argue with Mr. Baxter over the price of a book on the Appalachian Trail. Mr. Baxter gave a little lecture on something in the book called a "number row," which proved it was valuable, I guess. He was a little snippy, but he won. I had a half-second thought that, if I had to, I'd rather be snippy like that than be the professor guy, who looked around like he owned the world, and the store was beneath him.

Mr. Baxter was right about phone calls. People wanted to talk to him personally about rare maps or first-edition books. I heard him saying, "*gorgeous* map of Salem Harbor, 1790" and "Ricketson's history of New Bedford, near *perfect* condition" and "signed copy of Finch's *Outlands*." (That excited me because I had *Outlands* on my bedside table.) It wasn't just the femmy exaggeration I heard. I heard him *selling*. Maybe even lying a little bit, like about "near *perfect*." It made me wonder who he really was and how life really worked. I had always thought people basically told the truth and meant well. But maybe you had to exaggerate and lie to sell stuff and make money. Did people lie to me? Of course, I was sort of half-lying to a few people myself. Plus there was the Nate Flederbaum thing—not a lie, but a secret. I stuffed those thoughts in the back of my head and returned to work.

After lunch, my mother's friend Mrs. Budd came in. (Maybe they weren't friends, but they knew each other.) She was cheery to Mr. Baxter but her voice was strained, and she looked away whenever he said something back to her. She was surprised to see me there; in this tense, upbeat voice she asked how long had I worked there and what did I do? She asked Mr. Baxter if I was trustworthy. That was a weird question. Mr. Baxter just said, "Of course." Mrs. Budd spread crumpled bills out on the counter. Then, as she dug for change, she asked what grade I was in. I said I was a senior. She said, "Oh, so you're eighteen?" and I said "Yes."

Still digging, she said she was surprised that I could be eighteen before January of my senior year. Even though I didn't like myself for doing it, I told her how my parents waited to put me in kindergarten so I wouldn't be the youngest in my class. She kept digging, like she didn't hear. I decided I didn't care what Mrs. Budd thought. I'd already given away too much. Could she use it against me?

Mr. Baxter's jaw worked. The second she was out the door he shot me an exasperated look and rolled his eyes. I felt closer to him. I wanted to say something about Mrs. Budd, but Mr. Baxter was being well mannered about it and saying nothing. He went to the computer, and I just said, "More to download? I'll do 'em." I was pleased that I'd gotten good at working with online orders. "No," he said. He stepped around me and sat at the keyboard. "I can do it." He said it low and clipped. What was with him all of a sudden? What was it with everyone today?

So I asked, "Why would she care what age I am?"

He said nothing. I thought he didn't hear me. So I started addressing boxes and padded envelopes, matching each to its printed-out computer order and the books I had pulled. It was laid out on the floor like a kid's project. I was sort of proud of it. "I've been working indoors since I was sixteen," I said, "like anyone."

"Mm-hm," he said, not looking up. Had I said something wrong? Or was he afraid of what Mrs. Budd

45

might go and say? Maybe I wasn't supposed to be there for some reason, and I didn't know it.

He clicked away at the computer, but I didn't hear the printer. Then he got up, palmed another log, tossed it in the stove, and went back to the Employees Only room. The barn fell silent except for the fire crackling. A beam groaned. I could hear the wind in the pines, and sometimes a pinecone hit the roof and rolled down. The sun was "over the yardarm," as Dad would say, the light going. It was the most comforting part of the day; I wanted it to last forever. I inhaled deeply, and I thought: this is being in Wallaçonia, the papery smell, the stillness, the old charts, the view of bare trees and stiff, icy reeds, rippled by windows someone made by hand. I was embarrassed, though, to be eighteen and thinking of a childhood fantasy as though it were real. I felt like I'd wet my bed. But I had to have a place for my mind to go. I couldn't live without it.

Maybe someday I'd run a place like this. At the end of the day I would walk along the shore to a big, rambling house with windows overlooking the bay, where you could watch storms all safe, and the cliffs never eroded. A smiling little blond boy would greet me. I didn't picture a wife. I guessed it would be Liz. But she was away for a while, and my boy and I could make popcorn and watch scary movies all by ourselves.

Mr. Baxter was back at the computer, making notes. When he answered the phone he was terser. If he had to go to the shelves to look at anything, he'd dim the screen. Occasionally he'd look at me. I'd look back. I liked his terseness, like he might snap out an order. I remembered his shoulders and back under his coat that morning. But his mood wasn't like the morning, when he juggled calls, asked after people's families, and said, "Thank you *so* much!" and "It has been a *real pleasure!*" Was he still mad at Mrs. Budd?

Had I done something wrong? Did she think Mr. Baxter was, like, *touching* me? It made me think of his hands, like, caressing. In my head I made it Eric Cantler he caressed, not me. I made that thought go away real fast!

My phone went off. It was Mom, with an update. This time, I remembered to ask how everyone was. Dad was "worried, of course" but Aunt Lillian was "stable." She was back at the nursing home—not in her room, but in a hospital room in a different wing. Mom and Dad would stay in Falmouth another night. Mom asked how I was, and I said fine. They figured I was always fine.

I didn't want to go into how I was working for Mr. Baxter, but if he heard me and figured out I was talking to Mom, he'd expect me to tell her I was here. So I kept my answers simple—"Uh-huh," "Nothing," "Okay"—like I was talking to a stranger. It was sad, talking like that to my own mom, but there was no way I could start in about the job or Mr. Baxter or any of the other million things I was thinking about. I wouldn't know how to begin saying it, and Mom wouldn't know how to begin hearing it. So I said I was fine. It wasn't a lie.

She said "I love you" before she hung up. I knew what she wanted to hear, but, since I didn't want Mr. Baxter to know it was her calling, I said, "Yeah, me too."

A few seconds after I hung up, Liz texted me: "shopping tmrw? wherewhen?" I tried to figure out how to tell her I couldn't go. I could claim Mr. Baxter had just now hired me for tomorrow. My thumbs twitched over my phone as I thought how to begin. Just then, Mr. Baxter looked up and asked me where I was applying to college.

I kept on texting. "Oops," I said, "sorry, hang on a sec." He kept looking at me. I was delaying because I

thought he'd critique my choices. He always seemed to
know something better or more refined than what you
knew. I pretended my text was super important and
required all this concentration. I spelled out, "Might
have 2 go 2 Foulmouth tmw." So I also had to say
something about how Aunt Lillian was. It had to be
true but sound like there could still be an emergency.
I texted, "Aunt better not out of woods." Liz offered to
help. I said thanks, no, and tried to refine my explanation of Aunt Lillian's condition. I went so fast I
misspelled everything and had to start over. Plus, of
course, I was lying a little. I hadn't even noticed. I just
thought I was saying what I had to say to keep everyone from bugging me. And Mr. Baxter kept looking at
me. Finally I sent the text and answered his question
as offhandedly as I could. I named the four places I'd
applied.

"And which is your first choice?" Meanwhile, Liz
sent back a question mark and a smiley emoji. I told
him about the college in the Berkshires. It was a well-
known name, but it didn't seem to impress him. In
fact, he actually frowned. I named the two tied for second place and then my safety school, a big university
in downtown Boston. Without missing a beat he said
he thought the school in Boston should be my first
choice. I must have looked gobsmacked (I know it's
British, but Liz and I liked it), because he said, "I'm
wondering, what are you looking for *socially*?"

I was completely annoyed. No one had mentioned
anything "*social*" to me. "Social" meant going to parties, which I hated, and in fact it really meant
"sexual," didn't it? Mr. Baxter couldn't mean that. I
texted Liz, "oops gotta go." His remark hung in the air.
"What do you mean?" I blurted. He started in about
how a lot of college is who you meet. In the Berkshires
there was "frankly, nothing." I interrupted and said I
didn't want an urban environment. He said, "Boston

isn't *urban*. It's a small town." That pissed me off. Why did he have to correct me? That's how those types operated, embarrassing you with clever put-downs.

What was kind of exciting, though, was how know-it-all he suddenly became. "Look at what you have in Boston," he announced. He ticked items off on his fingers. I noticed he wore a school ring on one of them. "On the Red Line alone: Kendall is MIT; Harvard, Harvard, obviously; Porter Square, Lesley; Davis, Tufts." He angled his head and raised his eyebrows. "And that's just one part of one subway line."

I had my argument ready. My first choice offered opportunities X, Y, and Z, the faculty-to-student ratio was—

He interrupted. "Much of what you say is true of our local community college." He pointed to the chimney on the stove. "Would you open the flue a little, *s'il vous plaît?*"

What?? I stared at the flue and couldn't imagine what to do. My entire family and all our friends had been to four-year colleges. Community college was a *joke* to my family. If I made a dumb mistake, like almost dropping a firelog, Mom or Dad would say, "Off to community college!"

Mr. Baxter said they had great professors at community colleges here because many were retired from the universities he just mentioned, and they had programs in community colleges now, like semesters abroad, that were comparable to four-year institutions. "I think," he said, "you might be ready for something more than a Hogwarts/*Sterile Cuckoo* kind of place." He turned to check the computer screen. I took the old potholder I'd seen him use and I tried to fix the flue, and I wondered what the heck a sterile cuckoo was. The flue wouldn't turn, and I got more and more pissed off. He had to come and show me what to do, and I felt completely defeated. Certain guys I knew would know how to turn a knob, for Heaven's sake!

I just wanted out of this conversation. Once I decide something, I like it to stay the way it is, especially when it's something big and complicated. I just want to decide and be done with it. No reopening the case. And my parents would never buy that my first choice was equal to a *community college*. I could hear Dad: "Is that what Mr. Baxssster says?"

How did Mr. Baxter know all this, anyway?

"Where did you go?" I asked. He told me, but I didn't recognize the name.

"Little place in Pennsylvania," he explained. "Sweet but deadly. Makes me think *you* might be interested in more than some old stone and a view of the woods!"

Well, that was rude. I liked woods. I'd grown up in the woods here. I had made our woods into Wallaçonia. He wasn't even from here.

He nodded at the chimney. "You got it now?"

I said, "Mm-hm," kind of tensely.

"Maybe," he said, "I shouldn't be telling you what to do." He went back to the computer.

I knew the polite thing was to say, "Oh, no no. It's okay." But I was still thinking, *My safety school?* But what if he was right? My phone buzzed. I pulled it out. In response to my saying I had to go, Liz had sent a "k." I was afraid I'd hurt her, so I typed, "Maybe tmw 4 shopping," and I included two smiley emojis plus one of a gift box. I hit "Send" and then wondered if I should have typed a couple of hearts, too. But I couldn't do it as an afterthought.

Now I'd have to deal with Mr. Baxter. Okay, kids sometimes canceled stuff. But men kept their word. Damn! Plus, twelve dollars an hour, and he was counting on me. Maybe I could back out of Liz later, or find a way to do both.

"All righty!" Mr. Baxter said, clapping his hands twice. "Off to the P.O.! Let's seal everything up!" He joined me sealing the envelopes I had addressed and stuffed. I was anxious. While he was gone, I would have to deal with walk-ins. In secondhand places like this, people, like that professor, often wanted to negotiate. Mr. Baxter said if they wanted to haggle over anything under fifty dollars, I could take up to twenty percent off but should start with ten. Anything *over* fifty dollars, wait for him. I just hoped no one would ask. Already that day I'd seen another guy try to get a discount. He said, "Give you ten for this!" real loud and blunt, like a punch, like there was nothing anyone could say back. Mr. Baxter took the ten. Another was like, "I saw this for less at . . ." And one guy was like Mr. Baxter but femmier, and he said, "It's a first *edition*, not a first *printing*." Mr. Baxter explained that it was the same thing, but the guy didn't buy whatever it was. They all made me really angry, but the "Give you ten for this!" guy was the worst. I kept thinking of him.

I would tell anyone like that to wait for Mr. Baxter, but already I resented them. I felt threatened when people did that to Mr. Baxter. I hated to see him on the spot. Eric Cantler or the guys in my Exercise folder didn't get embarrassed. Or they got embarrassed over fun stuff, like someone ribbing them about a girl. (No one ever teased me about Liz.) Offer them ten bucks for a fifteen-dollar book, they'd say, "Sure!" Or they'd grin and say, "How about twelve?" and people would like them so much they'd be happy giving them twelve.

I carried the sealed envelopes to Mr. Baxter's car. It was worn inside, with nothing really in it. Mom complained how I left Starbucks cups and movie tickets in our car. Mr. Baxter's car just had a wool blanket on the back seat and a reflective red triangle folded up on the floor. The interior smelled damp and peppery. I piled the envelopes next to the blanket and closed the door. I stopped to look at the sunset over the marsh. The guys in my Exercise folder would totally dismiss that car. Too old and too simple. They'd know a much better kind and all the best features and attachments to get, or whatever you'd call them. And they wouldn't have the triangle. Those guys never thought about accidents, and accidents probably never happened to them.

Back in the barn Mr. Baxter was making a knot in his scarf. He put his coat on, tugged here and there to make it fit just so, and straightened his wool hat. "Could I trouble you," he asked, "to change a bulb while I am out? Up there, you see?" He pointed to a light that had gone out. "There's a ladder in back. You don't have a problem with heights, do you?"

I said no. I'm afraid of a lot of weird stuff, but I'm not afraid of heights. It was good of Mr. Baxter to ask, though. Being asked about my fears made me uncomfortable. One of my fears was people actually finding out my fears. But seriously, Mr. Baxter's thoughtfulness made me think for a second about a guy's goodness coming from somewhere other than how he looked (though Mr. Baxter looked pretty good). In school, I avoided fat or weird-looking or weird-acting kids because I thought they weren't good. I wasn't good, either. I had to keep my eyes on the athletic, good-looking ones, to see how it was done, to feel like, if I appreciated them, maybe I was a little bit like them, too. And I had to keep the Nate Flederbaums away.

Like I said, Mr. Baxter looked pretty good himself right then. The coat was stylish, I guess. Big lapels. Kind of jaunty. When he turned, I caught a look at it stretched across his shoulders again. "After I get back," he said, "we'll start downloading for tomorrow.

"Damn! What was I going to tell him about tomorrow? What was I going to tell Liz? "And if you'd watch the register." I nodded. I glanced at the register, and that's when I noticed more envelopes: not the padded kind we'd just sealed, but plain ones the size of a magazine. They were also addressed. Maybe that's what he'd been doing when he was so serious at the computer. It was like he read my mind. Just then he took a stride over and grabbed those envelopes and held them in his right arm, close to his chest, like a girl carrying schoolbooks. His other hand fussed with his hat. He pulled at his coat again, like a knight making sure his armor was in place. Last of all he patted his pockets. Then he turned and left, waving and calling, "Back soon!"

What about those envelopes? When he worked on them, he'd gotten quiet. I went to the back for the ladder. But instead, I went into the Employees Only room.

I stepped inside the door and stopped. It was chilly. There was just a little light from a square, rippled window. He didn't say I couldn't come in here. I could say I had to find something. I looked up. The room actually had two levels. The lower one had shelves of books with yellow slips saying they were set aside for this or that special person. I knew all about that. I went over to the bottom of the narrow, steep stairs and looked up. It was dim up there. I couldn't make anything out. Suddenly I climbed up, quickly and carefully. At the top, light came from just one, tiny window. I waited for my eyes to adjust, and all the time I kept an ear out for the door to open or the phone to ring. I could see that the shelves were crooked and dusty. Some summer things were stored there—fans, some flattened paper lanterns, and a weed whacker—and a few sorry, dusty paperbacks, stiff and wrinkled with water damage. The drawings on the cover were two-dimensional, like what a kid thinks the world looks like. The fonts were right out of Word. One was literally Comic Sans.

The first book was *The Cabin by the Lake* by M. M. Morgan. On the cover was a drawing of a cabin, all shut up, with a rocking chair on the porch. Around it were trees with straight, brown trunks and bushy tops in weird shapes. The other book was *What We May Do*, by J. B. Halperin, with just a drawing of a field. No fence or people or woods beyond, just greenery and clouds. The book was so stiff from water damage I could only peek in. The writing was sort of fake. Same with *The Cabin by the Lake*. M. M. Morgan said how he or she loved the cabin—"the best place in the world," "the best place ever"—but they never said why. Everything in the cabin was "old and worn" or "had been there for years." I liked the idea, but the repetition made the story seem unreal. Both books were published by a place called Lobster Pot Publishing.

The phone was ringing! I wanted to run and get it, but I had to put the books back just so. I figured Mr. Baxter wouldn't like that I'd been up there. Funny how he hid stuff that was so innocent.

I restored it all as best I could, then climbed down, ran out to the big, main room, and headed for the phone. The machine came on. I got there in time to hear a guy's voice, serious and soft, say, ". . . can come anytime. Just let me know. It'll be great to see you." He stopped. I just stood there. I didn't want pick the phone up. It sounded so private. Finally he said, "Take care. Bye." Another pause. I could hear him breathing. Then he hung up. Was this guy Mr. Baxter's boyfriend? I never knew him to have one. I didn't watch his house or anything, but after a while you know what you don't see as well as what you do see. Maybe he answered a personal or, like, picked this guy up somewhere. There were places, especially in summer. You'd see a guy riding a bike real slow. He'd have his shirt off—and I hope this makes sense—he'd have it off in a different way from normal guys with their shirts off. Normal guys are like, "Hey, look at me!" Guys riding bikes real slow have their shirts off like, "Let's make a deal." It weirded me out and disappointed me to think Mr. Baxter might have been taken in by a guy like that.

I put that idea away and thought what I would say about the unanswered phone. I'd say I was getting the ladder. I took the new bulb from the counter and went and changed the bulb. No one came in the whole time. I put the ladder back and went behind the counter, just to feel what it was like to survey a kingdom, to pretend it was my kingdom, even if no one came.

And there it was.

On the floor.

A magazine called *Hunk* in plain, bold letters. Bright yellow.

The naked, pumped-up guy on the front looked tough and mean and, well, naked. His butt showed— most all of it—and before I could stop myself I was examining it, my heart pounding. Online I looked mostly at models. They at least had shorts on. This guy had nothing. He had a cigar clamped in his teeth. He glowered at me. It kept coming at me, and I kept trying to grasp it. It was like he was daring me. And there was the tick of the clock to remind me I was here at Bay View, that I was Jim Wallace, and that somewhere out there I had a girlfriend named Liz. I kept staring. I felt queasy. I breathed through my mouth. I could almost taste the bitterness of the wet cigar. He might have been grinning, and he might have been sneering; I couldn't tell. He had a thick, black, trimmed beard, and he made this bulging muscle with his arm, like a map of Cape Cod on steroids, except his fist didn't curl in but turned out, artsy, like a duck head.

So this was what had been in those other envelopes. I thought of Mrs. Budd and how she was surprised I worked there. Was Bay View just a front? Did Mr. Baxter find a lonely place on the Cape and buy a bunch of old books, just so he could sell *Hunk*? Well, there had to be more. Right here. Right here in the barn. But where? Maybe some of them looked the way I wished I looked. But he was coming back any minute; I couldn't go looking. I'd already messed up those cheap old paperbacks.

And his "business proposition" for me. What was he planning? Isn't that what those types did? Lay traps for young guys? "Wouldn't you like to work in my store?" "Why don't you come in for tea?" Then they'd ask if you'd ever read some book about *that*. But they usually wanted big, handsome Eric Cantler types. Why did Mr. Baxter want me? Could he tell? Did he know something about me I didn't know about myself? Now I felt almost sick.

I looked up. Okay. He really did sell regular books. They were all around, and I'd seen him do it all day. He took online orders and sold antique maps for 500 bucks or more. He knew about first editions and little rows of numbers. But then, what about the guy who left a message? Was he Mr. Baxter's big Eric Cantler type? I imagined it was Eric himself who called. He'd come to Mr. Baxter's house tonight. While I was home alone, Eric would walk around Mr. Baxter's house nude, and Mr. Baxter would look at him and think how sterling and upright he was, and . . . *Jeez, STOP IT!!*

I just had to have more confidence, more belief in myself. I had to get rid of my inferiority complex, and then I wouldn't think stuff like that. I looked down at the *Hunk* guy again.

Okay.

Mr. Baxter would be back. He could *not* think I had seen *Hunk*. But before I fixed things, I could not help but look inside for two seconds. I saw more pictures of the cover guy, aroused, plus ads for videos and "devices," if you know what I mean. They creeped me out, even though I couldn't tell what some of them were for.

I had to think what to do. If I left the magazine there, he'd be afraid I saw it. So I'd have to say something like, "No one came. I didn't go behind the counter at all." I could set up the ladder again and pretend I'd been up there the whole time.

I had a better idea.

I sat down where he'd been addressing envelopes. If *Hunk* slipped off the table, where would it land? I put it in front of me and then pushed it with my hand. It went down into where the computer cables were tangled. I could even see an envelope down there that it was probably supposed to go in. Perfect! I left everything tangled in the dark, put the chair back, and then texted Liz: "shopping tomorrow ok what time?" I hit "send," grabbed the old light bulb from the trash, and by the time the bells jingled, I was back up on the ladder, pretending to struggle with it. "Up here," I said. "Sorry. Took longer than I thought."

"No worries!"

I didn't watch as he went behind the counter. I had a hard time looking at him. I had figured he was gay, as in, cozy and femmy. I wasn't like that, and that was okay. But to think he looked at those guys and, well, if he was a *Hunk* reader, then he sure wasn't the person I thought. He'd deceived me or imposed something on me. If I had to be there with him, I wanted to be as far away as I could. After I came down, I pretended I had some business in the back. He went to the phone and played the message. I could barely hear anything. It was all mumbly and the guy's voice was sad. Maybe he was in a place where he couldn't talk. With his wife? Or his girlfriend? I checked to see if Liz had texted back. When I finally had to come up front, I glanced under the computer desk. The magazine and envelope were gone. I said I'd been in the bathroom when the call came. Mr. Baxter just shrugged. I asked, "Was it a customer?"

"Old friend," was all he said. I couldn't say *how* he said it. I kept replaying it in my mind for clues, but I heard nothing.

So did he not care about books at all, but just about . . . ? Did he know I saw the magazine? Was the guy on the cover *that way*? No macho guy was *that way*. Was the *Hunk* guy making fun of me? "Hey, loser, you'll never be like this!" Did macho guys put out *Hunk* just to make money off weirdos? The whole thing had ruined the barn, the stove, the books, everything. Up till then, Bay View that day had felt like the safest place I'd ever been. Now, none of it was quaint or safe. It was empty, like that cabin by the lake. I wouldn't come back. How could I watch Mr. Baxter address envelopes, knowing what was in them? No. Tomorrow I'd go Christmas shopping with my *girlfriend*. What a normal guy does. Then I remembered what Mr. Baxter said about college, and my heart sank. Like him pushing Boston on me was related to *Hunk*. I'd seen those kinds of magazines in Boston. Well, I wasn't going anywhere near Boston. The Berkshires were perfect for me. Our home and our fireplace and our TV were perfect for me.

Except, what if he was right? What if there was one great thing I'd miss if I didn't go where he thought I should? But why should I care what he thought? What did he know about colleges? What did he know about me? Or did he think he knew something about me, encouraging me to go to a city? No. I couldn't trust anything he said now.

Okay. Tomorrow Liz and I would just go get lost in Barnes & Noble and Salt Spray Gifts finding something for Mom and at Snow's Hardware with its smells of rubber and paint getting something for my dad and finally at a little table in the front window of Nuts 'n Beans having hot chocolate before coming home and it would be snowing and my parents wouldn't come back tomorrow, either, and Liz and I would finally do something. I would leave Mr. Baxter and his dirty magazines and cheesy fake paperbacks. It wasn't me. It was all weird and deceptive and made me feel kind of sick.

I felt chills all over. I had to stop this. But what if it was my destiny? The deceptive part was about to happen again. I had to tell Mr. Baxter I wasn't coming tomorrow, so I had to make something up. Would he see through it? But now I had no choice. I stood there thinking there was no place in the world for me, and the words, "Mr. Baxter?" came out of my mouth.

"I think you can call me Pat," he said, looking up from the register.

I said okay, but I didn't. I could deceive "Mr. Baxter," but break a promise to "Pat"? So I didn't use either name. I just said, "I don't think I can come tomorrow." He looked at me, steady but surprised. I held up my phone. "My mom called, and things aren't going so well with my aunt."

And that's all I had to say. Then I just had to get through him sympathizing and asking for details (because his grandmother had a pacemaker, etc.). But I could fudge that. No one expects a kid to know a lot about his great-aunt. Well, there it was again: I didn't want to be a kid anymore. At least about some things. But I couldn't come back to Bay View, and I couldn't tell Mr. Baxter why, so that was that.

He said I should do whatever I had to, and he said he could imagine how my parents depended on me. I felt even worse. They *couldn't* depend on me. I would have tried to get out of going to Falmouth if they had asked. At last he let me go back to work. I couldn't wait for this to just *end*. A few minutes later I heard him on the phone:

"Well, I got your message." He was talking to that guy! There was some mumbling: ". . . quarter to ten . . . you can fill out a W-4 . . . till six . . . twelve an hour . . ." He was going to be my replacement! Who was it that Mr. Baxter liked better? Did that guy know about *Hunk*? Maybe so, and that's what Mr. Baxter wanted. I was just a dumb kid. "Well," he concluded, "it will be wonderful to see you again!"

I tried not to listen and instead thought how I had the whole evening ahead of me, and then tomorrow—off and away with Liz. But I couldn't stop wondering about the guy coming tomorrow. I wanted to see him and to know him.

The minutes ticked. I seemed to be pulling books in slow motion. I had to read orders four or five times and still I was unable to think where to turn to find a book or a map. I could barely concentrate on Mr. Baxter's words as I got ready to leave. He went on forever. He asked me to keep him "apprised of the college situation," and I said I would. I just wanted to go to that place in the Berkshires. No choices, no surprises, nothing to think about. I wanted to be a kid about this one last thing and say "I want" and have it happen and be okay. Well, I wanted to say "I want" about a few more things and have them happen. Like making love to Liz. Why did I have to listen to Mr. Baxter, anyway? What business was this of his?

I had my coat and hat on. I said good-bye. He was already turning out the lights. I can't explain, but I'd wanted to leave with the store still going. I'd wanted to stand at my parents' door and look back and see the light on and Mr. Baxter still doing stuff. I apologized again about the next day, and he said, "It's all right. An old friend was coming over anyway. Maybe you heard me speaking with him on the phone. So I have a replacement!" Oh. So I was out in the cold. The thing I feared all the time—to be sent outside, with no chance ever to get back in—was happening. He dinged open the cash register to count the money, and I turned to leave.

It was all the way dark outside now. I couldn't wait to get home, curl up on the living room sofa, and forget about today. I would heat dinner, block all the drafts with crocheted dachshunds, turn out the lights, and watch TV. There were good shows on tonight. No more *Hunk*, no books in the attic, no strange guy on the phone. Just TV and date bars.

I climbed to our house, which was completely dark. I hadn't left a light on for myself. At the back door, I couldn't see the key or the hole, and I thought I'd freeze before I got in.

When I was finally fed and bundled up under a blanket with the TV on and wind shaking the windows, I still couldn't forget what I had seen in Bay View. I couldn't forget how I felt: wondering what was inside *Hunk* and fighting not to look. I had to be ten times stronger than the guy on the cover. Like the marsh. People call marshes "fragile," but they're tough. They have to be, with the crazy changes in salinity and everything. A marsh is fragile only if you come at it with bulldozers.

Was Mr. Baxter fragile? He had weaknesses and needs. I guessed everyone did. Even my parents had secrets and disappointments, but they had each other. Not that they were so lovey-dovey, but each one knew the other one was there. Then I had two thoughts at the exact same time: I myself had Liz, supposedly, but there was one huge thing I couldn't tell her; and Mr.

Baxter—when he was alone and something bad happened, who did he turn to?

I was afraid that that would be me one day, alone and not knowing what to do. I had weaknesses, including the big one you know about, that felt impossible to overcome. I'd deceived everyone and planned even more deceptions. I couldn't bear to think about myself having needs. Needs seemed like awful things to admit. Any need I had would be impossible anyway. I'd say, "I want . . ." alone on the porch of a locked cabin or in an endless, empty field.

I went to the kitchen and made tea. I brought it into the dark living room, along with the last of the date bars. I wanted them gone before Dad came home. I snuggled under the blanket again, just one hand slipping out for the tea mug. This was supposed to be Wallaçonia—this, here, tea, cake, TV, blanket!—but the thoughts kept coming—*Hunk*, Liz, Mr. Baxter, lies, loneliness.

Then Liz called, asking when she should show up the next day. I couldn't explain, even to myself, why I had to be there to see my replacement arrive. I just told Liz I wouldn't know a departure time till morning. I said the uncertainty was because of Aunt Lillian. She said she understood. We said good night and "Love you" and hung up. I wished I'd never offered to go shopping. I wanted to go look in the "Exercise" folder. Instead, I found something else to eat and went back to the TV.

I fell asleep and missed a call from my mom. I woke up and listened to the message. She said nothing about Dad or Aunt Lillian. She just wondered if I was okay and asked me to mail the light bill. I got up and went to her desk. There was the Cape Light Compact bill with the lighthouse logo, stamped and ready to go. The wind whistled outside. I guessed that someday I'd pay bills.

I'd sort of failed to account for that when I made up Wallaçonia. When I was little, I was the prince of Wallaçonia. Now, I guess, they'd transitioned to a market economy.

CHAPTER 7

BASTARD

NEXT MORNING THE wind blew hard and cold, tearing at scraps of clouds. At 9:30 I was looking out the window every few seconds. I had to see my replacement, and he had to be on time. Liz was already on her way.

At nine forty-five, I heard a car engine outside our house and something huge appeared in the window of Dad's study. I ran to look. A black Hummer lurched down the driveway. Right behind came Liz in her dad's old Hyundai. The Hummer went down to Bay View and stopped, and the taillights went out. The door opened and a guy got out. The one who was better than me. I wanted to run down and ask Mr. Baxter to take me back.

I went to the dining room for a better view. The guy wasn't big but he was sturdy, with broad shoulders. He was blond and wore new blue jeans. He shut the door of the Hummer and turned to go down to Bay View. For a fraction of a second he lost his balance on the ice, and he did something sweet and un-hunk-like. He put his arms out, kind of elegantly, and recovered himself. I bet he'd had sex. Watching him be so elegant for a second, I thought differently about *be-*

ing a man. You could be a man and sturdy but not
so—what's the opposite of "elegant"? Stiff and con-
tained?

I'd seen guys make a big deal of doing soft, feminine
stuff like cuddling babies or kissing their wives or girlfriends, like they felt obliged and were also showing
off. What this guy did was trivial, righting himself from
a slip. It just came out of him, like a piece of art. I
would have fallen. This was who Mr. Baxter wanted:
elegant, strong, and sure of himself. Probably knew
more about books and maps than me. What did Mr.
Baxter feel for him? You look at a guy like that and
you think, "Sex." You look at me and you think,
"Whatever."

Our doorbell rang, and I jumped. Liz. What would
she think of me hyperventilating over this guy? Had
she seen him? Would she prefer him to me, like Mr.
Baxter did? I wished I could tell her about how he
slipped and recovered.

When I opened the door, she was shivering. I kissed
and hugged her extra hard, just to feel normal. Over
her shoulder I saw Mr. Baxter bustle out of his house,
adjusting his hat and scarf. I broke the hug and kind
of pulled her into the house, so I wouldn't have to see
him with the blond boy. She stumbled, and I caught
her. She didn't ask why I'd pulled. I heard Mr. Baxter
call out, and I had to steal one more look. He waved to
the blond guy. I could not make out their words echoing over the snow, but I heard his enthusiasm.
Suddenly they were together and they hugged. It was
like I'd waited for all my life to see this, but I had to
turn away and connect with Liz. I shut our door with a
whoompf.

"Cubs," I said, gulping air, my voice shaking, "you
want some tea or coffee?"

"Tea, please!" she said. "Have you been exercising?"

I told her I'd been carrying some stuff up and down stairs. She looked at me all concerned. I panted. I had that animal in my chest. For a second I thought, what if I start bawling? I made the moment pass, though. Was the blond guy maybe Mr. Baxter's son? Could he have one? Had he ever been married? Mr. Baxter with a sterling son. I watched Liz's small fingers unwrapping the tea bag, and all I wanted was those fingers on me, but I also wanted to be down at Bay View and be with the one I now thought of as my dad and his other son, my brother. Whoa! What? Mr. Baxter was *not* my dad! With his *Hunk* and his bustling? But no matter what he was and what this guy was, I wanted to be with them. But I had to go get presents. I'd promised Liz, Christmas was Thursday and I had to have something to give people. And Mr. Baxter had to see my car gone because I said I was going to Falmouth.

Coming out with my arm around Liz, I looked down at Bay View. Maybe I'd see my "brother" in a window. I'd call Mr. Baxter later; maybe the son would answer. It had to be a son or nephew, because Mr. Baxter had greeted him so effusively. Maybe he was the son of some friends. He was *somebody's* son, and right then I didn't feel good enough to be anybody's son *or* boyfriend.

We got in my car, and I checked my hair in the rearview mirror. Liz laughed and pulled at it. I tried to laugh the way a guy in my Exercise folder would laugh. I thought, *Mr. Baxter's son has nice hair.*

As I turned onto Goody Barron Road, my phone rang. ("Goody" is short for "Goodwife," which is what Pilgrims called married women. I wondered if Liz would end up as Goody Wallace. The thought made me feel hopeful and sad at the same time.)

It was Mom. She figured out I was in the car and told me to pull over while we talked. I just slowed down, but Liz was looking around at the traffic, worried about me driving and talking, so I pulled over and Liz mouthed, "Sorry!" and I mouthed, "It's okay."

Mom was fretting because I hadn't answered last night. Aunt Lillian was better. They would be back tomorrow. Mom and Liz called out hellos to each other; then we hung up, and I pulled out onto the road.

I had hoped they would be home when we got back from shopping. They'd met Liz before, obviously, but each time I brought her home, I felt like once again I was showing off that I could do this. I wondered, though, if they got it—how Liz made me special. Or was supposed to.

I wanted something to happen between me and Liz, but I didn't want to come back this afternoon, just the two of us, with Mr. Baxter and his son next door. Had he already asked the son to work tomorrow? When we got to Barnes & Noble I'd call and ask if I could come back. (I'd tell Liz something.) Maybe the son would answer. He'd become my friend. One day we'd be in the store without Mr. Baxter, and—

It started to rain. Rain at Christmas! I had imagined sitting at the end of this day in Nuts 'n Beans, looking out at snow or at bare branches in the sunset. Rain ruined everything. I took Liz's hand. Her fingertips were cold. Her other hand fiddled with the heat. This was more awful than rain at Christmas: having someone I loved be, like, a strategic problem. How could that happen to my friend Cubs? What pulled me to Bay View so hard that everyone was like an obstacle?

I thought how there were really two Lizes: Liz One, the beautiful, smart, funny girl who was my friend and who I loved; and Liz Two, who was a problem. Liz One would never in a million years think Liz Two existed. If she *did* know Liz Two existed, if she knew she was an obstacle, it would break her heart. It would break mine. It would break everything, and it could never be put back the way it was. I thought, *Everyone in my life is like that!* Mom One, who I loved, and Mom Two, the problem. Dad One and Dad Two. Mr. Baxter One, Mr. Baxter Two. Blond Guy One, Blond Guy Two. Everyone was a problem because I had stuff in my head I couldn't talk about. The situation was so bad that, in fact, there weren't any Ones. Until I said what I had to say, everyone was a Two.

Well, I had to get to B&N. I looked at Liz. I loved her. I did. Maybe this wasn't so bad. I wouldn't think about Bay View or Mr. Baxter or the son. I sped up. Liz placed her hand on my leg, and I slowed down again. "Sorry, Cubs," I said.

I know the situation between Liz and me sounds awful. But at the time I thought, *If I solve just one last little thing, we'll be free.* Like when you walk through underbrush. Like when you get stuck in beach roses, out on the marsh. They are wicked. One false move and your skin's scratched everywhere, and they catch your clothes, and suddenly you're pulled in ten different directions. Like the plants own you. You have to stop and undo the thorns almost one by one. Finally you undo the last one, and you run free. How I dealt with my parents seems underhanded, too, but I was trying to be normal. When I got rid of the last thorn I'd be the son they wanted. I guess there was also a Jim One and a Jim Two. I was Jim Two to everyone now, but I would be Jim One, soon. Just a few more thorns to go.

I even thought there was a Wallaçonia One and Wallaçonia Two. The first one was the kingdom from my childhood, where everything was the way I said it was. In the second one, it was like I'd lost a war, and the walls were collapsing in on me.

At the mall we stood under the B&N awning with the rain pattering down, while I called Bay View. Liz huddled beside me, putting up her hair. Mr. Baxter answered. He didn't sound that happy to hear from me. He asked about Aunt Lillian, and I had to fake it. "We think she'll be okay . . . they want to be on the safe side . . ." Liz looked at me as she fixed the elastic thing in her hair. I still didn't know what the matter was with Aunt Lillian. I said it was her heart and hoped I was close. Liz put on lip gloss, rubbed her lips together, and snuggled against me. I kissed the top of her head. She was so warm. Goody Wallace. How could this be wrong? Same question I asked when I looked at guys in my Exercise folder: *How can this be wrong?* I thought of the elegant blond boy. *How could he be wrong?* I pushed the thought away and inhaled the smell of Liz's shampoo. There were two kinds of thorns: practical stuff that hung me up; and thoughts that hung me up. With thoughts, I'd tell myself, *This'll be the last time I'll think that.* Or, *Now that X has finally happened, I'll never have to feel Y again.*

I asked about maybe working tomorrow. Mr. Baxter said, "Oh," and hesitated, which made me feel lousy. "You don't have to be in Falmouth tomorrow?" "No," I said lamely. Then he said, "Let me have a word with—" I didn't get the name. It was the son, I guessed. When he came back on, he said, "Jim? We aren't sure about tomorrow yet." My heart sank. "*We.*" The two of them were deciding if *I* could come back. I felt small. I turned to Liz. I clutched her and kissed the top of her head hard a few times. It was supposed to ground me again, but it didn't quite.

Okay, it *had* to be a son or nephew or some kind of obligation. I couldn't bear thinking they were two guys *attracted* to each other. If so, why hadn't *I* attracted Mr. Baxter? Except I didn't want to. I shouldn't want to. Except I did. I sort of *liked* that I wanted to attract him. I also wanted to attract Liz—and my parents. How could I earn all that love? When I didn't get stuff in school, Dad said I was smart but lazy. Was I lazy at love?

Thorns. See?

Mr. Baxter said I should check in later. "Or I could come by when I get back," I said. That made Liz look up. Now she'd ask about the whole thing. "Around three?" I added.

He said okay. I wished he had said it more enthusiastically. I could go there anytime I wanted. But I wanted him to invite me. I mumbled "Thanks" and hung up.

"Who was that?" Liz said.

I literally couldn't believe what I told her.

CHAPTER 8

ALL WET

IRONICALLY, I TOLD her the truth. I just couldn't believe how I said it. I said, kind of gruffly, "This guy, Baxter. Lives next door. Might want me to work in his store." Like I didn't know him or really care.

She just said, "Oh. Okay." After a pause she added, "I didn't know." After another pause she asked, "Is this something that you . . . ?"
"What?" I said.
"No. Nothing," she said. Then after another little pause, "I just didn't know if—"
"What?"
"Nothing. I guess."
And then we were inside B&N. I said we had to go our separate ways so she wouldn't see what I was getting for her.

As I went off into Fiction, I thought, *I can do this. It'll be okay.* It had to be. How could the other thing possibly happen to me? If I focused, I could beat it. I suddenly thought of the blond son at Bay View, and I felt elated. A present I'd get to unwrap at the end of the day. And it wasn't gay or anything. Just a mystery. Exciting. Not gay. Yeah, it would all be okay.

We each got what we needed; when we met again, Liz seemed to have forgotten about "this guy, Baxter." As we hunched under the umbrella and hurried over to Salt Spray Gifts, I held her close and massaged her arm.

Salt Spray had a sign on the door: "VISIT OUR NEW LOCATION, 520 ALEWIFE POND ROAD, SO. SICAS-SETT."

Inside we were surrounded by Christmasy smells— potpourri and perfumey candles. A brass band played "Away in a Manger" from little speakers. Everything was natural, like pieces of the forest and the beach— pinecones, driftwood, and shells—had come in to snuggle on the shelves. I thought about wind chimes for Mom. But she might not like the sound, and it might be a pain to put them up. With Mom, you had to stick with the tried and true. One Christmas some-one gave us this exotic jam, and she wouldn't eat it. She said, "I prefer the jam we always have. I like every day to be just like the day before." That's how she wanted me, too: exactly how I was yesterday and the day before.

Lily-of-the-valley hand cream was one thing she liked every time, plus I knew she was out of it. Still, I lingered over the wind chimes. I loved the idea that they made music according to how the wind blew. I tried to explain this to Liz. She knew my mom, though; she said there'd be complications we couldn't foresee. I knew that. I just wanted her for one second to get why I thought wind chimes were cool. In the end, of course, I went for the hand cream.

Unfortunately, Mom was not the only one out of lily-of-the-valley. Salt Spray had verbena, chamomile, and beach rose, but no lily-of-the-valley. The girl at the counter made a sad face, like she was a live emoji. But she offered to call the store in South Sicassett.

They had lily-of-the-valley. They would hold some for us, if we wanted to go over. I said okay, and Liz thanked her.

Liz had all these ideas for other things we could get Mom or other places we could get hand cream. She searched on her phone. I kept saying it had to be Salt Spray's own brand (not necessarily true) because I'd seen that sign for the store in South Sicassett, and I'd been thinking about Nate Flederbaum. That's where he lived. Where he might be home from school for the holidays. Where I might see what he was like now. Maybe he was sterling. I liked happy endings for other people, even though I couldn't imagine one for myself.

Liz said maybe Salt Spray distributed to other stores, and one of them might be close. She wanted to go back and ask.

"No," I said, "I really want to go to So-Sick. It's better to buy directly 'cause, you know. . . . Plus, there's this friend I have over there. I haven't seen him in, like, forever. I'd just want to say hi. I mean, we're not that close." Liz made her concerned frown, like she was mentally texting me a question mark. "It's just been a while," I said, "and I really want to!"

"All right," she said softly. Like I was getting worked up. Maybe I was. I just wanted to be near Nate, to think how I *might* see him, a sweet guy, come of age. I promised it wouldn't take long. Liz pointed out that So-Sick was halfway back to her house, and we could have met there if we'd known. I didn't say anything. I just wanted to get this thorn out.

The rain hadn't let up, only now it was freezing. As I drove, Liz kept holding her breath and saying, "Careful, careful." I liked thinking she said it because I was daring and dangerous. She really said it because she'd been taught definite ways to do things, like drive on ice, and she fretted if people didn't do them just so. I tried to control the car. There were a lot of blind curves. Finally the trees opened up and we saw the town hall, a clam shack closed up for the winter, and beyond it the docks and the bay. On our right were a few frilly little shops, decorated for Christmas. Salt Spray here was tiny. Inside, a chorus sang "I Wonder as I Wander." At the counter was this pale, sad-looking guy, dressed in a mother's idea of nice— pressed black pants and a V-neck sweater and an Oxford button-down. I had an outfit like that that Mom bought me, and I didn't wear it. He also had acne. He spoke to Liz, but he kept looking at me, warily, like I would hit him. When he stopped speaking his lips still moved, like he was having a conversation with an invisible person. In a country called Wallaçonia. He wasn't attractive, but I wanted to touch him. There was just no way to. They had the hand cream.

After the guy rang it up, he held the bag out. He still didn't look at me, but I took it and said, "Thank you." Then I said, "Excuse me." He started. "Would you know where a family named Flederbaum lives?" He stared at a point between me and Liz. "They have a son, Nate . . . ?" He shook his head. "No?" I said. "It's somewhere around here." Like a bozo I said, "South Sicassett," as if he didn't know where we were. Liz tugged at my arm. I backed away saying, "Okay, thanks." At the door I looked back one last time. He was watching, with this kind of pleading look in his eyes. He turned away and pretended to do something businesslike. Then we were outside, huddled against the store so we wouldn't get wet.

We tiptoed to the car, almost slipping and getting stung by the freezing rain. I convinced Liz to let me try one more time. We ran in little mincing steps over to this pizza place and asked about the Flederbaums. No one knew. When the convenience store next door didn't know, Liz suggested, in a helpful but tense voice, that the real estate agent on the corner had to have some kind of directory. We slipped and slid up to their door and pushed in.

The woman there had a phone book, but the Flederbaums weren't in it. She asked, "Are you familiar with South Sicassett? If so, you are aware that many residents choose to live here for the privacy and seclusion. They would not be listed—" She seemed suddenly to notice we were wet. "Would you step back, please?" she said. "You're dripping." She closed the book and took it back.

So I wasn't good enough to know someone in So-Sick. That made me more determined to find Nate. I could at least look at his house and sympathize, imagining him in there and his whole life of being picked on. I could *locate* him. I could be at rest. "Why is this Nate so important?" Liz asked, trying to stay cheery. I was sure it was hard for her with the rain coming down and the cold and what she thought was wasted time.

Around the corner from the real estate office was a cleaner's that looked closed, but I pulled Liz step by tiny step up to it anyway. I cupped my hand to the window and saw people inside in greenish-gray light. "Just one more," I promised. "I mean, we're here, right?" One last thorn.

Liz shrugged. Her hair was plastered to her scalp. I pushed into the cleaner's. She toddled in after me. There was an electronic ding-dong. An overweight black-haired woman with a flowery dress and a bright green coat and green purse was carrying on about something to the woman behind the counter. When the counter woman looked at me, the black-haired woman broke off and looked, too—like, to make a point of how inconvenient I was.

"May I help you?" the counter woman said. The black-haired woman looked back and forth, not knowing the one to blame for the interruption.

"I'm just wondering," I said, "if anyone can tell me where a family named Flederbaum lives. Here in—"

The black-haired woman's eyes blazed. "I am Freda Flederbaum," she said. She came at me like she'd steamroll me. "What do you want with my family?"

"Nothing!" I said. I was totally not ready for this. I backed up and bumped into Liz, who said, "Ouch!" I turned to see what "Ouch!" was. When I turned back, Mrs. Flederbaum was in my face.

"Why are you asking where my family lives? What do you want with us?"

"I just . . . I'm a . . . I was Nate's fr— I mean, I went to school with Nate, and I—"

"You know Nathaniel?" she snapped.

"Yes!" I said. That should help.

"Are you one of the boys who beat him up?"

"One of . . . ? No!"

"I bet you know who did!"

"I don't know anything!" She had me backed almost to the door.

"Like hell you don't!" she snapped. "You keep your lousy, stinking hands off my son!" I opened my mouth, but she cut me off. "You and your lousy, rotten friends!" She put a finger in my face. "I know what you did! I should call the cops! Throw your stinking be-hinds in jail! Go around ganging up on a helpless kid. Your parents should beat the daylights out of you. That'd teach you!"

Liz and I bumped into each other in our attempt to get out. She let out another "Ouch!" and said under her breath, "Let's please just get out of here!" I man-aged two more sentences to Mrs. Flederbaum—"I didn't do anything! I knew Nate in school!"—and then I was out the door, where I slipped on the ice and went down, wham, on my butt on the sidewalk. No elegant recovery for me!

Liz tried to help. Mrs. Flederbaum was standing in the doorway, oblivious to the rain, yelling, "You rotten, stinking kids can all go to hell!" A few people were looking. Then she actually spat at me. It didn't get on me, but it made me feel creepy, especially in front of Liz. But it also made me think Mrs. Flederbaum was so nuts I didn't have to pay attention to anything she said. I pulled away from Liz, slid on my butt over to a bike rack, and grabbed it and pulled myself up. The bell on the cleaner's door ding-donged. Mrs. Flederbaum had disappeared. What did you have to feel inside to scream like that? In a weird way I felt sorry for her. I felt ashamed of myself. I couldn't look at Liz. Maybe she believed Mrs. Flederbaum. Liz tended to believe parents, teachers, news anchors, or whoever. I managed to stammer, "I *never* did *anything* like she said. Honest." Liz said quietly, "I believe you." But the whole thing must have seemed ludicrous to her. Whose idea of a dream date would this be, *ever?* She had to know something was majorly weird about the whole thing. It was right in front of her! "It's okay," she said, putting her small, white hand out to me. "How can I help?"

We had lost the umbrella. Suddenly, and more loudly, Liz stated, "I am *not* going back in there!" For the first time we laughed just a little. We stumbled to the car, pelted by ice. We passed people and I wondered if they had heard Mrs. Flederbaum. Did they believe her? She couldn't have been talking about middle school, though. Someone must have beat up Nate recently. How bad? Was he in the hospital? Should I go see him? I wished I could make it better for him.

I felt beaten up now. I had landed on my elbow, and my butt hurt, and my shoulder. I was panting and my heart thudded. We had to chip ice from the car door handles to get in. I wondered if the guy at Salt Spray was watching. And thinking what? We finally got into the car. I sat aching, holding Liz's hand limply and staring straight into a curtain of ice on the windshield. All I could discern was blobby shapes and contorted colors.

I was almost relieved that I had to get out again to scrape the windows. I felt around on the floor of the back seat for the scraper. I wanted to be home, alone, and forget all this. Mr. Baxter and his son seemed far off now. I was so bruised and wet I couldn't have anything to do with them. How could I just fix all this? How could I fix what Liz was thinking?

I couldn't find our wide, new scraper with the long handle. I just found an old, little one that kept slipping out of my hand. It was worn at one end so the blade didn't scrape a wide, clear path but a wobbly trail I had to go over and over while Liz watched through the window, her brow making that little concerned tent. Finally it was good enough. I got back in, threw the scraper into the back where it came from, and tried to get in gear. I knew I'd missed a spot. Actually, I hadn't missed it; I'd ignored it. I'd thrown the scraper into the back seat just hard enough to let Liz know she shouldn't say anything. I felt lousy. I put the car back in park, took the scraper, got out, and scraped the part I'd missed. I wanted to cry, but I managed to get us moving without shedding a tear.

After a day like that, a car wreck would have been just perfect, so I did exactly fifteen miles an hour and stared at the center of the road. Liz sat quietly for a couple of miles. Finally she said something that stunned me. Looking out the passenger window, in this hard, cold voice, she said, "She's the one who beats him." I couldn't believe what I'd heard, so I said, "Say what?" Liz turned to me. "She's the one. And she's afraid someone will find out, so she accuses you.

I can't tell you how much I hate her!" Then she looked out the passenger window again and was silent.

I felt relieved, but I felt horrible for Nate. Could it actually be true? Now I was the one who wanted an adult to be right. Mrs. Flederbaum had sort of been right. There was a time in middle school when she would have been totally right. I never hit Nate, but I'd made him feel lousy, and that was almost as bad. But what Liz said. She was just angry. Maybe mostly at me.

Something caught my eye by the side of the road: a half-house.

Half-houses are this old-time Cape thing. Fathers built them for their unmarried daughters. The daughter married and had kids, and the husband built onto the house till it was a "full Cape." I didn't like to see half-houses. It meant some woman had lived her whole life there; no man ever came and everyone knew. Even though I was a guy, and in spite of Liz, I somehow thought I'd end up in a half-house. Mr. Baxter had a full house, because he'd married his books. That seemed like a good deal right now. You can't fail your books or your maps.

We slipped and fishtailed. I began to go over fifteen. I had to get home before Mr. Baxter's "son" left. I had to see him. We finally lurched down our driveway. The Hummer was still there. Pointing down to the barn, I said, "I gotta go down and see what this Baxter guy wants." I stopped, turned off everything, and put on the emergency brake. I was such a fake and a traitor.

"I'll come with you!" Liz said cheerily.

"It might take a while."

"For what? He offers the job, you say yes or no."

"Yeah!" I said. "But there's, y'know, paperwork and scheduling."

"You mean a W-4? That takes no time."

"I know!" Of course I did. I'd already filled one out!

"Besides, bozo," she said, rumpling my hair, "it's a *bookstore*. I can look at the books!" I took a deep breath. Her face fell. She looked away and said softly, "It seems you just don't want me around right now."

I didn't say anything. I checked my phone. Nothing. With all the ice, my parents were definitely not coming back tonight.

One last thorn. I took Liz's hand and tried to explain in my most honest voice how the thing with Mrs. Flederbaum had shaken me up, plus it made me worried about "my friend Nate." I added Aunt Lillian into the mix. What all that had to do with Liz coming to the bookstore or not, even I didn't know, but finally she said she understood. She brightened up. "I'll make hot chocolate for when you come back!" she said.

I kissed her cheek and said, "That'd be great, Cubs!" We snuggled up to each other and kissed several times.

I almost fell again getting out of the car. I saw Liz to our door, unlocked it for her, and told her I'd be back as soon as I could.

I couldn't get to the barn down the icy center of the driveway, so I climbed through the drifts on one side. I plunged my feet deep into the snow. It got in my boots, but I kept going. The barn drew close. I saw someone in a window. He was there! Now there was a fence. The only way to the barn from there was down the center of the driveway. It wouldn't be that bad. I hopped from the drift into the driveway, slipped a little, and when I tried to rescue myself elegantly, the way *he* had, I went down smack on my belly and slid into a huge puddle. The first thing I imagined was Liz seeing me out a window, and she'd come running. I wanted to scream. I couldn't, though, and that made me want to scream more. I nearly choked on the frustration.

I wasn't just a little wet. I was belly-flopped in ice water. I had cut my hand on the ice, and it was bleeding. I couldn't go home and change. The son would leave. I'd have to go into Bay View and stand dripping in front of them.

I got up, slipped and went down *again*, this time on my ass.

At that point (*damn*, it was cold! *damn*, I was wet!) I wanted to give up. Maybe this was a sign for me to go home. Tears stung my eyes. I stood up slowly and painfully. I had acted like people were watching, because they probably were—Liz on one side, Baxter & Son on the other. Water poured off me. I was soaked. I was frozen and I was shaking.

Some people laugh this stuff off. I had no idea what it was like to laugh stuff off. The world had kicked me, and I had nothing left. Stepping through the Bay View door, there was not one thing to make me look good. I was nothing, but I had to keep going.

Right away Mr. Baxter saw me and stopped in his tracks. "Goodness!" he said. "What happened to you?"

"I fell." I couldn't see the son anywhere.

Mr. Baxter told me to take my coat off. I did. I had grime all over and blood from a cut on my hand. I heard footsteps. *Not now*, I thought. Then he came out from the bookshelves and stood in front of me.

Wait.

The "son."

The "hunk."

My "replacement."

It was Nate Flederbaum.

All grown up.

Nate Flederbaum.

Right in front of me like a miracle.

CHAPTER 9

CRASHING IN

OKAY. SO.

Pat Baxter was friends with—maybe somehow even loved—the kid I had picked on in middle school. Of all people. This was a conspiracy! I wanted to say, "No. You *can't be* friends with Nate Flederbaum."

I kind of stared. Nate had lost his baby fat since middle school. He looked like he worked out. His butt was still round, but firm. The braces were gone, and his hair was short. It shone like Christmas decorations. Or Hanukkah decorations, I guess. His face was thinner and just so beautiful and serious and sad, with just a little overbite. He was all perfect and good in a yellow V-neck sweater and pressed khakis and suede saddle shoes with lines of salt on the toes. His blue eyes stared, but I couldn't meet them. Instead, I looked up and down his body. What was he like under those clothes? Bruised but strong. I thought of what Liz said. Could it be? He blushed and looked away. Blushing and in profile he was even more beautiful. I felt my heart pound, and I felt some kind of burden fall away. I was expanding and rising like a balloon.

I guessed maybe this was what I was supposed to feel with Liz, but I didn't very much. But for the moment, I was too dazed to worry about it.

Mr. Baxter told Nate to go get a bathrobe, blanket, and slippers he had in back. I tried to say I didn't have time. "My girlfr—" I began.

"Oh, and by the way," Mr. Baxter said, "Jim, Nathanael. Nathanael, Jim."

Nate nodded, barely looking at me. Now I was the boy in Salt Spray Gifts, unable to face Nate. He turned and went off among the shelves before Mr. Baxter could say more.

"We can at least wring those things out," he said, "and hang them over the stove." He got out some rope and tied it to two beams so it hung right over the stove.

I'd have to explain all this to Liz. But a weird thing was happening. Time was paused or was sort of stretching. I had no idea how long I'd been there. I was just slowly sinking into the warmth and Mr. Baxter being in charge and how beautiful Nate was. I felt bad about Liz, but I couldn't help it. Okay, this would be the last thorn to get free of. In a couple of minutes I'd text her.

Nate came back with the bathrobe and stuff. He didn't look at me; he just handed it to Mr. Baxter, who told me to change in the Employees Only room and wring out my clothes in the bathroom. Nate went back into the bookshelves, like a clam digging down faster than you can dig after it. I went to change.

I was so relieved to be dry that I didn't think of this as sexual—me undressing and putting on Mr. Baxter's robe, right next to my skin. I closed the robe tight so my chest didn't show. But my calves showed, and I didn't put on the slippers (too refined), so I felt my bare feet on the wooden floor, and I felt exposed. I brought my wet clothes with me. I'd slipped my underpants into my backpack. That would be too much to expose. Mr. Baxter palmed a log into the stove, his fingers spread, his hands strong. Then he hung my clothes over the stove. I looked around for Nate, but I neither saw nor heard him.

Suddenly Mr. Baxter demanded, "Is that *blood*?" He peered at my hand.

"Not much," I said. I'd only skinned myself. He took a couple of strides and pulled a first-aid kit from behind the counter.

I felt weird but kind of good just sitting there naked underneath the bathrobe, the terrycloth roughly caressing me. I stretched out my bare feet. As he brought the kit, I thought I saw Mr. Baxter stop a second and look at them. I thought of Liz again. How long had it been? Ten minutes? Okay. So. Ten minutes more. Max, fifteen. In a second I'd text her.

Mr. Baxter knelt and took my hand. I moved my skin a little against his. He dabbed my cut with hydrogen peroxide. He'd never been that close to me before. My hand rested on my knee as he dabbed; I could sense the distance from our hands to my dick. I started to get aroused. I put my legs together; then he was done. He handed me a Band-Aid and stood. I put it on myself. I wished for him to come back, but he had already taken the first-aid kit back behind the counter.

The kettle roared and bubbled. Mr. Baxter called Nate, who declined coffee, so we made it for the two of us. I saw no envelopes waiting to be mailed. Did Nate know about *Hunk*? Nate in his pullover seemed like he could stare right at *Hunk* and get what it was, but he wouldn't let it get to him. He could stare at me, too, and not let me get to him.

Was it fifteen minutes now? Outside it was dark. Five more minutes and I'd go. I didn't need to text. Liz would understand. Mr. Baxter asked how the day went and how Aunt Lillian was. I said we were still "concerned," but she was okay, and he didn't pry any further. That's a Mom word—*pry*. We never pried. To use another Mom word, prying was "unsuitable."

Mr. Baxter asked again how I got soaked.

"I was coming to say I can work tomorrow," I said hopefully. So I wouldn't have to see his reaction, I stood and felt my clothes. Still cold and wet.

"Oh," he said and called, "Nathanael?" So Nate got to decide? I got even more nervous. I felt my clothes again just for something to do. Just as cold and just as wet. I began to take them down. Mr. Baxter looked surprised. "My girlfr—" I began. Nate appeared. With a clap of his hands, Mr. Baxter suddenly decreed the two of us would work together tomorrow, "If," he added, nodding to Nate, "that's all right with you." Nate nodded. "Sure," he mumbled. Why did Mr. Baxter need his permission? Because he was beautiful. The beautiful ones run things. Nate turned to go back into the shelves. I wondered this so hard I almost thought for a half a second that I'd said it out loud:

WHAT THE HECK WAS HE DOING HERE???

Instead I asked, "Will there be enough work?" Was I so concerned about Mr. Baxter's finances? No. I was afraid he pitied me and was helping me hit the reset button.

"Absolutely!" he said with a little smile. "We are down to the wire!" Christmas was four days away.

Nate came out the end of an aisle, glanced at us, but not really *at* us, and disappeared again. Did he even recognize me? Was middle school not such a big deal to him anymore? Something about me was throwing him off. I shuddered at the memory of his mother screaming. Did she tell Nate about me? Or would she? And what about what Liz said—"She's the one who beats him"?

Suddenly the door jerked and the bells jingled. And in came Liz.

"Cubby, it's been more than half an hour!" she said. "I texted, and I called! I thought something terrible happened!"

My stomach sank. Liz was so sensitive about saying stuff in front of other people, and Nate and Mr. Baxter were strangers to her. Now I had to confess in front of everyone that I'd left my phone in my jacket and been thoughtless. Liz stared at the bathrobe, while I tried to explain what happened. I introduced her to Mr. Baxter, "the guy I'm—uh—working for," as I put it. He flushed, but he smiled appropriately, shook her hand firmly, said his name, and then stepped back. Nate emerged from the shelves, stopped, and stared at Liz with a blank expression, and she stared at him and blinked and swallowed. Nate cut his eyes at me. We had this moment—just a fraction of a second—where I thought he got my whole dilemma. Then he looked at Pat. I looked at them all. The room was full of Ones and Twos. I couldn't keep track of them all. I looked at Nate, and I thought again how beautiful he was. I was proud of him. After all the abuse, he had come out so beautiful. I was thinking this right in front of my girlfriend! I looked to Mr. Baxter, thinking he might make this all okay. He watched Liz with this still expression, like he was smiling inside.

Nate crossed right between us all and checked the computer, like he was going to have a normal, responsible day no matter what. Liz and I went to each other. "So, I fell," I said again. "I was frozen." I held up my hand. "I was bleeding." She reached up and arranged my wet hair and called me "poor thing," then went back to how long it had been. Nate and Mr. Baxter were whispering. About me and Liz? The room felt stifling. A knot popped in the stove. I squirmed. Liz saw and backed away. "No," I said softly. "It's okay." I rearranged my robe, like it was why I had to squirm. I just had to get free of this thorn. Except now I had Nate to deal with. For a whole day tomorrow. I looked at him, talking to Mr. Baxter. His lips moving. I had a totally inappropriate, inconvenient thought. I'd looked at guys and pictures of guys, and yes, I knew what guys did together. Genital-wise, okay? But I had never thought that much about guys kissing. I'd never thought about ever wanting to do that myself to a guy.

Until now.

Until I saw Nate's lips, as he whispered to Mr. Baxter. I remembered those lips. Nate had that little overbite, so his lips moved in a slightly unpredictable, jaunty way, right close to Mr. Baxter's ear. Mr. Baxter leaned into him.

I imagined them kissing. *Shit!*

"I think maybe I'd better go," Liz said, in a low, chilly voice.

"No!" I said. I began pulling my clothes off the rope, so hard that some of them fell. The rope bounced around. Nate and Mr. Baxter looked. My undershirt hit the top of the stove. He ran to rescue it. "Just hang on," I said, looking back at Liz and trying to keep my voice low enough so it would be between the two of us. "Just . . . my clothes . . . because . . ."

She came over to me. "Jim," she said, quietly but definitely, "there is something going on. I don't know what it is, and you haven't told me, but it's been going on all day. There have been phone calls and trips we have to take to Heaven-knows-where and screaming people out of nowhere and forty minutes of you *here* . . ." She looked around and repeated "*here*," as though she was still trying to figure out where we actually were. ". . . with not a word to me. And I am not going to ask what this is all about but I think that maybe I had better just go home."

"No, please," I said, glancing at Mr. Baxter, who was suddenly busy at the computer. (Nate was gone again, the clam digging down.) I was scared I would lose my girlfriend. Then what would I have? She headed to the door. "I'll call you!" I said, so our exchange would look normal to Mr. Baxter and Nate, if they were listening. She slammed the door with a jingle. I felt awful, but I had this weird, tiny glimmer: now maybe I'd never have to tell her. She'd just never speak to me again, I'd have to explain to people somehow, but then I'd go off to college and, presto! Out of the thorn bush. (And into what? What would I do at college? And would I take Mr. Baxter's advice? Where would I even be going?)

Neither Nate nor Mr. Baxter acknowledged hearing Liz's and my conversation. After she shut the door, Mr. Baxter looked up and smiled, quite genuinely, and said, "Pretty girl." I managed a grin and said, "Thanks." I threw my clothes back over the line, kind of haphazardly. Then I sat and took a sip of coffee. For a while, the two of them worked in silence. Another knot popped. Finally Nate brought Mr. Baxter a handful of books and orders and said, soft and low, "I'm done." He put his jacket on without looking at me. Mr. Baxter reminded us both about tomorrow. Nate nodded. When he left, I couldn't tell if he closed the door normally or maybe slammed it a little. Two of them mad at me. Great!

Mr. Baxter worked quietly on as though me being there was the most natural thing in the world. I reached up and felt my clothes. They seemed almost dry now. I went and checked my phone. Nothing from Liz. I came back, took my clothes, and went to get dressed.

My clothes were still plenty cold. I started shivering and couldn't stop. I hugged myself hard. Mr. Baxter counted money and shut off the computers. The lights were off except up front. He put an elastic around a bundle of bills and another around credit card receipts. "Have you thought more about our talk last night?" he said. "Berkshires versus Boston?" I was still shivering. There was so much stuff I didn't know how to ask.

"A little," I said.

He pointed at me. "Put that stuff in the dryer when you get home!" he said. "Anyway, I hope you don't mind, but I did go online for some research. The place in the Berkshires—sixty-some percent of your classmates will be from within a hundred and fifty miles. Eighty percent from 'the Northeast.'" He shut the register. "Boston, of course, is a different picture." He went for his coat. All the new information disconcerted me, but I also liked that he had done so much just for me. It was like putting on the hydrogen peroxide without being asked. Still, I had made my college decision, and now this. I mumbled that we'd have to see if I got in anywhere. "Oh, of course you will!" he said. "You're around a three-point-five, right? GPA?" Mr. Baxter said. I nodded. "How about extracurriculars. Did you rejoin the choir?"

I stared at him. I had quit choir after freshman year. It took up a lot of time, and doing all that stuff wasn't going to help my one big problem. But how did he know?

"I talked to your father a while back. He hoped you'd get back into choir with college coming up." Yeah, Dad had pressured me about that before school started last summer. Mr. Baxter had his coat on and was tying his scarf. I zipped up but didn't put on gloves. "College admission people," he said, "like that kind of thing."

I mentioned I was in the Science Club and had presented last spring at a science fair in Hartford. "That's good," he said. But he said it like science fair wasn't quite enough.

Outside, the freezing rain made prickly, crackly sounds in the bushes. The cold went through to my skin and made me shudder. I marched in place to get warm, but it didn't help. "Gloves?" Mr. Baxter asked and smiled like he felt sorry for me. For more than being cold. For a second I thought he might hug me. "You'd better get home!" he said. I nodded. My teeth chattered. He locked up, then paused. He looked at me and smiled broadly. It seemed no matter what I did or said, he still liked me. I smiled back, then looked away.

He led the way up the driveway, choosing each step carefully. Everything was insanely slick. I heard the wind in the pines, fighting through. Sometimes he would choose a place for his foot, try the ice, gauging like an expert, and then choose a different place. I followed, putting my feet pretty much right where he put his. Suddenly he took a long stride up. I felt he was leaving me behind, like I couldn't make that same stride. He turned and reached a hand back to me. "It's especially bad there," he said. I took his hand. He pulled, shifting his weight like he knew what he was doing, and suddenly I was up and over the slick patch. "You okay?" he said. I nodded. Of course. I was always okay. I tried to remember just how I had felt taking his hand and holding onto it. I could still feel it. But he had gone on, easier now, the way more level.

At his mailbox we said, "See you tomorrow." He pointed at my clothes and said, "Get those into a dryer!" He knew I would. He was just telling me what he'd do for me, if he could. I said I would, then I picked my way toward our back door.

The choir thing reminded me of Mr. Groff, my freshman English teacher, who coached intramural cross-country and told me I should go out for it. I'd said I was no good at sports. He said, "Anyone can run." He told me about a guy who'd never done any athletics and ended up on varsity cross-country just by sticking with it. My first thought was, *I bet he was good with girls, too.* I told Mr. Groff I'd think about it. The next time he asked I said "Too busy" or something. He looked sad. As he walked away, I wished I knew how to accept stuff and refuse it at the same time. To take stuff but not be taken. To be sterling and upright and still be me.

I said no a lot. I thought that if I "showed initiative," as Mr. Fusco, our guidance counselor, put it, the messed-up parts of me would show. If I stepped up, people might look too close and ask questions. "He looks so nice in that track suit. You'd think the girls would be all over him!" Or they'd laugh. "Jim *Wallace?* Doing *athletics?* I guess they *will* take just anyone!"

But if I was on varsity cross-country, what good would it do? Ironically, doing sports wouldn't make turn me into one of those guys in my Exercise folder. Winning a race or singing a solo would just remind me that nothing could change the screwed-up things I felt inside. So I did nothing and hoped, and I did stuff like Science Club, where it's all intellectual and anyone can do it.

As I approached our back porch I heard a crunching sound, like footsteps. I realized I had just heard a car door shut. A voice, tough but tired, said, "Mr. Wallace?"

There was Liz. She came over and wrapped me in a huge, hard hug. "I'm so sorry, my friend," she said. I hugged back and drew her into me and kissed the top of her head. I felt a surge. We were kissing on the mouth, and in between kisses I was saying, "No, I'm sorry. I'm really sorry." I kissed hard, and it felt really right. Relieved and horny kind of work together.

"Why don't we go in?" she whispered. I just kissed her more. I was completely aroused. Liz pulled away and laughed. "Go on in," she said, her eyes twinkling. "I think you should put those clothes in the dryer."

My heart thumped. I knew where she was going. As she turned to the door I trailed my hand down her back and gave her a little pat on the butt. She looked back and smiled. I reached around her to fit in the key, and she turned and locked her arms around me hard.

We beelined to the laundry room. I kept chatting while I stripped. I wasn't nervous about stripping. I wanted to stop Liz from asking more about Mrs. Flederbaum and Nate. I had to remember, she didn't know that was Nate down at Bay View; plus, she thought I'd agreed to work at Bay View just that day, and I'd made it sound like I barely knew "this guy, Baxter." At this point, there were Ones, Twos, and maybe even some Threes and Fours, whoever they might be, all over the place. Pretty soon, though, none of it would matter. I was down to my underpants. These boring old gray boxer briefs. But they left no doubt I was excited!

Liz came over and kissed me. I kind of engulfed her in my arms and kissed back big and hard. I was so grateful. All the worrying and wondering and guessing and second-guessing and lying and hating myself would be over. I'd be one thing, I'd know what it was, and so would everyone else. I slipped my hand under her sweater, kneaded her breast, and pressed myself against her. She looked down. "You aren't going to dry those?" she said.

"Sure," I said. I stripped off my underpants like nothing and tossed them in the dryer. She knelt down.

And that was how Liz and I finally got to do what everyone does, what everyone talks about, and what everyone expects. And now I would become what she and I and my parents and everyone wanted and expected: a strong and normal and dutiful and sterling and upright young man, everyone's hero, on my way to a great future. Nate and Mr. Baxter were good and nice enough, and I would always be an "ally," but I would leave them behind.

She took my hand, and we went to the living room couch. (It turned out we both had rubbers. I thought it was sexy using hers and having her put it on me.)

It was strange and thrilling, touching her just casually in places I'd never touched anyone, her letting me, me owning those places, and her touching me in places no one had touched me. Everything warm and so sensitive. And how she smiled when she did it. How I smiled. It was like the whole universe was watching and was proud. That made being naked even greater. My whole body felt what was actually happening, plus how good I was now.

I felt my heartbeat—and hers—but the whole thing felt calm, too, like something greater than us took over and held us. It had been a huge thing to think about all those years, like having to climb Everest alone with no parka and equipment or whatever. I had worried so much about my body, thinking it couldn't do anything real, and now the time had come and I knew what I was doing. We both did, and I actually felt in charge. It felt great physically because I felt like I *was* someone.

It transpired pretty much the way I'd heard (and heard and heard and heard), but it was present and intense, like in slo-mo and HD. Her eyes, all still and liquidy, looked up into mine, trusting me, enjoying me. *Me.* I could look back at her for only so long. Then I shut my eyes, but shivers still ran through me, making my breath come in gasps. Then I looked again. Beautiful Liz, my friend, just as she'd always been. I was in her. We were together. We could never be apart now.

She was so alive and responsive, so different than my hand or anything I'd used before. It was kind of animalistic. I saw how she really cared, how much this meant to her. And I was doing it. I was on track. All that other stuff was just some little part of me like it was some little part of everyone, probably, that didn't matter. I stroked her hair and asked if it was okay. She smiled and made a couple of readjustments. Typical Liz, practical: what I loved, what I was thrilled and proud to be inside of. It was sort of apparent she had done it before, if you know what I mean. I wondered who with. Images of some guys we knew flashed in my head, but I didn't need them now!

For a second at the beginning, I'd actually been afraid I'd think about my Exercise folder or Mr. Baxter putting peroxide on me. But amazingly I didn't. I felt Liz wanting me. And I felt me loving and wanting her and how easy it was, finally, like a day when the clouds are low and the water is gray and suddenly the sun comes through, the clouds break up, and the water shines with little sparkles off the points of the waves, and you watch, hypnotized.

Liz did give herself a little help. More than a little. But I'd heard that was normal. I'd imagined doing everything for her, though. I imagined Eric Cantler did everything for his girlfriend. But I guessed I shouldn't be greedy.

When we were done I held her so tight, like I was liquid poured all over her. "I love you, Cubs," I breathed, and I felt the vibration in my chest as she sighed, "I love you, too!"

And calmly, joyously, in the back of my mind, I thought, *I did it.* I was *able.* I was sterling and upright.

I went and flushed the rubber and then came back and pulled a blanket over us. My arms engulfed her. Goody Wallace. My life was happening now, the way it was supposed to. I buried my face in the side of her neck. I told her again that I loved her. For a second I thought how pleased my parents would be, except I couldn't tell them directly. But they'd like knowing their son could love normally. Suddenly, I thought of my Exercise folder. My breath caught. I knew Liz had felt it. I'd delete the whole folder, as soon as I could. I didn't need it now. I'd block all the URLs I knew.

It might be harder to delete stuff from my own memory—Nate's lips, Mr. Baxter's grip, his shoulders in that coat, me naked in his bathrobe—but I would. I didn't need that stuff now.

We said again how much we loved each other and how beautiful it had been being close like that. She laughed at me taking the rubber off and almost spilling. My Cubs. Forever. I was aroused again. We actually did it a second time. I was a little more confident and more vigorous. She flushed really red and smiled at me, her eyes half open. We had found it, and it was ours for all the cold, smoky nights with wind in the pines forever, and all the bright, blustery, salt-smelling mornings in the world. Still, from the edges of my consciousness, certain thoughts came back— Nate, peroxide, *Hunk*, Eric. I had to be alone to sort them out and delete them.

There were no more date bars, but I did make tea. We pulled a blanket down from the back of the couch and huddled under it with our mugs. We asked each other if it felt good and were we okay, and we both said yes, it was beautiful and we were okay. I had to be okay. Better than okay. Not to sound crude, but I'd just gotten the thing every guy wants. It was like this mysterious stranger had visited me but had now moved on.

Liz hadn't planned to stay. Eventually she said, "Well, Mom's waiting." (Sometimes when she said that I wondered, *Waiting for what, exactly?*) She looked at her phone and said, "She's texted, like, five times about road conditions."

I was kind of relieved, actually. I felt the need to get back to Wallaçonia. I couldn't really celebrate with Liz what had happened to me. I had to be by myself. She wouldn't understand that I was a frog turned into a prince. She'd thought I was a prince all along. A tear came to my eye. Was she right? Or was I just a frog in a prince costume?

I kissed her several more times. She kissed back, long and deep, then broke and rolled onto her back and slowly sat up.

She got dressed. I pulled my pants out of the dryer and put them on without any underwear. I'd always wanted to do that. To really have earned it. I put my arm around her and pulled her close as I saw her down to the back door. We kissed, and I got excited again. She said, "You have to work for that guy tomorrow, huh?"

"Yeah," I said and rolled my eyes.

"That blond kid is kind of a weirdo."

I felt a clutching in my chest. "He's just quiet!" I snapped, not looking at her.

She kissed me and grinned. "I say he's a weirdo!"

I shrugged. "Well, you don't know what he's been through—" Oops!

"Why? What's he been through?"

"Um, well, I dunno. That's just the point. We don't know."

She tickled me and said, "Weirdo weirdo weirdo!"

I squirmed away. "Whatever!" I said.

I said it too strong because I was annoyed. Not just by the weirdo thing. It had just occurred to me that Liz could *not* find out that the weirdo's mother was the wicked witch of So-Sick. I'd just done the most intimate thing possible with my girlfriend, and now I had to withhold information from her. How did that happen? And I was doubly annoyed because I wasn't completely sure why I had to withhold it, and I wasn't completely sure she couldn't figure it out for herself.

Liz looked hurt and I took her in my arms.

"I'm sorry," she said. "Is he some special friend of yours?"

"No!" Damn! Another lie. Kind of. The last one. I promised. "I'll call you tomorrow," I said, and I held her tight and rocked her. She apologized for calling Nate a weirdo, and I said it was okay, and I apologized for my reaction.

I walked her to her car with without putting on my jacket. She said I should have it; I just shrugged. I hoped Mr. Baxter was watching. No, I hoped he wasn't. He and I had had something, and now we wouldn't anymore. I was normal now. I kissed Liz again. She closed the car door and revved the engine, and the taillights bathed our yard in red.

She pulled away, and at last everything went dark and quiet. I walked slowly back, feeling the cold, feeling all the parts of my body work together, easily. I went in by the back door, locked up, and turned off the porch light. Mr. Baxter, putting peroxide on me. What would it be like at the store tomorrow? Would I feel better than him? That would be mean. We could be equal. Sure. I did like guys, too, in a way. I'd just found my love, and it was a girl. And she was my friend.

I realized the dryer had stopped.

I felt my clothes, then restarted it. I closed the house up, crocheted dachshunds and all. I had flushed the second rubber. As it swirled down, I thought how I had finally joined the human race. I stood on the cold tiles trying to make it as important as I'd always thought it would be. It came up a bit short. The condom disappeared. My stuff was gone. Would there be a time we'd do it and I'd be a dad? The water rose, clear, and the tank hissed. I turned out the light and went to my room.

Mr. Baxter showing me the way, making footsteps, reaching out his hand, taking mine, pulling. All of it natural and honest. *There* was the real man. I looked around my room at the shells and driftwood and guessed I shouldn't need any of it anymore. I felt empty and unprotected. I shuddered. Wallaçonia would get a new name now, and a booming economy and lots of glass towers and Ralph Lauren shops.

I couldn't delete my Exercise folder. Those guys had been through a lot with me, and I still needed them. Instead I actually opened it up and went through the photos, silently saying to each guy, "I'm like you, now. I've done what you've done." Then I realized what I was doing, and I quickly closed it.

I shucked my clothes, turned out the light, and crawled into bed. I had loved. I had done what I was supposed to do, and I did it with my friend I loved. Now all the songs and movies were about me, about us, and nothing could take that away. Except that, already, in spite of the wonder and relief I felt, the importance was draining out of what I did. Apparently there were bigger issues in life than flushing rubbers down the toilet. As I lay there, wide awake, I felt those issues looming.

Well, there was one I could handle right there. I went online and I searched "percentage women achieve orgasm."

I found out we were pretty much okay.

Then I had another terrible thought, so I quickly searched "flushing condoms septic system." It looked like I was okay doing it just the two times. At least I hadn't tied a knot in it (CO_2, dontcha know). Still, on the night I finally lost my virginity, I lay there awake and alone, not thinking about my girlfriend and how beautiful she was and how much I loved her, but about some crazy fantasy where our lawn was all torn up and Wallaçonia was drowning in shit and my mom stood in the middle of it all, picked out my condom and said, "Well, this must be the problem! What on earth is it?"

CHAPTER 10

FRONT

OVERNIGHT, THE STORM broke up. At dawn, low, purple clouds scudded, tinged with gold. The creek rippled in the wind, and the marsh waters and the icy spartina glistened. As I got out of bed, my ass and elbows hurt from the day before.

I looked down at myself as I peed. The fact that I'd "done it" didn't feel real. It didn't seem like it had changed me. I felt my worries and doubts brewing just out of sight. There was the college thing. Was Mr. Baxter going to start in on that today? How would it be, Nate and me working together? I was disappointed that, when I thought about Nate, I didn't care about him as much as I did before. I still hadn't dumped my Exercise folder and I still didn't want to. I could appreciate guys and love a woman, couldn't I? I might let that thorn stay stuck.

In the kitchen I chewed a raisin bagel, sipped coffee, and watched the sky brighten. I loved Liz. We were together for real now. Would we get married? Then I thought about Nate. I could sort of sense him, on his way. Probably because I was still ashamed of what I did to him in middle school. But then, when I thought of his blush, I felt something move in the same part of my body that moved last night. I felt his blush right in the center of me, worming around beneath my diaphragm.

I went upstairs to my computer, to the URL for the guy naked on his bed, so proud of who he was, offering himself. What had I offered, last night? Another lie? No! I did love Liz. A part of Liz. A big part. The real part. Liz One. I closed the window, took out my phone, and texted "Love you working today last night was great ur beautiful." I felt less like a crazy person. Or a heel. I meant what I said. Every thorn of it. Looked like I was in that prickly bush no matter what!

Next, Mom called. They were leaving Falmouth and would be home in an hour. I pretty much had to tell her where I'd be when they got home. I told her about the job at Bay View. I hated how I made it sound the same way I made it sound to Liz, like Pat happened to ask and I was doing him a favor. Mom said, "Oh. Well. That's fine." I should have said something before. Anyway, good thing I didn't have to tell Dad. She would.

What should I say to Nate? And when? He was so grown-up now, and beautiful. I went into the bathroom and played with my hair. I was conscious of my body again. I wasn't beautiful. I thought maybe my face showed what I'd done to Nate. What I might be doing to Liz. Maybe Nate had forgotten middle school, but I could still see his face the day I was picking on him about something and Rich Reed came out of nowhere and grabbed him around the neck, hard. I remembered Nate's head hitting the wall, and his red face. Nate's face for those few seconds, plump and panicky, his glasses crooked, him wincing, then his complete lack of expression—like because he couldn't fight Rich, he was pretending it wasn't happening. I hadn't meant it to happen, but I didn't stop Rich. (No one stopped Rich.) I had wanted to see that confused, ashamed, angry look on snotty Nate's face, but when I actually saw it I was ashamed.

Now Nate was trim and built up. That round ass. I couldn't help it. It meant something to me, to a deep part of me that couldn't be separated.

Had he told Mr. Baxter what I did to him? Would Mr. Baxter be disappointed in me now? Walking down to Bay View that morning my feelings changed every two seconds: happy, worried, relieved, anxious, plus a lot of hating myself. Liz texted, "Good luck I love you too maybe get together tonight." I texted back "Ok have 2c if units back."

Ten to ten. I knocked. Mr. Baxter let me in. I stopped cold. I saw the most amazing thing. The lights weren't all on yet. It was still a little dim and ghostly, so for a second, I saw Nate before me, kind of grown-up, but at the same time like he was five years ago, ready to trot up to me and ask something in his annoying voice. Little Nate had gotten serious and slimmed down. But I saw that Big Nate still hurt. Little Nate was now strapping, Big Nate was still vulnerable. I looked at Mr. Baxter. He raised an eyebrow at me. What had he been like at thirteen, or eighteen? It was hard for everyone. And I thought my own response to the hardness had been insufficient.

When Little Nate trotted up to me I didn't say, "Go away!" I tried to convince him the thing he said was dumb. I wasn't nice to him, but I didn't send him away. I guess I liked him and wanted him with me, in spite of his annoyingness.

I watched him, there in the shadows of the bookshelves, and he watched me back.

What if I had been nice, just once? Everyone thought I was weird anyway. What if one day I had just been nice to Nate? Kind. And then maybe the next day. And the next?

But no.

Somewhere under it all, I knew he liked me. And I knew just *how* he liked me. And I was drawn to him in return, and I couldn't deal with it. Nate Flederbaum had actually been my first experience of love. And fear. And hurt. And the day came when I said something extra mean, and he turned away. The next day I came up to him, and he ignored me. I was hurt and relieved. He never came to me again. In time I missed him, sort of. I had destroyed something I didn't know I had. I had destroyed that tiny little leaf of love. It never had a chance. Who would dare?

The lights flickered on all around the barn. There stood Big Nate in another pullover and button-down shirt and another pair of chinos. The classical music came on, and Mr. Baxter motioned us toward the computer. He was scrolling through online orders, page after page of them. "Whoa, Nellie!" he said. He began printing, and all three of us got to work. Just before ten, the phone started ringing.

I thought I wouldn't be able to stand a whole day trapped at Bay View Books—never seeing enough of Nate, never being able to really talk to him. He was even more beautiful than yesterday—so sad and thoughtful with his hair shining. I looked at him and kept getting flashes of Nate back then. "Hey, Jim. Knock-knock . . ." "Jim, didja get number nine on the homework . . . ?"

I had to find a way to tell him what I'd realized about the two of us. Maybe that blank beautiful face could smile some more.

We went up and down the aisles pulling books. Several times I was near him and Mr. Baxter was out of earshot, but I couldn't bring myself to speak to him. Meanwhile, Liz and I were kind of sexting back and forth. I was excited but a little annoyed when she kept asking about tonight. I typed, "Units back have 2c," just as I came around the end of some shelves. Nate was right there. He stared at me with those blue eyes, his face still and more perfect than mine could ever be. I saw the anger, his mother's anger. He blinked, his eyelashes golden, and I saw that he had the clear eyes of a decent person, but as those eyes suddenly cut away from me, I thought he was also afraid. My bullying had hurt us both, but he was a better man for enduring it and not giving up. Maybe I'd hurt myself more than him.

I said, "I have to talk to you, later."

"Okay," he said. I saw the hint of a smile. Maybe a significant look in his eyes. He remembered. I wanted to say, "Don't be afraid" and "I'm so sorry." I wanted to put my arms around him. I couldn't, but I did get a little "swelling" between my legs. Jeez, what was I? Some kind of freak bisexual maniac? I hit "Send" on the text to Liz.

I didn't want to hug guys too often. I wanted to glimpse, to be them, to have what they had. And I had what-if games that I played at night. What if I went to So-and-so's house and he was alone and we went walking in the woods and he said it was hot and we took our clothes off? (In Wallaçonia it was a tradition for boys to hike naked together, starting on their thirteenth birthdays. When I was about thirteen, I got a real friend to do it with me once, out on the marsh. He got totally red and giggled and pulled his underpants back up. I did, too. We sort of stayed friends, but he didn't come over again after that.)

But hug a guy? All that day I fought the urge to put my arms around Nate and say I was sorry and tell him it would be all right. He'd freak. I'd freak. Liz would freak, if she knew. No, she'd stand there staring and not understanding, because none of her friends had bisexual sex maniac boyfriends secretly hung up on guys they'd picked on in middle school.

On the other hand, watching Nate, head cocked, fingers walking across the spines of books as he looked for a title, I wondered, was he even like me? But what was I like? Was he like Mr. Baxter? What was Mr. Baxter really like? I thought I heard a soft thing in Nate's voice and saw it in his elegant gestures. He was standoffish, but not in a rude or bored way. He was haughty. He didn't trust me or maybe didn't trust anyone, but he wasn't surly. He was up-right-looking and wanted to be loved, I just knew, but I also bet he could unleash a rant just like his mother could.

When I spoke to him, what would I say? When would I say it? When Mr. Baxter went to the post office? Customers might come. After work, would his mother want him home? How could I just *stop everything* and have a minute to breathe and slowly start to say everything I had to say?

He turned away now. I stared at the nape of his neck, golden and soft. I wanted to protect it. Cherish it. He couldn't see how beautiful he was, but maybe I could make him see. I tried for a closer look. I wasn't afraid. My parents, my house, the marsh, the bookstore, Mr. Baxter—they all went away. But not Liz. I had made love to her. I pictured her neck, soft and pale with downy hair. It moved me. But Nate's neck grabbed my heart. I wanted to consume it. I wanted to smell him. I didn't want all this to be true, but it was.

He turned back. I looked away. I had a girlfriend.

He and Mr. Baxter spoke in little bits I never quite caught. Eventually I said, "So how do you two know each other?" They exchanged a glance. "I know Nate's family," Mr. Baxter said. The end of the word *family* went down, to cut off more questions. Nate looked at me. I thought I saw the ghost of a smile. Did Mr. Baxter pick the Cape because his friends the Flederbaums were here? Would I have to meet *her* again? I asked

Nate where he had applied for college. Again, he and Mr. Baxter looked at each other. I guess Mr. Baxter had involved himself in that, too. Nate's list was impressive, including a couple of Ivies, and he smiled at me again, a little, but he didn't elaborate.

"That's great," I said. My list was lame by comparison, so I started by saying how bad the college guidance guy was at Lower Cape. There was another look between Nate and Mr. Baxter. I just wanted the day to end so I could get Nate alone. He was so moody, though, that I was afraid he'd "forget" I asked and take off in the Hummer.

I fidgeted as Mr. Baxter locked up. Going uphill I counted the steps. The Hummer was parked above Mr. Baxter's front walk, so Nate and I would have to walk on a little way by ourselves. My knees were weak with anticipation.

The Hummer looked huge in the light from our house. My parents were home; Mom had already texted. I wasn't so excited to see them or to explain my job at Bay View. But I did look forward to our home going back to normal. I texted Liz that I had to be home with them, and she said she understood. She said I should call if I needed help. She always said that, but I thought of it in a new way now. She didn't just say it; she did it. I saw. I remembered it all now. You asked Liz for help, and she gave it. "Want 2b with you bad," I texted back. "Tomorrow?"

At his mailbox Mr. Baxter thanked both Nate and me. He said there would be no need for us tomorrow—his regular person, a woman from town, was coming—but it had been wonderful of us to help as much as we did. He shook my hand and said he'd see me again soon. Then he hugged Nate. Nate hugged back with one arm. Mr. Baxter said to him, "I'll see you eventually," probably because Nate was going back to his private school. I watched Mr. Baxter go up to his door.

Nate stared off at the stars. Then we looked at each other. "Now?" I said. Nate shrugged, and we started walking. We came to the Hummer. Man, those things are huge! What were the Flederbaums thinking? The thought of Nate driving it was ridiculous and at the same time a little, well, sexy. Nate—built up but elegant—wrestling a Hummer through the snow.

"Get in," he said. He bleeped the doors open.

We climbed in and sat facing front. I was kind of intimidated—leather everywhere and enough little lights and controls to fly a damn plane.

"I wanted to apologize," I said, "for middle school. For how I treated you. I still think about it, and it was terrible. How we all treated you. Me especially, though. I shouldn't have."

He turned his face just a little toward me, then stopped, then turned it front again and stared out the window. He had just the hint of a smile, but it faded quickly. In the light from our house I could see his pale eyebrows raised in surprise.

"Well, no one would make fun of you now!" I added. I allowed my eyes to go up and down his body and take it in. "I just wanted you to know that I was sorry for—"

"You didn't make fun of me," he said, still staring out the windshield.

Oh. I stopped. Was all forgiven?

"You *persecuted* me," he said.

My heart gave a ginormous thud. I felt trapped, held down in the huge, plushy seat, with this massive control panel between us and him at the wheel.

"Every. Single. Day," he said. "When I woke up, I wondered who was going to say what today. 'Spastic.'" His voice shook. "'Loser.'" He took a deep breath and swallowed. "'Kike' . . ."

A tear ran down his face, but he kept his quivering lips together. It must have hurt him horribly to say those words, especially the last one. I'd never said it, but I thought I knew who did.

He clenched his teeth and inhaled. "I just wanted to be your friend," he sneered, and I couldn't tell which one of us he was sneering at. "Of course it would never happen!" He cast a sidelong glance at me. "You so handsome, and—"

"Me? Hand—??"

"And me like this disgusting little ball of fat—"

"No!"

"—but you didn't have to—"

"Please!" I said. I reached over and put the palm of my hand against the side of his face. He ducked a little, but he let me do it. I slipped my hand around and cupped the back of his head, so it would seem more brotherly. Again he pulled his head away, then relaxed a little and let it touch my hand, then pulled away again, then relaxed. "Don't cry," I said. "It was our fault. My fault." "Huh!" he said. The heel of my hand felt the stubble at the top of his jaw. My breath left me. Little Nate with whiskers. And pubes. With hair under his arms. He turned his head away.

"But you proved us all wrong!" I said.

"Every. Single. Day. 'Spastic.'" He spit it out, staring ahead. "'Pussy!'" Suddenly, real fast, like he was having a little fit, he reached behind, grabbed my hand and threw it back at me. "Ow!" I said. He'd actually twisted my arm. And yet I couldn't get over the way his warm skin had felt against mine. "Sorry," he muttered. He wiped his eyes. "It's stupid. Go on. Get out. Go your *merry* way."

Okay. So to stay, I had to raise the stakes. "They'd all say 'beautiful' now," I offered. It excited me to say, and it got him to look at me. I took in a deep breath. "At least *I* would. *I* think you're beautiful." He turned his head and stared, eyes searching, hoping, I guess, that I meant it and might say more. My head spun.

There was something I *so* wanted to say. This was the moment to try it. I could explain it. It didn't have to mean—

"I like handsome men," I said. The corner of his mouth turned up in the hint of a smile. Maybe Nate Two, the obstacle, had become Nate One, a real Nate that the real Jim could love in some way. I had the bizarre thought that my parents were just a few yards away—and Mr. Baxter. And I liked beautiful women, too. I loved them. Loved one. . . .

Yet I did mean what I said, and it didn't matter what anyone thought. I held Nate's gaze and nodded. The truth of what I said would carry me through. I rubbed my arm. I liked that it hurt a little.

His eyes cut sharply at me and asked, "Jim, why are you here?" He was angry, but I was grateful for a serious question. We seemed in that moment to be grown-up men.

"To *apologize*," I said loudly. I twisted toward him in my seat. "I mean it. It was terrible, what I did, and even though I don't deserve it, I'm asking you to forgive me."

He grabbed a tissue from one of a million little compartments and wiped his nose. He wiped each eye with the back of his wrist. "What did Pat tell you?" he asked.

"Mr.—? Um, nothing . . ."

He leveled a finger at me. "Don't you say anything against him."

"No! I mean, what would I say?" I pictured *Hunk*, splat on the floor.

"Just don't." He wiped his eyes again.

I tried to relax into my leather throne. "How do you know him?" I asked, as gently as I could.

Nate sniffled. Soft and low he muttered, "Like he said, my family knows him."

"But, um, *how*?" I really wanted to say, "Did you hear me say 'beautiful' just now? What did you think?"

Tucking the tissue away he said, "Why should I tell you?" He stared out the windshield again, his jaw thrust out. "You don't know me," he sneered, cocking his head and stroking a tuft of blond hair with his finger. "I'm some loser you persecuted in seventh grade. Now you're 'sorry.'"

"You're no loser!" I said, loud and kind of pissed. It was funny and nice how in-charge I felt.

He was a formidable opponent, though. Curling his lip he said, "I don't need the guy who picked on me to say 'sorry.' I am going into the army. The Israeli Defense Force. IDF. After I graduate high school."

"No!" I said. "No, don't!" The thought that anyone would harm that beautiful golden face. I'd called that face handsome. I'd finally told the whole truth about something. It couldn't go away!

He turned the key in the ignition. The dashboard lit up. "I have to go," he said.

"Can we talk again?"

He shrugged. "Sure." He started the engine.

After a pause he took out his phone. I dictated my number, and he texted me so I'd have his. I told him it might be a few days before I could get together, because of my aunt.

"Sorry to hear," he said. "What's she got?"

"Heart," I said. "I'll be in touch, though." I didn't know what else to say, so I said, "See ya." I climbed out.

"Hey!" he said. I turned. In a dull voice he said, "Arm okay?"

"Yeah, sure," I said.

He nodded. Then he set his gaze on the road ahead. I shut the door behind me.

He put the Hummer in gear and lurched away, tail-lights turning the drifts red, until I stood alone. For a little while I stood in the cold, kind of amazed, kind of pleased with myself, but nervous that I was about to fall from way up high down into a great big mess.

I began to crunch uphill. I glanced toward the marsh, as though I might see Mr. Raccoon. Then I heard another crunching sound. I turned just as Mr. Baxter said, "Jim?"

He had no hat, and his scarf was not tucked in. He had no gloves; his hands were whitish and didn't seem so big. He was panting.

"Hi," I said. I felt myself smile.

"You know Nathanael," he said, steam trailing out of his mouth.

"Just from middle school," I said. How much did he know already?

He nodded. "He's a special guy."

"Yes," I said. As always, it seemed, I couldn't say everything. "I mean, you know, he seems to be . . . kind of quiet."

"Yes. Well . . ."

Maybe he thought Nate had told me stuff about him, so I explained that I had been apologizing for picking on Nate in middle school. Since it was cold and my parents were waiting, I tried to make it sound trivial. "That's good," said Mr. Baxter, meaning, I guess, that it was good I apologized. I felt bad for not giving him the full picture. "Anyway," he said, "What I wanted to tell you is, I'm off to my niece's in Woonsocket tomorrow, but I'm coming back Thursday. I'll be in the shop Friday, and I wonder if you could come then. People see books their friends got, and they want their own. Happens every year. I'll pay you for everything then."

I said I would be free, unless something happened with Aunt Lillian. "Excellent!" he said.

He left with a wave, and I went on up to the house. Mom was at the door. She smiled and said, "Seems you and Pat had a lot to say." I shrugged and gave her a quick hug. In the living room, Dad read the newspaper. He didn't say anything about Mr. Baxter. Good. Dad was not going to be a problem that night. I asked how Aunt Lillian was. She was back at the home, in "skilled nursing." We were going to Falmouth "as a family" on Christmas. Mom said "as a family," like, "You're going, and that's that." I went upstairs till dinner.

I got on Facebook and looked for Nate. He wasn't on there. I tried "Nathaniel." Nope. Maybe the crazy mother forbade Facebook. For the heck of it I went to the Bay View page. "Don't forget! We're open Friday!" Mr. Baxter had asked if he could post a picture of me as the "new assistant," and I'd hesitated till he backed down. I didn't go to Mr. Baxter's own page. I'd already put in a friend request he hadn't answered, and if you weren't his friend, all you saw on his page was the barn and a blurry photo of him cropped from something bigger. Next I went to Liz's page, because there'd be stuff I had to like. She'd changed her cover pic. Instead of *Les Miz*, it was another picture of us, from a party held on her friend Erin's boat Labor Day weekend. So I had supplanted the guys with guns!

That night, after we watched TV, I got in bed and texted with Liz. The same-old same-old, plus some sexual stuff: me feeling the front of my pants; her mostly puckering up or licking her lips—and one cleavage shot. I wanted to sign off, though, so I could stop and think about Nate. Pulling that sweater off. Letting me hug him. Like a brother. Anyone would understand that. I hadn't deleted my Exercise folder yet, but I didn't look at it right then. The day had been complicated enough. At the same time, I didn't want to get out of that day. I had told a big truth, and no matter what dominoes were going to fall where, I liked it.

Outside the moon shone brilliantly, and the ice on the marsh blazed in twists and turns between the dark clumps of vegetation.

I looked at my phone. Liz had sent one last text.

No. Okay, who . . . ?

Nate. Texting me two words:

thank you

I stared at those two words and massaged my arm.

CHAPTER 11

CRACKING

CHRISTMAS EVE I WENT to Liz's in Brewster. There were so many relatives and so much food and both of us in good clothes and sweaters that nothing much intimate could happen. We kissed a long time in the kitchen hallway before I left. I wished I could stay. The thing with Liz worked. I felt the same things again that I had felt making love to her, and I hadn't looked at my Exercise folder in three or four days. I had texted with Nate. We talked about getting together, but we had nothing definite. Before I left Liz's I promised we would do something that weekend.

Christmas with Aunt Lillian was okay. She looked at me on and off like she was trying hard to remember me, but just couldn't. That had to be terrible—wanting to remember someone but just not being able to. Why be alive at that point? What a thought to have about my own great-aunt!

Friday morning, working the key into the lock of the front door of Bay View, Mr. Baxter said, "I want to talk to you about Nate. *Nathanael.*"

Uh-oh. Here it was—the bad stuff I did. Maybe I wouldn't be staying to work that day.

"That's with an *a*, by the way. *Nathan-AY-el*. It's really with an *i*, but he unofficially changed it." The lock turned and he pushed. The sleigh bells jingled. In one move he reached for them and took them down. I was startled. It was only the twenty-seventh; was Christmas over? "He knows we are having this conversation, by the way."

Whoa. Was my picking on Nate in middle school going to be handled so officially?

We did not switch the computer on right away like usual, but Mr. Baxter lit the stove. "He also knows you're here today. I told him he could come tomorrow; then he goes back to school."

"We could both keep working weekends," I said. "I could, anyway."

"No no," Mr. Baxter said, as the newspapers caught. He handed me the kettle. "No need. Today will probably be the last hurrah till spring."

I went to the bathroom with the kettle, wondering what he meant. He had talked before about the "economic climate," but I hadn't paid attention.

I came back and put the water on. He pulled out the coffee and the filter cone. "Nathanael," he said, fussing with a brown paper filter, "does not go to school here."

"Right," I said.

"He hates it here, so his parents sent him to Benleigh, in Wetherford, out by Acton, Fitchburg, that area. That is how I know him."

We sat by the stove. My mind raced about Nate not being able to stand it here. He couldn't have left because of me, could he?

"I used to work at Benleigh."

And then it all made sense. "Let me guess." I said. "College guidance."

Mr. Baxter smiled. "How ever did you know?"

"So . . . that's a pretty great job," I said. "Why did you leave?" Suddenly I wished I hadn't asked. Why did single gay guys quit teaching jobs at ritzy private schools? He had done something with a boy, and the boy told on him. I'd heard stories like that. There was a case at one fancy prep school where a teacher took pictures and videos of male students. I remember reading about it and wishing I could be so good-looking someone would want to take pictures of me. Stupid. So Mr. Baxter did something with Nate . . . ? "I mean," I said. "I'm sorry. You don't have to tell me." But then, how could Nate be his friend now? Nate might forgive, but not the Wicked Witch of So-Sick!

"Oh, no," he said. "Nothing like that." I felt myself go red. "Well, a little like that, but I could still be there, if I wanted." The water boiled; he stood to make coffee.

"I went to Benleigh," he said, "right out of college. I had grown up on a prep-school campus, so it was like home. I knew what to do, what not to do, what *never* to do. I thought I'd pass my life there. I wasn't college guidance at first. I taught English. And I married a colleague." He raised an eyebrow and smiled at me. "Don't look so stunned!" he said.

So, I was supposed to have gotten that he was gay? What did he think about me—and Liz? My stomach sank right out the bottom, practically. I put my head in my hands. "She taught English, too," he said. "We got along so well. Soul mates. Agreed on everything. At first. Laughed at the same things. Very important."

God! It was like going down a list—check, check, check, check!

"Took long walks. Sunsets and, you know, so much *approval!* From everyone. How could it not be right? Didn't they all know better than I? Everything was a sign. Things were finally going the way I'd dreamed. I'd finally got through all the adolescent this and that.

116

And I was lifted up." He cleared his throat, paused, and then said, in the tenderest voice, "She was a writer." He shook his head very slightly. "You haven't heard of her. She wrote these sweet romances"—his smiled, and the way his voice, like, caressed the air, I thought of the back of Nate's neck—"under different names."

Ah-ha! M. M. Morgan and J. B. Halperin! He had kept those books all that time, keeping his wife with him. I understood. I couldn't lose Liz. Or even think of what would come after.

He handed me a steaming mug and then sat. "We published her books, together. Lobster Pot Publishing. She was from Maine. It was our big project. Made us feel very together. I did the covers. A little amateur painting." My heart felt like it would fly apart. Mr. Baxter sitting up late, making gentle strokes with a brush, trying to paint his wife's dream. Would that be me and Liz? "But I believe you understand that I am not 'the marrying kind,' as they used to say a billion years ago."

I nodded. "Yeah," I said. I took a deep breath. "I wondered about that." Whoosh! I hadn't planned on saying it, but I couldn't help it.

"Wondered about . . . ?"

"Marrying." My voice cracked. I felt myself break out in a sweat under my layers.

"But, well, maybe you don't know that expression," he said. "It's very retro. It means—"

"I know," I said. I was looking at the floor, shoulders hunched, holding my hands between my knees and flexing my fingers. I sort of lost the next few seconds. I felt like my whole self was suddenly dissolving. I must have looked bad, because finally Mr. Baxter leaned toward me and said, "Jim?"

I took huge breaths, one after the other. I felt this awful knot digging in under my diaphragm. He waited.

Finally I said, "I like her a lot," and I blew out this huge gasp and started to cry. I felt like I'd been shot. Now he was crouching by my chair, looking up at me, which made the whole thing true and real and terrible. "I don't . . . I don't know what to tell *anyone!*"

I was so afraid he would say, "Well, you have to tell everyone, right now. Get out your phone." But he didn't. He knelt by the chair and said, "No, of course you don't. It's very complicated. You could say a whole paragraph and the next minute it wouldn't be true."

That was so exactly what I'd been thinking that I wanted to hug him, but I didn't think it was okay. He sat Indian-style on the floor in front of me, and that made me want to hug him even more.

He put his hand on my knee, firmly. "But I will tell you," he said, "it helps to say what you *think* you know."

I put my head in my hands. "I can't!" I said. "What? How . . . ? What do I *say?*"

"Try telling me." His voice soft again, like a caress. What made his wife love him. I hugged myself hard so I wouldn't hug him.

"But . . . the store . . ." I said.

"Oh, screw the store!" he said. I believe you could say he said it "stoutly." And he smiled.

"You have to open up!"

"There's nothing in the world that can't wait a few minutes, Jim."

That made me calm down a bit and breathe normally. He took away his hand but kept looking up at me, kindly and patiently. Here was someone right in front of me who'd maybe been through the same things I was going through, and I was terrified. And kind of relieved.

So I began telling him, starting with feelings from childhood and middle school—back when I returned safely to books and hot cocoa and the marsh and Wal-

laçonia. In the midst of all these awful feelings I ached
so much for all that. I told him how I might have felt
about Nate and then Liz and the Exercise folder, talking all the way with lots of "maybe" and "sort of" and
"you know" and "I guess" and "I want" and "but I don't
want." I described guys I saw as "undressed" or "in
bathing suits" instead of "naked." I said they were
"good-looking" instead of "hot" or "sexy." I talked fast.
I was worried about the store opening. Sometimes I
mumbled and he frowned. An interested frown. I shiv-
ered, so he brought a blanket from behind the
counter, put it around me, and said, "Go on." He
reached for his coffee and sat with it. I took a sip from
mine. He kept his eyes on me. He didn't look at the
door or react when the phone rang. He just listened to
me. Soon I couldn't say any more. I felt like I could
barely sit up. I tried to smile. I asked him, "So what do
you think?" It was like Wallaçonia had been overrun,
my parents captured and even killed, and I was flee-
ing, slogging out through the marsh to the sea, never
to see anyone again. Then Mr. Baxter waved from a
ship in the bay and reached for me. If only I could get
to him. "C'mon!" I said. "Say something!"

He smiled warmly and said, "You're brave to tell me
this." That made me want to run away, because it
meant he took it all for true and real. "You may not
know everything you know, yet," he went on. "Your
head might be a mess of contradictions. It's hard. But
I remember a lot of the moments you describe. And it
does help to tell what you know is true today, doesn't
it?" It took such effort just to nod. I still felt sick. He
wasn't telling me to confess to Liz, but the more he
didn't say it, the more I knew I had to.

I took a deep breath and wiped my eyes. "You were
telling me about Nate and this private school?"

"I was telling you about my *wife*," Mr. Baxter said,
and I felt awful. Me and Liz, years from now, still go-

ing. I thought I would pass out. "We had a child," he said. He paused as though swallowing something and said, "Excuse me. I have a daughter. Risa. And then Saralynn, my wife, said her books *lacked* 'something.' It turned out the books lacked the same thing the relationship lacked. What we didn't feel for each other. *One* of us, anyway, didn't feel . . ." He began this combination of shrugging, shaking his head, looking up, looking down, waving his hands like even now it was still incomprehensible to him. "Feel something for someone." He stared at the stove. It occurred to me— here he was, thirty- or forty-whatever years old and still not knowing what he knew, like me.

But I knew what his wife meant. I had noticed, in the few words I read upstairs, that the writer was not getting something. The thought of her wanting to write a good book and not being able to and the two of them not feeling enough for each other made me feel nauseated and dizzy. I didn't want to hear any more, but I kept my eyes front and tried not to show it.

"According to her, part of the proof was Risa's crying. She cried all the time. Because she knew Mommy and Daddy weren't 'really together.' I knew, I mean, by then." He stared intently ahead, like he was trying to decide whether or not to step off a cliff. Finally he said, "She took Risa. To an artists' colony. In California. Big Sur. This was the summer of 1997." But he kept glancing back at that cliff. "I visited, though I couldn't go on the grounds. Outsiders were forbidden. Sara had had more revelations. I had, too. By then she knew about me. It had come out. And Risa wasn't crying in Big Sur." I watched him closely. I had never heard this edge in his voice before. "I moved out. I still thought we might be, you know, a family again." His voice shook. He took a deep breath. "But there came that day. 'Say good-bye to Daddy.' The moment you have to let go, the moment you have to turn and . . .

and go." He froze almost and stared at his hands. It was like I could see a little baby reflected in his eyes. But I was confused. Were we in California now, or at Benleigh? It seemed something was skipped over.

"On the plane," he said, "I felt her with me. Inside me. Risa." His bunched fingertips touched that place below his diaphragm. "A little kid who didn't know what was happening. I knew Sara would take good care of her. No matter what Sara's 'issues' were, I could count on her for that." For a while he stared. At last he sat up straight and smiled a little.

"I was at Benleigh alone now. Nothing meant anything. Everything was dulled. Fall didn't smell like fall. I registered no smells. Isn't that odd? I had to apply for single housing. In a dorm. I moved. Carrying boxes. I reread one of her books, *The Cabin by the Lake*. It was a completely different book now. About the love she'd wanted. The man was like me, but at the same time not. More powerful. All-consuming. But nice. Like me. She wrote it under the name 'M. M. Morgan.' 'Morgan' was her maiden name. She wrote about the man I should have been, and I never saw it."

I thought about being "powerful." The man who had hired me, the man who had told me what college to go to, the man who had dabbed my hand with peroxide and who listened to me. He was powerful. But not the way Saralynn wanted. What did Liz want? Could I ever give it to her?

"The second one, *What We May Do*, was about how her life had actually turned out. The man was sweet but couldn't *possess* her. Was ineffec . . . whatever . . ." He folded his arms and looked way. After all he'd done for me, if he cried now, could I do the right thing?

"It's okay," I said suddenly. He looked at me, startled. I pointed to where he'd put the peroxide on my hand. The Band-Aid was still there. "Effectual," I said.

"Very." He smiled and said softly, "Thank you. Anytime." He reached over and patted my knee, twice.

I still felt queasy, my head near disintegration or meltdown. I wished we'd discuss something else. This was like a test, to see if I could stay with my friend. With myself. Like being on a train. I wanted to get off at Wallaçonia, but I had to hang on and ride with him, ride with myself. I could see what happened to him happening to me, though: marriage, kids, house. Why not? Liz was my *friend*. It was what you did. The approval, like he said, from everyone. Plus, we'd had sex. So what if I thought Nate Flederbaum was beautiful? So, so beautiful. So moving. I took a deep breath. The smell of old wood and paper and a fire in the stove: that's what I fought for when I fought all my fantasies of guys and tried to be normal. To have fantasies instead of books and maps and dunes and the marshes and the glasswort and spartina.

"She wrote it under my nose. I proofed it. I went . . . I mean, I *publicized* it. And all the time, it told the story of how she had married wrong and what she wanted instead. I liked men. Yes. But I had loved her. We were friends."

I sat shivering. I didn't have to do what he did, did I?

"I was devastated. I suppose it helped me let go, but. . . ." He paused, then became animated again. "Anyway! I was alone. I was coming out. To myself and about three other people!" I drew air in, deep, deeper, and let it go. He rubbed his hands together slowly, fingers spread. "I moved into an apartment in a dormitory full of 'impressionable' young men, and perhaps you understand this: *They know.*" He glanced at me as though getting my okay to go on. Did he assume I was part of his club, the way Dad assumed I was part of his? Except Dad wanted me in the Normal Boys' Club; Mr. Baxter wanted me . . . where? In the club I'd always been in? Why couldn't I just be in my own club?

"They talk. And you hear. And the ones who *are* 'inclined'"—quick look at me, but I wouldn't look back, wouldn't say, *I'm all in*—"they know, too. They may not know what they know. They just know you are their *oasis*." Was I going to find out that Nate was one of those "inclined"?

"Meanwhile," he went on, folding his hands and pressing them to his mouth, "you are meant to be counseling and 'helping.' Like a regular guy. 'Travis, great game Saturday!'" He shook his head. I had wanted a man to tell me I'd played a great game. If I'd gone out for cross-country, maybe one would have.

"Was Nate," I asked, "one of those guys? Who didn't know what he knew?" Because if Nate was, then maybe, just maybe, I could let myself be.

"Nathanael was very aloof. He barely looked at me. He studied and lifted weights and dressed in those sweaters, just like the other day. And I behaved perfectly toward him and everyone." He straightened up. "Any meeting with a boy took place *in my office*, with the *door open*. In good weather, we went outside—*on the quadrangle, in full view*." He emphasized these rules with chopping motions of his hand. "No woodsy walks. No 'Come up for some tea.' But I did have a child of my own, far away, whom I'd held at birth, whom I'd changed and fed." He checked his watch and went on. I wanted just one customer to come make the day normal again.

He folded his hands, and with his elbows on his knees leaned toward me. "You don't know yet, but when you have a child and are separated, you ache for her, *toward* her, as if your body is trying to grow limbs to reach for her." His hands made claws that kneaded the thin air. "I felt sick. My head hurt. I ached for her, and I ached for the kids I saw every day. Some without parents. I mean, parents off in Vail or Saint Martin who dumped their kids on us. It was my job to ache

123

for those kids. I did nothing improper, ever. You had faculty with their hands all over students—pats on the back, roughhousing with the jocks. Not me."

Not me, either. I'd never really touched anyone till Liz.

"But, as Neil Young says, 'Comes a time.'" I must have done a double-take. "You think I don't know *Neil Young?*" he said. "Good Heavens!" I blushed. "Today we'll put on *Rust Never Sleeps.* Oh, it's so good!

"At any rate, eventually, there was a young man. We will call him 'Teddy.'" I breathed easy now, knowing that for a few minutes we would *not* be talking about a failed marriage. "Fifteen and beautiful. And, as far as I could tell, perfectly straight."

Mr. Baxter saying "straight" startled me more than if he'd said "gay." He divided the world in two, like he had brought down a gate between the two of us and everyone else. If Nate could be on this side, too, it might be okay. Except Nate was going to Israel. Without Nate, I couldn't be on Mr. Baxter's side of the gate.

"I'd been good for years, keeping my hands and even my eyes off kids. There'd be noise in the hall, I'd come out, they'd be in athletic supporters and whatnot. I looked *nowhere* but their faces. They would have *nothing* on me."

I nodded. I'd done it, too, promising myself that today in gym class I'd let myself look three times, then next gym period twice, then once, then not at all. Then before I knew it, I'd looked at twenty guys, and I'd have to start over.

"On breaks and odd weekends, I'd go to Boston. I 'hooked up,' as we say, online, and then? Time goes by. Years go fast. Something else you have not discovered."

"I have," I said. "One day you quit choir, and before you know it, high school's over."

"Well, you can sing in college." The phone rang; he did not go for it.

"Yeah," I said. "This sounds weird, but there's something about singing at fourteen." I placed my hand in the center of my chest. "A . . . perfection. A just-rightness. I don't know. That I still want. Singing at eighteen isn't the same. It doesn't make up for—" He nodded and smiled. I didn't have to say more. I was eighteen now, and it felt like everything was over. The age of grace seemed like fourteen or fifteen, a time that had passed without my knowing. Eighteen, nineteen, *twenty* felt old. Eventually you were disappointed.

He resumed. "One winter day Teddy caught me at the door of my apartment. He had to talk. Normally Teddy was, you know—" He stood and did this imitation of a loose-limbed jock, running his hand up over his chest. "But not that day." He sat. "He was distraught. Hugging himself." Here Mr. Baxter hugged *him*self. "And I could see he'd been crying. He said, 'Something's happened; I don't know what to do.' Well, I wasn't going to say, 'Hold everything while we find an empty classroom,' and it was January, so we weren't going outside. My precautions were silly anyway. My colleagues had students in their apartments all the time. So I said, 'Come in.' But!"—he held up a finger— "I left that front door open! We ended up in the kitchen, but I left that front door open!"

But I was still thinking about that normal, masculine boy, Teddy, teary and saying, "I don't know what to do." I loved him for it and wished I knew him.

"He had just been told his parents were getting a divorce, and . . . I'm not sure you'll know what I mean, but there is something beautiful about the first deep grief in a young man. You see them slight and vulnerable and wrestling with all their might. Then you see them grow before your eyes. Even as he stood in my kitchen sobbing, he was beautiful. His chest heaving. Drove me to distraction."

He paused, like, "You know what I mean?" I nodded slightly. I couldn't say out loud yet that I found sad guys beautiful, nor could I explain why, but Mr. Baxter could, so I knew that what went through my head was real.

I wondered when I would have my own "first deep grief." Maybe I'd *been* having it—for years, just all covered up and let out in little bits. I'd lost opportunities, I'd lost the guy I wanted to be, and I'd nearly lost the guy I was. The first time I'd cried over any of it had been today.

The phone rang again, and again Mr. Baxter let it go to voicemail, but he did go unlock the door. "I think for days like today," he said, "we need a sign that says, 'Yes, We're Open; Please Go Away.' He came back to me, threw another log into the stove, and went on about Teddy.

"All I've been describing to you was, in fact, my job. I was Teddy's dorm master. He was supposed to come to me for these things. No one said I couldn't put an arm around his shoulder.

"But what I did or didn't do is not the issue. Arm or no arm, the issue is what someone decided she saw. And before you know it, I got called in by the head of school." As he said this, Mr. Baxter sat up straighter, hands in his lap, as though he were not a teacher but a kid, being called in by the head. "Personally, she didn't think anything was wrong. She wanted to 'nip this thing in the bud.' She said the person complaining was 'a bit strange,' and immediately I knew who— this faculty wife in my dorm. She was always coming after someone and taking them aside and being oh-so-concerned about something inane. Just going on and on. Like on *Saturday Night Live* . . . the Girl You Wish You Hadn't Started a Conversation with . . . ?"

I laughed for what felt like the first time in days. I did a quick imitation of Cecily Strong—"Pat, wake up! Look around you!" He grinned and relaxed his called-before-the-head posture. That might have been the first deliberate gay thing I ever did. The sketch isn't gay, but the way I did it was. It's funny. Liz was my friend partly because I could do jokes and imitations like that with her. She laughed and joined in and didn't think it was weird. If I couldn't have that anymore, what would I do?

Mr. Baxter leaned back and crossed his legs. "This woman always had some idea that something insanely important was going on—drawing me aside and muttering, 'Pat, are you aware . . . ?' *And* . . . the head told me a little detail. She said it was reported to her that I had 'persecuted' Teddy. Not 'abused,' but 'persecuted.' I'd heard this woman use that word." I held my breath and stared at fire. I had heard that word, too, from Nate.

"The head said she believed me, and she promised this wouldn't go any further. I told her over and over how much I appreciated it, and even after she let me off the hook, I kept telling her in fifty thousand different ways that I would never ever *ever*, et cetera, et cetera. But I wondered if maybe the damage hadn't been done. Who else had this woman told? I saw my chance just to get out of that life. Forever. All the making sure I never did this and never said that and never looked at X and never looked at Y. I could finally, finally, finally *stop* it all." He made the downward chopping gesture of his hand again. "I could be free. I could breathe. I could say what I was. Out loud.

"Once upon a time, I had thought that one day I'd get out of there and move to Boston, but I wasn't so interested now. I'd had my flings or whatever you'd call them. Discreetly. Driving long distances after dark. Coming back at three a.m. and getting up to be in my office at nine. By then, we could get married. Here, at least. There were two women at my school who did. But I hadn't been able, you know, I hadn't found. . . ." He stopped and picked lint from his trousers.

"But!" He flung his arms wide and looked around the store. "I dreamed a dream." He took in all the books. The *Les Miz* reference made me think of Liz. I had to talk to her. I came down from the almost giddy feeling I'd had doing Cecily Strong. "We spent summers on the Cape when I was a kid, and I knew this barn—this specific one. I would dream it was my bookstore. A week after submitting my resignation to Benleigh, I was down here with my niece, and I saw a 'For Sale' sign out front. Providential. I knew Nate was from here. I'd met his parents at school. So they became my investors. Not that Nate doesn't know, but I'd prefer that remain confidential." He paused and then said softly, looking away, "Their terms were very generous."

I nodded and watched the flames. I thought about Mr. Baxter driving after dark and coming home at three a.m., and also about him being a kid, worrying all the time, like me, worrying, worrying, then once a year zooming past a barn in a flash and all the way home imagining a bookstore there. It's the kind of thing I'd imagine. But not, I realized, the kind of thing I'd actually do. No Bay View for me.

"At any rate, I saw you and Nate talking. He told me that he knew you before, and so I figured it was time to explain things. I want you to know me. I want you to know that I would tell you the truth. And I guess you know you can tell *me* the truth." I nodded and wiped away the beginnings of more tears. He smiled, stood, and gave me a pat on the shoulder. "Maybe we had better get things opened up now."

I stood, too. "But Nate ignored you," I said.

"Excuse me?" he said, glancing back as he went to the computer.

"If Nate ignored you, how did his parents know who you were and what you wanted to do?"

"Oh," he said briskly, "it didn't matter what he thought of me. I met the Flederbaums at Parents' Weekend, and we talked Cape Cod. One thing led to another. They were much friendlier than their son was." That was hard to believe! "Although I have come to appreciate him." He sat and turned on the monitor. "Let's see what we've got online."

There were online orders, and more calls came, but it turned out not to be a heavy day. He had probably wanted to talk to me more than have me work. As we printed out our fulfillment list, he said, "Do you like Nate?"

"I guess," I said. It was hard to know what to tell and how, because no one was saying if Nate was actually *that way*. What was I supposed to know or not know, ask or not ask? Whatever the case, I wanted to talk to Nate again, because of that "persecuted" thing. He was the one who blabbed. He saw Mr. Baxter with Teddy, and he was jealous. I knew it, because I knew what it was to be the one on the outside, seeing someone I wanted suddenly belong to someone else. I could see the door to Mr. Baxter's apartment closing. Closing on Nate, even though he really left it open. Closing on me, even though I wasn't there. I felt for Nate, so wronged and abandoned. He had to speak. He had to tell someone something. So he told that annoying woman, because she wanted to hear. She probably told him she was his best friend. Then she reported the whole thing to the head. Mr. Baxter knew; he had to. And he was protecting Nate. But how did they get to be such friends?

And I still wondered: what about Mr. Baxter talking to Dad about my extracurriculars? A lot was going on that no one was telling me about.

One of our chores that day was taking down the Christmas decorations. I felt sad boxing them up. The place looked so bare. During Christmas, you can pretend there's nothing to worry about and nothing to do. But when the decorations come down, you have to deal again. I had a heavy heart.

Mr. Baxter asked again how *I* knew Nate. I told him again about being mean to Nate in middle school. Mr. Baxter laughed. "Oh, those years are a nightmare for everyone," he said.

"No!" I said. I started over. "No, sir, I mean really *mean*. Like, you wouldn't want to know me."

"Well, I doubt that!"

I told the quick-and-easy version of my apology.

"All right," Mr. Baxter said gently. "I hear you. I do. But Jim, I assure you, in any case, I would always want to know you." He held my gaze for a moment. Then, before either of us could get too uncomfortable, he suggested we get to work. He just didn't want to know how bad I was. Maybe that was his Christmas gift to me, like excusing a debt. Quickly I said, "Same here," and then I was off amongst the shelves. As I went, I thought how I had never quite had a relationship like this with anyone. Maybe this was being grown-up. Maybe having a talk with Liz was grown-up.

Around noon, Liz called. She asked about getting together that night. My stomach fell. I gasped and sucked some saliva the wrong way, and so I coughed. "Are you getting a cold?" she said. I said, "No." I felt dizzy. Would we talk about *it*? It felt like we had to. I agreed to go to Brewster after dinner. I spent the rest of the afternoon in a daze. Stopping for coffee was no fun. My leg jiggled, and I felt short of breath. I sipped and burned myself. Mr. Baxter brought up the college thing again, and I didn't hear a word. Finally he said, "Anything wrong, Jim?"

"Nervous, I guess," I said.

He said, "You're under a lot of pressure." I nodded. "You know, you don't have to go explaining to every—"

"But I do!" I said. My leg jiggled faster. "She's my girl*friend!* I love her!"

"Oh," he said. He was quiet. I had kind of vomited it out. He looked at me steadily. "If you do, you do," he said. His voice was soft. This was how he had spoken to Teddy. Maybe I could be Teddy. Maybe we could all live together, free and beautiful in the Exercise folder. I felt awful for Liz. I felt like I might vomit for real, but I also felt excited. I finally got to say it to someone who knew me. Maybe she'd understand. Maybe it wouldn't be so bad.

Last thing before we closed up, Mr. Baxter handed me my check for the week. He switched the lights out and then said, "Oh. You know, I never got to wish you happy birthday." I must have looked surprised. "Your license, when you filled out your W-4. I saw I missed it by just four or five days. There's a present coming, when I get to it."

"Oh, thanks," I said. It was almost too sweet. I couldn't tell him that he didn't have to, that he'd given me so many presents. Though my voice shook a little from nervousness at being cared for like that I said, "So, like, birthdays, gun control, fracking. Wake up, Pat!" He grinned, and we locked up Bay View for the night.

As I picked my way up the hill, my phone vibrated. Text from Nate. "Want to get together?" I went all tingly and light-headed again. I almost fumbled the phone texting back, "Sure." And then, "When?" I don't remember saying good-bye to Mr. Baxter at his mailbox, though I must have. All the way home I kept my eyes on the phone.

When I walked in, the kitchen was bright and smelled of turkey soup and warm bread. "I want you to know," Mom said, "we're going back to Falmouth Saturday, just for the afternoon. It would be nice if you could spare the time." I sighed and said, "Okay." She muttered, "No need for the dramatics!" I kept my eyes on the phone and prayed Nate wouldn't say we had to get together Saturday or never. "By the way," I said, "I have to go to Liz's tonight."

"Oh," Mom said. "Is it some party?"

"No," I said, before heading upstairs. "It's not a party."

CHAPTER 12

"I THINK..."

WE LAY ON her bed, holding each other in the dim light from her desk lamp, twisted the other way. I remember saying, "I think" and "I guess" a lot, and a lot of "Maybe," "Probably," and "I don't know." I remember concluding, "Lots of ifs, ands, and buts!" and laughing a little, and she didn't laugh, and I didn't conclude. She picked at the bedspread with her fingernail, so delicate. I stopped and started over and stopped and started over. Her breath was slow and tremulous. She'd look at me with soft eyes, and I thought, *How can those eyes be so soft?* I could fall right into them and bathe. Then she'd look back at where she was picking but not look, not see. I thought about each word, *Is it really true? Really* really *true? How can it be? And if it is, how can I be here?* For years I'd felt certain things. I'd thought certain things, or I'd thought I thought them. I feared the day was coming when I'd look back and say I'd known them all along. But that night, actually saying those things to Liz—"Attracted to guys," "Well, more like *drawn* to guys," "Looking at guys on the beach," "Envying guys on the beach," "Think I might be more into guys," "Something in me,

call it envy or . . ."—it all sounded wrong. Not enough
or not important. Or too much. Like announcing they
had found bodies under the Captain Penniman House
or our house on Wrestling Cove. "A Town in Shock."
The announcer would say it "shook this peaceful sea-
side community to its core."

Bodies asleep forever under a half-house.

I'd be taken away.

I remember her head on my chest, wanting security, jumping with each beat of my heart. The rest of
the house didn't exist. Her mother and her kid brother
Randy didn't exist. My parents and my school didn't
exist. Pat . . . existed, but he couldn't help. No one
could help me set the next word and the next word in
place. This must have happened before. I hadn't dared
Google it.

She placed her hand over my heart, gently and
firmly.

I said "I wish" and "I hope" and back to "I guess."
Those deep eyes searched the dark side of the room.
With each step I took into what was supposedly the
real truth of my life, she blinked or bit her lip or made
a tiny, plaintive noise, but she didn't say anything.
But when I said I loved her it looked for a split second
liked she'd been stabbed by a thin, thin blade that
went deep. I absolutely meant it, though. I did love
her. I hated doing this. Every word I made up was like
my skin coming off. Her weight as we lay there felt
good on me, made me strong and responsible, but it
also suffocated me. I wanted to push her off and say,
"You know what? Forget everything. I made it all up.
December fool! Let's watch TV . . ."

I couldn't go back, though, so I tried to tidy everything up as much as I could. I didn't mention the
Exercise folder or Nate or my Eric Cantler obsession. I
just kept the simple sentences coming, repeated two
or three of twenty ways, preceded by "I guess" or "I

wish," and followed by "but," like those machines that lay down repeating patterns of bricks to make sidewalks.

"I feel things for guys, but obviously for girls, too, for you, obviously," or, "I guess the best way to describe it is: I feel moved by guys. I dunno. Compelled? Envious of? They just answer something in me. Probably because I never felt like much of a guy myself. Or not like enough of one. Just not being good at sports or. But obviously you answer something in me, something much more, a big something, a *huge* something!" There. A tiny smile from her. Gone. It must have taken a lot. Like a drowning person fighting to get half a second of air. Or letting the undertow win.

She sat up, her sweet-smelling hair falling down to my chest. "You don't have to keep saying how much you love me in spite of everything," she said, softly but definitely. Tears glistened in her eyes. Her voice shook. "I know you do, and it just makes it harder. Okay?"

I nodded. Though she had risen I felt a tremendous weight. There was so much unsaid. I reached up and stroked her hair. Her mouth tightened a little. She didn't move. She lowered herself, maybe sort of collapsed, next to me. "Forget about me," she said. "Just say what's happening to *you*."

"Cubs!" I said, going up on my elbow and arching partway over her. "How can I possibly forget you?"

"There," she said. "There you go again."

I opened my mouth but just stared at her. I hadn't planned anything except lots of apologizing, lots of putting myself down, and lots of reassuring her. And I guess I wanted her to reassure me. And maybe have sex again and maybe make it all not true. Now I wondered if I'd ever have sex again. Had I thrown everything away for—well, not for a lie, but for a truth I didn't understand?

She pulled her hair back, turned her head, and asked me, scowling, "Is there *someone?*" The scowl quivered and dissolved as she added, "Is that what this is about?"

I took a huge breath of relief and said, "No. No one at all, no one specific." She watched me, brown pools harder now, their glint like sword points. "What?" I said. "You're the only one, and that's totally, absolutely true. It just is."

"Not one of those guys at the bookstore?" She said it with a sad little smirk, like it couldn't possibly be.

Suddenly I resented it. Still, I stiffened myself and said, "What?? No! I mean, I find Nate, you know, nice-looking. Enough." She made a face. "I mean," I said, "that *is* kind of what I'm trying to tell you. I know you think he's a weirdo. Maybe you think they're both weirdos. I don't even know if he's, you know, the way I am. I barely even know what way that is." I felt horribly guilty, because at that point Nate and I supposedly had a Nuts 'n Beans date for Sunday. But of course nothing would happen. I just felt guilty about the reason—or one of them—that I had made the date.

"The other guy's more attractive," Liz said.

"Who, Pat? Liz, he's, like, thirty-something. Forty, almost!"

She shrugged and looked away. "I'm just saying what I think. He's more attractive. The blond one's a weirdo, like I said. Secretive. That's what I don't like." She shuddered.

"I'm not like that!" I said.

She frowned at me. It seemed like she was in some other place suddenly, tossing stuff back at me. "Who said anything about you?"

All I could think was, yes, Nate was secretive. And weird. Some of the guys at school I thought might be gay had that same secretive-haughty thing going on. Fruity. Like, too ripe; you bite into it and it's slimy and

David Pratt

too sweet and collapses. I dreaded being that. Why couldn't I just be a normal guy? Be normal, love Liz, and like guys, too? Why didn't it seem to work in reality? Would I ever touch another guy? Or would I just go on mentally wanting something about them? What would it be like the day I touched a guy like that? Would I like it?

Finally I asked, "What do *you* think, Cubs? I've been talking all this time, and I don't know what *you* think." I took a deep breath and braced myself. I was ready for anything. "Betrayal," "lying," "deceiving," "using," all of it.

She put her hand on my arm and played with the cloth. She swallowed. I looked down. My elbow was scrunched in the eye of one of her teddy bears. I tried to move it but couldn't very well.

"I guess . . . I don't know what I think," she said. "I know what I *did* think." She tugged at the cloth. "I *did* think I knew that I wanted to make love with you. To be close and have that bond, that *commitment.* I just wanted the time to be right. There was never any question about you. I didn't *think* there was. Then, last Saturday, I *thought*, this is it." Her hand stopped. She stared and stared at the folds of my shirtsleeve and breathed tremulously.

"What?" I said.

She shook her head, like a kitten shaking off water. "Nothing," she said. She let go of the shirtsleeve and turned partly away from me. "It was beautiful, how we fit together."

"Yeah," I said. "It was." I said. It seemed so long ago. The next time I'd touch anyone like that seemed impossibly far away.

"And I *thought*," she said, taking a huge deep breath and blowing it out, "that I couldn't wait to see you Christmas Eve. But I felt something missing. I told myself, it was all the people, the big *occasion.* And you

137

were sweet and attentive. Polite. Like always. But it was different. You weren't quite here. I got scared." She turned partway away and drew her knees up a little bit. "For the first time, ever, I started to wonder who you were. I'd never wondered that before. I'd never thought, *What's he thinking?* But that night I wondered, just a little, if you were who I thought you were—or if you were . . . ? And I thought, *Why did we make love?*" She wiped the corner of one eye with the sleeve of her turtleneck. "I thought it was because, you know, we were *in* love and wanted to have that thing, that, like, sharing. Being one thing. And I wondered . . ." She took another huge breath, like a gasp. "Did it have . . . ? I dunno!" She sniffled and wiped her eye again. She drew her knees up further.

There was this crocheted afghan on the bed. I pulled it from under me and put it over her. She took it and pulled it around her. She rubbed the corner of it back and forth across the tip of her nose. "Did it have what?" I asked.

She shrugged. "Nothing! I guessed . . . maybe it was true. Boys can love you, but they don't understand these things the same way girls do. Some crap like that." She paused. She turned her head halfway to me. "But I thought, *No. We always understand things the same way. Always!* Whenever anyone said that boys always do this or that inconsiderate thing, I always thought, *Not Mr. Wallace. He doesn't do that.*" She began to cry, her mouth stretched out in that way that's so awful to look at and her shoulders shaking. "I thought, *I'm so lucky; I have the one who doesn't do that!*"

I felt so lousy. I could barely touch her. I had no idea what to say. She had relied on me way more than I thought anyone would rely on me. She had relied on me, and she had loved me, and I thought I was unreliable and unlovable, but I'd somehow gotten lucky with

Liz. She somehow saw my shortcomings, and I guessed she didn't mind. God! What a horrible way to think about someone who had really and truly loved me!

"Now you tell me how you feel about guys. And the first thing I *thought* was, maybe you were trying to prove something. To show you could do it."

I felt even more miserable at that idea, but I didn't protest. The hardest thing that night, I guess, was just letting Liz say what she thought. Letting Liz say what it was like to be Liz right then. "It was awful to think that," she said, shaking her head. She turned another little way to me, legs tucking up some more. "But I knew it couldn't be true. The Jim Wallace I knew could not do that. He could be confused, he could make mistakes, and even if he did one thing and said another, it would have to be because he genuinely believed in each thing at the time he did it."

I couldn't help but smile. "Way too much credit, Cubs," I said, and I felt my own tears come.

She rolled all the way around. She almost did this little sideways dance, trying to pull her knees all the way up and keep the afghan around her. "Plus," she said, and I saw her struggling to control her face, "tonight, at one point, I stopped listening to you. I just concentrated on your breathing and that heart going a mile a minute. I could tell from your breathing and your heart that you were for real. Your breath and your heartbeat don't lie." She wiped her eyes with her sleeve. "I know you have to be up against something big." She played with my sleeve again. "Do I like it? Do I understand it?" She shrugged. "You're my friend. I'm still going to ask, 'How could this have happened?' I can't help it. I counted—"

She cried again. I scooted a couple of inches over to her and put one arm around her while the tears ran down. "I counted on things," she wailed softly. "I thought what we did meant one thing, and then—"

I opened my mouth.

"I don't mean those times, the good stuff," she said, holding up one hand. "But all that time, I thought a certain thing was happening—to me. And to you, too. To us. But some whole other thing was happening." She nodded. "I do," she said, and nodded more. "Yes, I do. I feel used." Her voice was lower and louder now. "I thought I had, you know, not much to offer. Dead dad and the first one to volunteer for bake sales." She scoffed. "Then Jim Wallace suddenly wanted me. I had something. I had something. I *felt like* someone. Not Velma Dinkley toting stale cupcakes!"

"That's terrible, Cubs!" I said.

She sighed and looked over at her dad's picture on her desk. He was holding her kid brother in his arms and smiling at the camera. She stood to one side in a frilly bathing suit, grinning. "He would have liked you," she said. "That's what I thought: *Dada would have liked him.* Silly. I guess. I was just silly. How could I—?"

"No, Cubs," I said softly. "You are never silly. Never ever. And you're not Velma. You're Daphne. Definitely."

"I believe you do . . . *feel* something for me. Maybe you need time. I don't know." She drew back her hair, tossed it, and adjusted it flowing down her back. I wanted to touch it but didn't. She tucked a piece behind one ear and looked at her dad again. "This is like some joke the universe is playing," she said.

Now, that annoyed me. I said, "Yeah, that's what I thought it was. A joke a day for eighteen years." She looked at me and her face hardened, but she didn't say anything. "I was gonna beat it, though," I said. "I was gonna show it. But I can't. It's bigger than me, Cubs, I guess." For the first time the thought flashed through my mind that this might not be my death, but a new life. The thought was gone quickly though, crushed under a lot of guilt and failure. Liz had turned back over, facing away from me.

Very softly she sighed and said, "I guess." I felt drowsy. Then I thought, *I never have to do this again. It's almost over, and no matter what happens now or how I feel, I never have to live through this moment again.* But Liz would. Liz would huddle with that afghan and hear my little announcement over and over. But she'd get another guy, wouldn't she? Easy.

What would she tell her mother and her girlfriends, though? "He thinks he's gay or something." And they'd say, "You know, I wondered." "It doesn't surprise me. He's not very, you know . . ." "He works for *Pat Baxter!*" "You know what Mrs. Budd said . . ." "Oh, that poor, poor Madelyn Wallace! And poor Jack! He's the *only son!* I can't *imagine* what *they're* thinking . . ."

I just wanted to be back in Wallaçonia, long, long ago. Or maybe I still *was* in Wallaçonia, a lonely kid, ignorant of everything. I tried to hold Liz gently. She stiffened. "Do you want me to go?" I asked.

"It doesn't matter," she said in a small voice. "Yeah, maybe."

"Are you thinking about your dad?"

"Of course I am," she said. "Always. Poor Mom. Randy won't talk about it. She tries to make him remember, and he just says, 'That was a long time ago' and goes and plays a video game."

Randy was fourteen. At fourteen I was picking on Nate Flederbaum and staring at guys in the shower, each naked body a judgment, a verdict.

"Maybe you should go," she said. She patted my arm, like, to seal it. I was both relieved and crushed. Even though I'd come planning to break up, I'd had this image of staying all evening. It wasn't even nine.

141

I felt weird having to see her mom downstairs and make small talk. Seeing Liz suddenly be perky and make small talk, too. Her mother looking at her face, at all the redness, and frowning. The relentless, repeating sound of Randy playing some game in the den. Liz's mom wanted him to come to the kitchen and say good-bye to me. I said, "No, please," but she insisted. The first two times he pretended he didn't hear, so the whole thing took forever. I felt exhausted, waiting while Liz and her mom just looked at each other kind of helplessly and hopelessly.

I knew somehow that Liz's mom had counted on me, as a guy. Everyone counted on guys, like in *Les Miz.* That was the definition of a guy: someone you counted on. Maybe if you were gay, you were sent to some place where no one counted on you. You were given up on. But Pat could be counted on, every time. For more than I could ever have imagined.

Liz's mom asked about Aunt Lillian. I still didn't know what exactly she had. Randy finally appeared, said, "'Bye" to me, was corrected, said, "Good-bye, *Jim,*" with an elaborate bow, asked, "Can I go now?" and left. Liz and her mom looked physically wounded. I'd said before that it was Aunt Lillian's heart, so I just repeated it and embellished it a little. Jim couldn't be counted on to *really* know, to really *do* anything.

We kissed each other on the cheek before I left. I told her I was proud to have a friend who was so generous when I had been dishonest and confused. She put her finger to my lips. It felt good, but I gently took it away. "You were right, though," I said. She glanced toward the kitchen, afraid her mom would hear, I guess. She'd have to explain to her. Now I was a problem. I looked into her eyes, and I said, "I pretty much believed everything I was doing, at the time I did it." She pressed her lips together and nodded. Then she glanced toward the kitchen again. I figured I'd better go. I repeated how I had to see Aunt Lillian tomorrow, though what I was doing tomorrow or any day didn't matter now. We hugged quickly. Then she pushed away and said, "Good night, my friend," her voice going down at the end, like it was the last thing she'd say to me, at least as my girlfriend. We broke, and I went into the night and inhaled a huge, huge gulp of cold air.

I felt like my mind, my body, and my mouth had all been saying different things. But sometimes they did agree. One thing I knew: I just didn't want to be alone. That wasn't completely true. Right then, I really did want to be alone.

At home, as I went through the living room, my mother said, "You're home early. Is everything all right?" I didn't think I had the energy to answer. I wanted to get to my Exercise folder. "It's fine," I said. I realized as I made my way upstairs that I'd sounded kind of like Randy.

"Jim . . . ?"

I stopped, took a second, and tried to moderate my voice. "Yeah?"

"Would you come back down, please, a minute?"

I went down and stopped in the doorway to the living room. There the two of them watched TV, Mom with a comforter over her knees, Dad sunk in his chair, the tree glowing and presents still stacked in the corner. The whole room said, "You can't be that. You can't." Had I just lost my best friend to something I couldn't follow through on? Did I just have a bad habit I should be able to fix? What if I couldn't? Should I go see a therapist? What would happen with the next girlfriend? Or would it be . . . ? I surreptitiously checked my phone; I was afraid Nate would cancel Sunday. The TV droned. Mom cleared her throat. Dad didn't look.

"You sent off all your college applications, didn't you?"

"Of course! Like, two weeks ago."

"All right. No need to snap. I just wasn't sure." She smiled and held up both hands with her fingers crossed. They were crossed for the college out in the Berkshires.

I managed a smile, then went back upstairs. I undressed, sat down, and opened the Exercise folder. I stared at one guy after another. If I could be them, I would not have to look at them. That had always been the story. Now, though, I could just for about two seconds imagine a life where I let go of the Exercise folder, but the thing it spoke to would still be me.

In the morning I saw an email, sent at 2:40 a.m., with the subject line, "What we talked about."

Dear Cubs:

After you left, I thought of a million questions I should have asked. I was so sad and shocked and angry and I still am. I cherished you, Jim Wallace. I still do. I think I always will. I loved making love with you, but it seems you have to do something else. I wish I could go with you on that journey. That is what friends are for. But maybe you have to take it by yourself. I mean it when I say I love you, and I know you mean it when you say you love me. Let's talk soon. I hope you are okay.

Your friend,

L.

My head swam over what to write back. I could see that I wasn't coming out of any closet, like they say. I was coming out of a maze. And going straight into another one.

I had to write something before we went to Aunt Lillian. I itched all over thinking about it. Finally I plunged in. I peeked at my Exercise folder almost between every sentence.

Dear Cubs –

I love you, too. What you wrote is beautiful. We will talk and see each other soon. Thank you for all your thoughts. They will help me a lot on my "journey," as you put it. Which I hope will include you as much as possible, if you want. I love you again, Cubs.

"Mr. Wallace"

I was going to add "I'm sorry," but I didn't. Whatever I did before or after, right at that moment, I was *not* sorry. Sitting with my tablet, looking out to where the decaying peat gave way to the sparkling cove, and beyond, to where the cove finally opened into the great, blank sheet of the bay, I actually felt good. But that good feeling came at the expense of my best friend feeling bad, and there was no way I could help that. Did she and I really have to be over? What if she didn't find someone else? I tried to think of something to add to my email to make things better. Finally I just clicked "Send." Then Dad called from the bottom of the stairs. It was time to go see Aunt Lillian.

On the way to Falmouth, Mom sat in back and I sat up front with Dad. He talked about the potholes we'd see if this winter was harsh, and how there'd been awful potholes in the roads after the blizzard of 1978. I just said, "Wow" and "Really?" I wanted to move over and nestle against him, but it would have been weird. We were quiet for a while, and then he said, "How about you? How's Liz?"

"She's fine," I said, before I could even think about it.

CHAPTER 13

"I WANT!"

THE HOME WAS called Sea View, but you couldn't see the ocean from it. To get there, you turned off Route 28 just past Waquoit Bay and drove past souvenir shops and food stands. In summer the stink was awful, but now they were closed up. In summer the Sea View sign would have baskets of flowers on either side. Now, the baskets swung in the wind with a few bent, brown stalks.

Inside, the smell got to you right away. They had cutglass dishes of potpourri everywhere, but this high school cafeteria smell was right underneath, plus vomit and, frankly, poop. In, like, seven varieties. People went around like they didn't smell it. Maybe they didn't after being there so long. Maybe they didn't hear the old woman crying, "Help me!" No one did anything. Or maybe they did, but she didn't know, so she kept crying, "Help me!" I guess she was crazy, and it didn't matter. But how do you go to work, knowing someone will be yelling "Help me!" all day, and it doesn't matter if you do anything? I felt sick, like when Mr. Baxter was telling me about his wife. Like when I had tried to tell Liz, "I don't know . . . sometimes . . . I think . . ."

In a way, having this hopeless, poop-smelling place was a comfort right now.

Aunt Lillian was in "skilled nursing," which was more like a hospital than where she was before. On the way to her room we passed skinny women in nightgowns clinging to the wooden railings that ran down the hallways. In the reception area, people sat around tied into their wheelchairs, opening and closing their mouths and rolling their eyes and grunting. The radio played the Eagles. Did anyone but me think that was weird?

I was afraid to see Aunt Lillian. I was afraid she would look dead. I was afraid she would *be* dead. I was glad when a nurse came up to us and took over and escorted us to the room. "Lillian, honey! Look who it is! It's your *family!* Isn't that nice?" If the nurse talked like that, everything was okay, right? Aunt Lillian looked confused, but she put her arms out to us, bony and veiny. The veins on the backs of her hands were dark purple, like you were seeing the blood, and it might spill out any second. Her eyes were watery and unfocused. Her face was creased like a totem carved out of wood, and her lips were chapped. The inside of her arm was purple and yellow where her IV was stuck in. The dressing was crusted with dried blood. She looked up at Dad and smiled a little. She was so much smaller than the last time I saw her. She was disappearing. She seemed to know who Dad and Mom were, though she mostly looked like she just wanted someone to hang onto. "You want me to crank up the bed, hon?" the nurse said. Aunt Lillian looked confused. The nurse cranked. Aunt Lillian's eyes widened. "Let me get you another pillow," the nurse said. Now Prince was on the radio outside. "Little Red Corvette."

"You remember me, dontcha?" the nurse said, arranging the extra pillow. "I'm your friend, right? I'm your pal." She smoothed Aunt Lillian's hair and turned to us, beaming. "We're pals," she said.

"Well, I can certainly see that!" Mom said, cheerful but kind of strained. Aunt Lillian tried a smile, the way she was supposed to, but it faded, and she looked sadder and more lost than ever.

I stepped up on cue and said hello. Aunt Lillian pointed and asked Mom, "Who is he?"

"You remember Jim," Dad said. He put an arm around my shoulder, a rare event.

"Who?"

"*Jim.* Our *son!*" Yeah, your failure son. They had no idea. Neither did Aunt Lillian. Their conversation, if you could even call it that, reminded me of my texts with Nate, trying to pin him down for a Nuts 'n Beans date: "How about Sunday?" "Sure." "What time?" "Anytime." "Afternoon?" We had finally agreed on Sunday at four o'clock.

"I don't know any Jim!" Aunt Lillian snapped indignantly. But then she looked around and made these whimpery little gasps, like she thought she should know, like everyone expected her to know, but she just had no hope of ever remembering. "It's okay," I said. "Really." I felt bad for her. She didn't mean to do this *to* us. She was old and sick and the loud nurse was cranking the bed and pushing pillows behind her. When things got bad, I could go to my room. Aunt Lillian didn't have a room or her own home or anything. She used to have a home, on Skunk Tail Road. In spring it was cool inside and smelled of cinnamon, and wet wool and cookies and pine at Christmas. There was a picture of my father as a little boy, and an old-fashioned flour sifter, and she grew avocados from pits in water glasses. I guess that house was cleaned out and sold at some point. I thought I might remember. We got some stuff from it. Mom was suddenly saying, "Careful of the antiques!" all the time.

Aunt Lillian's fake home here was bright, and everything was tan—tan blankets, tan walls, tan trays for tan food she wasn't eating, tan coffee in a tan cup. The TV was a huge, blind eye. There were crumpled tissues everywhere.

"I'm their *son!*" I said. I felt funny saying it. I wasn't any kind of son Aunt Lillian would know anything about. "I used to play on your living room floor!"

She stared and nodded slowly. Her mouth opened and closed, like a fish's. It was hard to tell if she was trying to say something or to chew nonexistent food. The nurse asked her if she didn't want to sit in the tan recliner. "You want to get up, Lil?" No one ever called her that. She looked panicky, but the nurse got her up anyway. My parents stood back. The radio switched to Bieber singing "Where Are U Now?" A man called out, "I want!" A few seconds later, he said it again, "I want!" He said it over and over and never finished.

Mom asked the nurse to grind up one of Aunt Lillian's pills to feed it to her, because it was "the size of a *horse pill.*" She tried to make Dad interested, but all he said was, "Yup, yup," like he might be agreeing or wishing she'd be quiet.

"Well," Mom muttered, "I guess I have to take the initiative!"

"We're going to sit here!" the nurse told Aunt Lillian.

Aunt Lillian said, "I don't want to sit down!"

"We'll sit you down here, Lil," the nurse said. "You can talk to your family. Won't that be nice?" Aunt Lillian kind of fell into the recliner. "Oopsie-daisy!" said the nurse. She fastened Aunt Lillian into the chair with a tan belt. Aunt Lillian waved her hands in slo-mo, as though she wanted the nurse to stop. Or wanted everything to stop.

Mom went out to the nursing station about the pill. She took Dad with her. "I want!" the man called. "I want!"

Everyone was gone. I hated this. What if she tried to get out of the chair or started crying or had some kind of attack? I hoped she'd just ignore me. After all, I couldn't be counted on.

She looked out the window, and her lips moved. Her eyes were all quivery and wet, like some blob in a Petri dish you'd touch with a needle, and it would spasm. Those eyes awful to look at. I remembered when she brought me those toys on her living room floor: wooden cubes with letters and colored rings. Boring for a kid like me who had all electronic toys, but they were old and reliable and had always been there, like the spicy smell of her house. Like Skunk Tail Road, a road going on forever. When I was little, I thought if we kept going down Skunk Tail Road, we would come to a big house that I'd seen in my dreams. The thing I would eventually call sex would be in that house, but in those days it would just be sunlight and cookies.

Suddenly she looked at me. Her lips moved. Finally she said, "I would say this is a *prison*, isn't it?"

"Yeah, I guess it is," I said. I reached for her hand. The man yelled, "I want!" Her hand just rested in mine, dry, cool, and motionless. She stared ahead. She was so small, like a kid almost. She looked like she was shrinking right in front of me.

When she spoke I was startled by how loud she was. "I'm never getting out, am I?" she asked.

"Sure, you are," I said. I glanced toward the door to see if anyone might be coming.

She shook her head and said, "No. Never." Her lips moved more; then she looked up at me and said, "You can't let me die here. You have to take me away!"

For a second I thought of abducting Aunt Lillian, going somewhere away from colleges and girlfriends or ex-girlfriends and guys who might be this or that and parents who might want or not want this or that. As nicely as I could I said, "Let me check if they're coming back." I went out to the corridor. I could hear Mom: "You're making her swallow a *horse* pill!" In Wallaçonia, Aunt Lillian would live in a cabin with a picture window and a real view of the sea, with a nice, quiet nurse twenty-four/seven. There'd be music she'd like: *South Pacific* and Benny Goodman.

When my parents came back, Aunt Lillian suddenly pointed at me and told them, "I want him to take me away!" I tried not to make a face, like *Can we please leave?* Mom tried to calm her down. They told her she looked better and she was going to get better still. She looked bewildered. She pointed at me again. "I want him to get me out of here."

"Tomorrow, Aunt Lillian," I said. "Tomorrow we'll get out of here." Mom looked startled, but Aunt Lillian actually calmed down. Dad smiled a little, but nobody said anything about what I said, not even on the way home.

We drove back past the shut-up clam shacks and souvenir shops. Pink streaks sat low in the sky. My heart felt heavy again. The stink and the glare of the nursing home stayed with me, telling me, I think, that everyone had to grow up and move on and make scary decisions. Or have them made for you. Or have stuff just happen for no reason at all. And no matter what you did, you couldn't stop it from ending in a stinky tan room with an invisible guy crying, "I want!" There hadn't even been pictures on the walls. No one could be bothered. Or it wasn't allowed. I wanted to get as far away as I could. The car wasn't fast enough. I pretended we were driving through Wallaçonia instead. But Aunt Lillian couldn't get away. She would die there, like she said, on a day just like the day before, the guy still yelling, "I want!" I couldn't think about it. I could only be relieved that we had pulled free of the clam shacks, and we were away, away, away, down Route 28, into Wallaçonia.

My parents did a little debrief about Aunt Lillian— Mom did, mostly. After that they didn't talk much. I checked for messages from Liz or from Nate.

Why had Aunt Lillian asked *me* to get her out? Maybe since she didn't know who I was, she thought I was magical. Maybe she understood somehow that *I* wanted to get out—of a lot of stuff. Decisions and obligations. The silence at home. My nice, safe silence. Eventually I would have to speak up and break it.

I thought about reconfirming with Nate, but I didn't want to risk him canceling. I looked out at dark woods and salt marshes rolling on and on. Night fell. I thought, *Just one more night in Wallaçonia.*

At home, a package lay on the doorstep, wrapped in brown paper, sealed with a gold Bay View sticker. Mom and Dad didn't notice it. I took it up to my room and opened it. Inside was a sorry-I-forgot-your-birthday card from Mr. Baxter and three books: *The Cabin by the Lake* by M. M. Morgan; *What We May Do* by J. B. Halperin; and a blank book, bound in leather, with "JHW" stamped on the front. I tossed Saralynn's books on the bed and stood caressing the cover of the blank book. For the first time in I-don't-know-how-long, I felt like someone was truly with me, in his heart, and I was with him, and things were good and might be even better.

I sat down to write some thoughts in the blank book. Not much. I just liked holding it more than anything. I forgot the two Saralynn books lying on the bed. Later, when I pulled back the comforter to get into bed, they slid and fell. I went to pick them up and saw writing inside the cover of one of them.

"To Jim," it said, "in memory of the day you courageously went looking for what you did not know. Best wishes, Pat."

A part of me that I rarely felt began not just to like but to love a part of him I had not truly seen before. What to do with that feeling, I did not know. But it gave me no place to go but forward.

CHAPTER 14

FOR BEING BAD

SUNDAY AFTERNOON AT Nuts 'n Beans and the Flederbaum Hummer was nowhere in sight. I went up to the window and peered in where it was bright and people went about their business. No Nate. I felt sick thinking I might not see him again. I wanted his smile and his softness. His forgiveness. His bruises. I wanted him to know he was actually beautiful and unbruised. I wanted him for once to feel beautiful and owe that feeling to me.

Meanwhile, I had to figure out how *not* to look like a doofus being stood up. I went and leaned on the gate in front of the store and hugged myself against the cold. I looked around like I didn't care. I didn't check my phone because there might be a message from Liz. Dark began to fall. At four-fifteen, I turned and with a jingle went inside just to make double sure before I left.

He was sitting all the way at the back with his jacket on, no coffee or anything. He looked up suddenly and just raised his eyebrows. I tried to explain that I had been there all that time, but he didn't act interested, and he didn't say that oops-there'd-been-a-mistake. Apparently he sat where he wanted when he wanted. But who meets someone at a café and sits in the back? I think he knew it was weird, the way he frowned and chewed his lip. He wished he'd done the normal thing, and now he couldn't.

I asked if he was going to have anything. I'd look dumb and self-indulgent slurping a *grande* capp while the quiet, upright guy foreswore all drink. Fortunately, he wanted a chai. I had planned to pay. I had never been able to buy anything for a beautiful guy. Telling him I was going to pay for him turned me on. But he refused. He handed me some raggedy bills. He did let me go get it, though. While I waited for my name to be called. I tried to think how I was going to begin. Turned out I didn't have to. When I came back and set the mugs down and dumped sugars and stirrers, even before I sat he said, "You spoke to Pat." Just flat like that. Kind of accusatory. Was this an interrogation? I thought we were going to be two guys hanging out, breaking the ice, me saying something sweet and he'd blush, etc., etc.

Well, guess not!

"Pat spoke to *me*," I said coolly.

Nate's lip curled. He flipped a stirrer around and around with his fingers. "Did he tell you why he left Benleigh?"

So, I'd say "yes" and then be told I didn't really know? Was there a Baxter-Flederbaum tag team messing with my head? No, Pat was discreet, but he didn't lie. He was Mr. Integrity; that's what I loved him for. But Nate? My eyes settled on his chest. Between his chamois shirt and thermal T-shirt, I can't say I saw it *tremble* exactly. But I saw his breath came un-evenly, like he was working on something difficult. I couldn't reach across the little table and *hold* him, but I thought I could hold him with my voice. Gently I said, "He told me he always wanted to be on the Cape. That he loved that barn and—"

155

Softly and briskly Nate asked, "What else did he tell you?"

"Um, I guess there was some incident at Benleigh—"

"*And* . . . ?"

"Look," I said, "were you him? This 'Teddy' guy?" No, of course, he couldn't be, but everyone was so touchy about the whole thing, I was anxious to get some one piece of info straight.

Nate wrinkled his nose. "Who's Teddy?"

I explained.

"Oh!" He scoffed and shook his head. "Larry Kingsley. I don't know why we have to use *pseudonyms*." His face turned a little sad. "No, I am definitely not Larry Kingsley. 'Teddy,' huh? Pat Baxter, proper down to the last whatever." He fell silent and twirled the stirrer.

"*And so* . . . ?" I said.

"*And so*, I was the one who squealed!" Leaning toward me, his face flushed, he said, "I was the one who turned him in! Pat!"

"Okay," I said, trying to sound as gentle as I could. "I wondered. But you're friends now."

He nodded and pressed his lips together. I can't remember what he changed the subject to. Weather or tourists or something Cape-like. Finally he said, "You don't want to know why?"

"You mean, why you turned him in? If you want to tell me, sure." Holding him with my voice wasn't working. I felt like I had an emotional boner and couldn't get off. "You don't have to." I almost reached for his hand. "I wouldn't want you—"

Looking down into his tea he said, "I liked Larry." He got even more flushed. "I wanted him to like me. For one day. One perfect afternoon. We'd talk." He shrugged and gazed off into a corner. I saw a path, in fall, going off over some meadows, where he wanted to go with Larry and never could. "Every day I looked, and tried not to look." He shook his head. "But he never—I mean, no, never, not at all." He made a sweeping gesture, palm flat. "Not once." He hunched forward, both hands now under the table. "Then his parents got divorced. I wanted to do something for him that would really *mean* something."

He looked so sad and lost and beautiful, just like what Mr. Baxter said about Larry, standing in his kitchen. "I know what you mean," I said. All the guys I had wanted to help and be alone with and be best friends with on all those meadow paths. But Nate acted so self-sufficient. I didn't know how to sympathize with him. I imagined him lying in his bed at Benleigh, longing to hold Larry, like Mr. Baxter longing for his daughter. Like me, lying in bed at six years old, five in the morning, thinking of things I could do for this boy in my first-grade class who was on crutches.

"Finally I tried saying something to him," Nate said, curling his lip and looking away. His fist rested on the tabletop, inches from me, clenching and unclenching. His other fist was in his pocket. "It was like . . . like he didn't even get that I was talking to him."

I knew that, too. I'd tried to talk to the boy on crutches. One afternoon, we were getting on the bus, and I did what I'd dreamed of for weeks. I offered to hold his crutches for him while he got on. He said, "Just get away, will ya?" The other kids laughed. They imitated me offering to hold the crutches. All the way home to Wallaçonia I sat while they said, "Hey, Wallace! *Can I hold your crutches, ple-e-ease*???"— knowing my feelings were wrong. And the boy with the crutches laughed with them, and I sank down and thought about my shells and books and tried not to cry.

"But Larry wanted Pat." I said.

Nate nodded, but his nod was mixed with a shaking of his head, as though "yes" and "no" and headshaking done in bewilderment all got mixed. In my head I told Liz, "See? You can never say 'yes' about anything and you can never really say 'no.'"

"One time," Nate said, "in the middle of it all, the divorce, Larry spent the night at Pat's. I saw him go in, in the evening. And come out the morning. In the same clothes."

Whoa! I didn't know that. If it was true, I understood, though. I wouldn't tell that part either.

"I convinced myself it was my 'responsibility' to report it. I told this faculty wife. I liked her, sort of. Everyone thought she was an idiot, and everyone thought I was a weirdo, so I, like, felt for her, I guess. I told her just so I'd have *someone*. I said, 'It should be *reported*.' And she agreed." He sighed. I imagined how his heart broke, seeing Larry come out of Mr. Baxter's door in the morning. Not that they did anything. I believed Pat about that. But the fact of spending the night near someone. How guys look asleep.

I remembered my cousin staying in my room. At dawn his broad, bare shoulders and back. I got up and wandered through the house until my parents got up. When my cousin finally came down, Mom offered him all kinds of things for breakfast in this enthusiastic voice she never used with me.

Just the thought of Larry, under a blanket on an older guy's couch. I watched Nate's face, regretful, aching. I could imagine him making the whole thing up. I don't mean lying. Just making it up. A lonely boy building a tragedy out of Legos. His imperfection. Larry's perfection. Snap 'em together.

"She went to the head," Nate said. "I thought Pat would just resign. And Larry would need someone, and we'd go for a walk, or, well, I don't know. Then an article came out in the school paper. The *Montis*." He actually smiled at me! Jeez, he was beautiful! "It's Latin for *hill?* Because the campus is on one? Imagine admissions, though: 'Mr. and Mrs. Smith, you and little Johnny might enjoy a copy of the *Montis!*'" He grinned generously, then slowly he clouded over again and chewed his thumbnail.

"The article said how Pat would leave at the end of the year. I was sweating. It was me! I was responsible! I had to pass him every day, two or three times, and he didn't know I was the one." He sighed. "I had to tell him. I was never more scared in my life. Finally, I made myself go to his apartment, made myself knock, and babbled something like, 'Oh, I hear you're leaving.' He said, 'Come in.' I came in and sat down, real carefully, like I'd spread a disease. He said he was fine and talked about the bookstore, how he'd always wanted it. He was a nice man. I wanted to die. Everything was happening at once in my head. I hyperventilated. I was crying. He came over and put his hand on my shoulder and said, 'It's all right.'" Nate blew out a breath. He kept his gaze down. I was so overcome by a wish to help and hold and whatever else, maybe that's when I really started knowing I was gay. As much as I had felt for Liz, my desire to care for Nate right then, to care for his masculinity, seemed like the thing people really meant when they talked about love.

"I told him, 'I'm so, so sorry,' and he said, 'It's okay. It's natural.' I told him he didn't get it. I said, 'I'm the reason you're leaving!' He looked surprised. He said, 'Well, then, I should thank you! I'm finally getting my dream.' I kept saying, 'No, no, it's worse, it's horrible,' and so he said, 'Nate, do you *like* Larry?'" He sighed and slumped and wiped quickly at his eyes. "I bawled," he said softly, shaking his head. "It was the biggest relief of my life. Like the sun came out." He looked at me, eyes uncertain. "I felt lousy, but I was relieved. You know?"

"Yeah," I said. My hand was twitching. I so wanted to touch him, grab him, and frankly, French him from there to the middle of next week, even though I'd never done that to a guy. At the same time, I still couldn't believe we might be the same. "I was practically convulsing," Nate said. "He said, 'It's okay to *like* someone. You like Larry. Maybe it's the first time it's been this strong. Then you saw him with me. You felt betrayed and abandoned. You felt so violated, you had to tell, had to say it, and you found the only person who might possibly care, and you told it to them the way you experienced it.'

"Here I'd been thinking ever since I met Larry that I was bad. That Larry was put there, put on earth, right in front of me, to show me how bad I was. And what I got for being so bad was Pat understanding. I told Pat the story of Evil Nate. He's like, 'You know, 'Nathaniel' means 'God has given.'" Suddenly tears were coming down Nate's face and his whole mouth was quivering. "I thought, if my parents could hear that! Well, they never would. And then he gave me that smile, you know? Like, when he's about to teach you some life lesson you can't get out of?"

"Yup!" I nodded and smiled, though I was almost starting to cry myself.

"He said how no one knows much about Nathanael in the Bible, except he was truthful. 'You came here to tell me the truth,' he says. 'So you have to stop saying you're so bad. It's not true. What's true is, you are new at this. The emotions are big.' Whatever. He said it: 'Larry can't do what you want.' He let me lie down, right there, right on the sofa where Larry had been. Suddenly I was the one. Like, the accepted one.

"I still wanted Larry to see me, talk to me, let me help. But now, if I felt shitty over Larry and shitty over

160

who I was, I'd be walking on the quad and see Pat, and he'd say, 'Hi,' and I'd know I had a friend—who knew."

"So," I said, "If you don't mind me asking, does your family know . . . that . . . you . . . ?"

His face got still as a stone. "Not really," he mumbled. Then he looked up at me. "I told you I'm going into the army, right?"

"Yeah, "I said. "I mean, how? The Israeli—"

"They don't know yet."

"Your family? But, the Israeli army, how do you do even do that? How can they not know?"

He explained in a lot of detail about what was actually called the "Israeli Defense Force," or IDF, and how foreign-born Jews could join. He talked fast and mumbled, and I couldn't totally keep up. It seemed there were different "paths" to join the IDF, and the paths had Hebrew names I kept forgetting. Nate would take the path for people who weren't fluent in Hebrew, but he would "serve shoulder to shoulder with regular Israeli soldiers." That sounded like it came off a website, and in fact it did (I looked later). But he sounded definite. He would tell his parents soon. He had to, because, to get into the IDF, he had to prove that they were Jewish. He also had to learn more Hebrew. He'd been studying it from podcasts. He had applied for college but would get a deferment. Service in the IDF was just fourteen months. He sat silently a moment and twirled the stirrer. People came and went and I heard the steam on the espresso machine go off. Nate's tea was gone. I had a puddle of cold cappuccino and dried foam.

Finally he said, "So why did you do all that stuff to me?" He smiled sadly and blushed.

I was so unprepared I said, "Huh?"

He repeated the question.

"I guess I was . . . afraid," I said. "You . . . liked me, maybe?"

To my total shock he nodded and looked right at me and said, "Looked up to." While I caught my breath, he went on. "You were one of the smart ones. You knew all the answers. So I'd think up these dumb questions to try to trip you up. I thought it was fun. When you got pissed, you were even—okay, maybe 'sexier' isn't the word, exactly, but you had this kind of *stare*. You sort of still have it. Sexy. Yeah. Sort of." I felt myself blushing. I put my hand up to my face. I said "Wow" or "Jeez" a couple of times. The idea that what I called mean was sexy to Nate . . . I felt totally freakish and wanted to hide. The place I could run to, the place I could escape to—the new Wallaçonia—was his body. "Nate," I said, "can I just *touch* you?"

"*Touch* me?" He glanced around. "Here?"

"I care about you, and I care about saying this! Can I?"

He hunkered down more and from the way his shoulders worked, he seemed to be sort of wringing his hands or something under the table. "So what were you afraid of?" he said.

"Maybe I liked you, too," I said. "I said mean stuff, stuff *I* thought was mean, but I kept talking to you." He looked around again to make sure no one was hearing. "And you kept talking to me. We had some-thing. But I also kept my distance. I couldn't—"

"Be friends with fat, fairy Nate with the braces?"

I stopped. He had me. I was shocked. Plus, what did he mean about "a guy like" me? "Hey," I said, "I looked at guys, too! I had guys that I, okay, maybe 'worshipped' is too strong, but guys I wanted to be. Wished I knew them. Then you came along." I smiled. "Pudgy with braces and a pain in the ass." He smiled, too, but it faded. "Always coming after me. And I guess I knew we were, you know, maybe alike. But I *couldn't* be like that!

"But today," I said, "you're the one I'd want to look like!" He tensed. His eyes went back and forth. I'd said it too loud. Hey, it was exciting to say! Everything was new and an experiment now, like a kid in a candy store (on the Cape it would be an ice cream parlor, though). I lowered my voice and went on. "I mean, handsome, and the way you're built up—"

"So I should forget about before?"

"No! You can't. No one can. And I'm sorry. But if you think I felt secure and, you know, superior or whatever, if you think I had it *easy*—"

"I know, I know," he said. He readjusted in his chair. "It doesn't matter, anyway."

"No, it does!" I said. I wanted to keep talking. I wanted someone finally to know my story, dumb and yucky as it was. I also wanted to know about Nate, about him getting beat up. I wanted to be the guy for him that he had wanted to be for Larry. I told him about looking for him and finding his mom—minus her craziness, of course—and what she said about guys beating him up. It was a little like stepping on a land mine. His cheeks flushed and his nostrils flared. "You *stalked* me?" he said.

"I always wanted to apologize, for a long time. I just wanted to know, you know, where. . . . I asked at this cleaner's and your mom was there. She thought I was some guy who beat you up. Did someone? Beat you up, really?"

All kinds of expressions crossed his face, like he was reacting to a whole movie in his head. He looked angry, pleading, heroic, but mostly he wore this strong-sad look. He started flipping the stirrer again. His nails were trimmed, like, perfectly. I tried to get him to look at me. Suddenly he said, "Let's go somewhere." But he didn't move.

"We can sit in my car," I suggested.

"I want to look in your face," he said, very low, "when I explain." He flipped the stirrer. Then he looked up and said, "I'm deciding whether or not to tell you something."

One last sip and he got up, took his coat and scarf, and walked out. I followed pretty fast, but I didn't see him out on the street. It was all the way dark. Finally, I saw the Hummer on a side street. He leaned against it, shivering. I ran up. "My parents are up in Cambridge," he said, "till late." He turned and climbed into the driver's seat. I assumed he wanted me to get in the passenger side. Good thing I crossed around back, though, because suddenly he pulled away. I had to run for my own car and follow as best as I could. By the time I was in gear, the Hummer was gone, but I basically knew the way to South Sicassett. Eventually I found his taillights ahead, threatening to pull out of sight and leave me lost.

CHAPTER 15

NAKED

HE PARKED IN his driveway, shut off the Hummer, and headed up the porch steps. As I stumbled out of my car, I called, "Are you gonna lock yourself inside, too?" He stopped. I came panting up after him. He unlocked the back door and went in. I followed and closed it behind us. I went after him through the kitchen as he pulled off his jacket and sweater and, coming into the dining room, threw them over a chair. The dining room was nicer than ours—big cabinets with lots of cut glass and china with silver edges. The chairs were tall and carved. I felt for a second like I was in Europe.

In the living room, his back still to me, he unbuttoned his shirt and pulled it off.

Uh-oh! I had this idea that gay guys could be kind of bim-bam-boom with sex, and yeah, thinking about that could be exciting, but I wanted to make love.

He threw the shirt on the floor, then pulled off his undershirt the way guys do, crossing his arms, which I think is kind of hot. His bare torso stretched and his head disappeared, and in the light coming from the porch I saw the blond hair under his arms. I felt proud and turned on that little Nate was grown-up. He whispered, "Ow!" and stopped a second. Then he pulled the undershirt the rest of the way off and tossed it aside. I watched the curves and bulges of his shoulders and arms, outlined in light. He stood with his hands on his hips and stared at me. It was exciting but annoying. What was I supposed to do? Was this about having sex? I undid a couple of buttons of my shirt, then stopped. Still he stared. I stared back. His shoulders and upper arms were downy and rippling. He had a little hair in the center of his chest, a flat, rippled stomach. He had his revenge, all right. He was what I had dreamed of, seeming to offer himself the way I had always hoped, but something was off. I came up closer to him. I was standing two feet from Nate Flederbaum, his bare chest heaving, his lips parted, and I began to see, on his chest and his shoulder, and then on his belly, blotches of yellow and green.

"Nate!" I said. "Holy shit!" I placed my hand on his abdomen. It was warm, and it was sweetly soft and hard at the same time. He tensed. I tried to make my words soft as gentle as my hand: "Who did this? Does your mom think—?"

"This is what it's like," he said. "This is what it was like, every day."

"Nate, I never did anything!" I caressed all his bruises. Then I stroked his hair.

"You made some of these," he said, low and evenly, "even if you didn't. Shame on you!"

I felt sick. He was right, even though I burned inside at how unfair it was that I had to pay now. It was five years ago. I was thirteen then, a totally different person. Plus, he'd brought me here and taken his own clothes off. Not to sound like I was thinking with my dick, but when someone does that, you have expectations. You at least expect a person will be nicer when they're naked. Well, his body was beautiful, but he was more a soldier now than ever, keeping intruders out of his beautiful country. "Did guys from around here do this?" I said.

"Yeah. She thinks."

"They did it at Benleigh?" I imagined Mrs. Flederbaum storming into the head's office and making a scene. He shook his head.

"Where, then? Who?" Who had damaged such beauty? It horrified me. I touched him because I wanted him to have his beauty back.

He glared. His head jerked up toward the ceiling, and he spat out the word, "Him." I didn't get it right away. He jerked his head up again and said, "*He* did it."

"Your . . . not your dad!" I said. "How? You're strong enough to—!" I was trembling. I thought I'd fall apart with the craziness and injustice of it all.

"You don't," he said, "when it's your father." His voice cracked. He bit his lip. "He found something. In my room. Plus, this friend from Benleigh called. He made fun of the way the guy talked. All day he made fun. Then I went up to my room. And there he was. Holding the thing. The magazine. He was shaking. His whole body. I'd never seen him like that. I'd never seen anyone. I just kept saying, 'Please, please.'" He coughed and the crying spluttered out. "'Please, Dad. No.' I thought, if you looked your own dad in the face and *begged* he *couldn't possibly.* . . .'" Now his face hardened. His lips twisted. "Boy, was I wrong!"

His stomach convulsed, caving in, his muscles becoming more defined. In a soft, high voice he said, "I don't remember it hurting. I don't remember when it ended." He paused, drew a deep breath, and said, "He hasn't said anything since. He didn't hit my face. He knew better." He had recovered his kind of snide voice. "But one time, in front of my mom, I took off my sweater and my shirt pulled up . . . ? She saw this."

167

He pointed to the bruises. "She grabbed my shirt and pulled it up higher. She demanded to know. Again and again. In this voice she has."

I almost said, "Yeah, I know!"

"I said it was 'some kids around here.' She screamed at *him* to do something. Go to the police. They fought. I said no, it wasn't that bad. But today she was talking about the police again, stroking my hair, saying, 'My poor *tateleh.*' I think she suspects. What he did. I bet she suspects why. It happened before. A couple of times, maybe." He shrugged.

I had to protect him. I had my arms around him, and I pressed my face to his warm neck and kissed and then couldn't stop, except to breathe, "Oh, Nate!" I couldn't think of anything else. Or, I could think of about a thousand things. But I just repeated his name and stroked his hair and kissed the neck I'd been a thousand miles from and now I was touching. He put his arms around me, lightly. I was kissing him on the mouth. And again, harder. And he was letting me! I opened my mouth. Wow, the soldier sure knew how to respond! I'd never had someone's mouth *wrestle* with mine before. His tongue dug and thrust and pulled. We were speaking to each other, shouting, telling stuff with our kisses. My chest felt about to burst. For the first time, I knew I had a soul, and I knew what I was doing was right, and I had to go on doing it, no matter what anyone said, because my soul was speaking. I would obey. I'd figure out the million and one things that would happen now. I was invincible.

We broke, panting, and I just held his face against mine. I felt his heart and his breathing; they said in science class, those are the two things that never stop till you die.

All the stuff I'd done, the stuff I'd imitated but never felt like I was really doing it—now I *was* really doing it, to a guy, without thinking. I felt loved. Not so much by

Nate, but by the world, universe, whatever. He took a deep breath and held me a little tighter. I poked at his ear with the tip of my nose. He jerked his head away, then he brought it back. I touched my nose to his earlobe. I wanted to suck it, but I didn't dare, so I just kissed. He kissed me once, behind my ear. I ran my hand down his back. "I'm so sorry," I said.

"Don't be," he said, suddenly. He kissed my neck. "Don't be, man."

"You're very brave and very good," I whispered.

"Huh. Thanks," he said.

"I can feel how good you are." His heart was knocking away, and my own was thumping pretty hard. I worked to catch my breath. His fingertips picked at a seam on my shirt. It was just so sweet. I really got now why people make love. You *feel* so damn much for someone, you just have to. I kissed him again. I didn't worry if I was doing it right, like with Liz. I didn't worry if any part of me was inadequate. I was being who I was. Everything about me and what I did was good. I was so driven, I really got what it all was *for*. Finally he stroked my hair. "You mean . . . so well," he said, panting, a weird thing to say in the clinch, but it made me feel bigger, like I was growing and becoming solid and real right before my own eyes. He kissed me again. "There is no one," he panted, "who would come back four years after he wronged you and do what you did. It's kind of, like, the sexiest thing ever." He laughed a little. "Really!"

"Well," I said, clutching him to me and whispering right in his ear so I thought I could feel the hairs on my lips, "there's not a lot of guys who'd appreciate it. Can we maybe lie down?"

He looked around and said, "Um, dunno." He had a bunch of reasons for not going to his room. The main one was his mother would know, I guess because of the sheets. He said she'd know if we used the couch, too. We decided on just the living room floor. He undid his pants and shucked them. He turned out the only light, so I couldn't see if he was aroused. I sure was. I rushed to catch up with him. Now he stood, legs spread, hands on his hips. In the light from the porch, coming in the living room windows, I could see the outline of his broad shoulders and muscular calves. He left his underpants on, so I left mine on, too. I wanted him to take mine off. I'd always wanted that, for someone to take my underpants off when I was aroused.

We got down on the floor—I heard and felt him wince from the bruises—and we made out some more. The carpet was rough against our skin; he kept shifting around. I pressed the front of my shorts to the front of his. He pressed back, then retreated. "Do you think we could be naked?" I asked. He hesitated and said, "I don't know." It took a lot of strength, but I said, "It's okay if we don't." He waited a bit and then said, "I've just . . . I never . . . you know—"

"Me, either," I said. It was true that I'd never done it with a guy, plus I wanted him to feel better and the two of us to feel closer. "It would make me proud to do it with you."

He laughed suddenly and said, "Why?"

"Because," I said, laying a hand on his chest, "in here you're such a beautiful man."

"Oh, come on!"

"I saw it the first day! Kinda silent and pissed off, but beautiful." That got a laugh, and I saw his shoulders and chest relax. "Plus," I added, "who goes to meet someone at a coffee shop and waits *inside* in the *back*?"

"Okay, okay. Sorry. I was, whatever, shy, I dunno."

I stroked his hair and said it was okay. Then I leaned down and kissed him.

"You know what?" he said softly. "Oh, um, I don't know if I want to say this."

"Anything Nate Flederbaum tells me," I said, "is kept here." I took his hand and placed it on my chest. "And never goes anywhere."

His fingertips played with my chest hair: "Like, in secret, sometimes I think I might be beautiful. Inside. But I would never tell anyone. It's my little secret with myself. Now I guess it's our secret."

"And it's true," I said. I took his hand and kissed it.

There was a pause. I felt how nervous he was about the underwear and all that, so I just held him, and he held me. I tried not to think about anything but making him feel safe. I didn't think right then how he could get killed in Israel. I told myself, he was American, and they must have special protections or something. Still, the thought of anything happening to his body made me touch him even more gently. I didn't say anything. There was nothing to say.

We kissed on the lips, once, twice; then he put his head back and opened his mouth. I was on him and kissed him deep for a long time. While we were kissing he worked his underwear off. He didn't take mine off; I had to handle that myself. We embraced again and said each other's names and gently touched each other. "Oh, nice!" he whispered. "Yours, too," I said. I slipped my hand around to his butt. He did the same, and we pressed together. He gasped. I wanted to say some kind of dirty stuff, but I didn't think he'd go for it. I didn't quite want to say I loved him. *In* love, yes, but saying even that might be too much. "How do you feel?" I said. He said, "Good." We kept pressing together, then we humped, then he wanted to slow down a bit. I wasn't sure how to tell a guy it was safe to have an orgasm. You feel so like a baby. Could he do it? I played with him just gently. He returned the favor. We got into a rhythm. Our breathing sped up, and soon

171

we were whimpering and gasping, "Oh, yeah," and, "Yeah, go for it," and going nuts and not caring.

For a long time we held each other and panted. I said, "Thank you, that was beautiful," and he said, "Likewise." Then, suddenly, he asked, "What's your name? Your full name?"

"James Howard Wallace." He repeated it, softly, his eyes on the ceiling. "You?" I said.

He smirked. "Isaiah Nathanael Flederbaum."

I repeated it and said, "It's beautiful."

He made a face. "Dude, are you joking? 'Flederbaum?' 'Flying tree'?"

I grinned and tousled his hair. "Is that why I can't find you on Facebook? I should be looking under 'Isaiah'?"

He shook his head. "Look under my Hebrew name," he said, sounding very official. "Type in 'Yehonatan F.' Hey, you want a Hebrew name? We can type 'James' into the Hebrew Name Generator."

So we ended up, two naked, messy guys, cross-legged on the Flederbaums' living room floor, hunched over a laptop, bare knees and shoulders touching. He typed "James" into the Hebrew Name Generator and clicked, "Let's Ask God." I got my choice of "Jeremiah" or "Yirmeyahu"—basically the same thing, but we agreed "Yirmeyahu" was cooler. Then he showed me the IDF site. That took a while. Then I asked him what music he liked, and he had never heard of Low Anthem, so I played him a couple of their videos.

We listened to this song of theirs, "To Ohio"—which happened to be all about finding and losing love—and slowly we put our arms around each other and touched our heads, and after a minute or so, our breathing came together. When the song ended he said, "I guess my parents'll be back," but neither of us moved. After a bit he turned his head and said, "Bathroom's in there, if you want." I went, and I felt a little sad cleaning up. I tasted a little bit that I thought was his, and I whispered his name—"Isaiah, Nathanael."

When I came out, he was there leaning against the wall, arms folded. He went in without a word and closed the door. He did smile as he went past, though.

In the living room I dressed quickly. It spooked me being alone, surrounded by the parents' stuff. What if they did walk in? Nate came back, smiled at me again, and got dressed himself. He winced and said "Ow!" when he put his undershirt back over his head. I hugged him. "It's okay," he said.

"It's not okay," I said. "If I was your dad"—my voice caught in my throat. "If I was him, I . . . I would be so proud. I *am* proud. Maybe it sounds weird, but I am. I am proud to know you, and I am proud that I *knew* you, even then."

"Well, yeah, that is weird," he said.

"Well, it's true," I said. I guessed it was time for me to go. He was thinking about his parents, and I was thinking about mine. Night had fallen. They were probably worried, or they'd say they were. "You go back to school . . . when?" I asked. "Sunday," he said. "I'll text you." I nodded, a little disappointed. I hoped we might see each other again, but with his crazy family and everything, I guessed it had to be this way. "We can hang out when you come home," I said. "Before you go . . . over there." He nodded. I hugged him again. He hugged back lightly, but like he meant it; his mind was just on his dad. He had a lonely journey to make. I had been allowed to help a little. We'd given each other our first experience loving another guy. We'd given the thing we'd wanted to give for years but had no idea how. Now I had to go.

I turned and headed slowly for the back door. There was one thing I was still wondering. At the back door I stopped. He had his hand out. "Nate," I said. "Why are you joining the army?"

"I might," he said, very slowly, "need a home."

"A what?" Stupid me, I didn't get it.

"He said, if anything like this happened again, he'd
. . . throw me out. I don't know what she could do. The
rest of the family's in either Austria or Washington
State, so I'd have no—" He winced and tried to hold
himself perfectly still.

"You could come to me!" I said.

"I might stay over there," he sighed. Then he
coughed, but I realized it wasn't a cough but a splut-
ter, from trying to keep from crying. His head bowed.
His shoulders shook, and I put my arm around him.
He made mucusy-slurpy sounds and an awful, low
wailing like an animal. His tears wet my jacket. He put
his hands on my arms. Then, almost as suddenly as
he'd started, he took a deep breath and gasped, "I'm
sorry." He said it once and wiped his nose, and it was
all over. He pressed his lips together and glared, like,
at himself, as he stepped around me and opened the
door. He put out his hand. It was weird and cute. All
that kissing and bodily fluids, then a handshake.

Outside was colder and silent. As I looked back at
the house my phone buzzed in my pocket. Nate's sil-
houette disappeared from the back door. I pulled out
the phone. Text from Liz: "how r u?" I put the phone
back without answering. I didn't know how I was.

Nate hadn't told me how to get home, and I hadn't
asked him. I guessed I could follow signs to Route 6,
and then it would be one exit. I entered our address in
my phone, but I turned the volume off and just drove
randomly for a while, taking turns just for the sake of
taking them. A lot were dead ends. Finally I turned the
phone on. The mechanical voice kept saying, "Recal-
culating" over and over. When I finally saw a sign for
Route 6, I was relieved. I drove toward the light and
turned.

CHAPTER 16

THE MAKER OF THE WORLD

SCHOOL STARTED AGAIN, my last semester of high school. I blew off a lot of stuff, cut a class or two, went to Providence and Boston with friends and even New York, where we saw *Pippin* and went on the High Line. Everywhere I went I'd stop suddenly and think, *I did it. Just like other guys. But not like other guys. I am officially different.* Sometimes I thought it triumphantly, but I also worried. What did it really mean, being different? What would happen to me? I knew I was ready to leave the Cape. I just wasn't sure a nice little college way out in the Berkshires was the answer. But it had seemed so right, and everyone was counting on it.

Liz and I tried hanging out now and then, but it always got awkward. I didn't stop thinking she was attractive. I even desired her, but what really made me breathe funny and go a bit dizzy was the thought of being with Nate again, us breathing together, me saying things to make him feel loved.

But there was one more thing Liz and I had to deal with. We'd already planned to go to this dance, the Winter Informal, soon after New Year's. We decided to go ahead with it because, hey, we were still friends. Liz said, "I mean, nothing *HUGE* has been decided," and since we were used to being together and I could still look at her and want her, I believed what she said and went with it. Plus, most everyone thought we were still a couple—they still saw us talking in the hallways (but somehow didn't notice sometimes when Liz was crying), and if we were walking along she took my hand, "just as a friend," and I let her—and we didn't want to have to answer lots of questions about why we weren't going to the informal or why we went with other people or went solo, plus how would that even work? Would we dance together at all? Or just one dance? Or what? So we went together, "as friends." That's what we told ourselves. We didn't think about how going together had basically the same problem: were we going to hold hands in front of other people? That was friendly. How about kissing, and what about slow dances? I thought about that stuff, but I didn't bring it up. I guessed we'd just . . . whatever.

We met in the school parking lot. Liz came with her friend Alisha, who I think knew what had happened. I felt tired even before going in. I'd felt tired at home getting dressed. Liz gave me a quick peck on the lips and took my hand. I held on. The gym was hung with these big, shiny, droopy snowflakes. They had this local band, You Could Be Swept Away (it comes from beach signs over on the Atlantic Ocean side), which was, like, half Eagles cover band but played their own stuff, too. We danced a lot with other kids so we didn't have to think so much about kissing or not, but slow dances with other people seemed weird, so we sat them out or danced together but not actually hugging. Eventually Liz asked if I wanted to take a break. I did—just not with her. Not with anyone. I just wanted to go home and stare at my maps.

We walked out, down past the cafeteria, around the corner by the wood and metal shop, darker and more locked up than I could ever have imagined rooms in my high school being.

We were alone. She put her arm through mine and then put her head on my shoulder. I must have sighed funny or looked funny because she suddenly stopped.

How do you tell someone you take to a dance that they can't touch you? Or can touch you only in certain ways? She *was* my friend, right? Of course. We shouldn't have come. We should've made up some excuse "Cubs," I began. I couldn't call her "Liz" yet.

She put her finger to her lips and looked up and down the empty hallway. I did, too, though there was no reason. She put her hand on my arm.

"Cub—" I was going to call her "Cubble," another one of our variations, but I stopped myself.

"What?"

"We *are* here as, y'know, friends. Right?"

She paused and then nodded.

"'Cause, what I said before, at Christmas?" (What *had* I said? It was like a dream.) "That's, I mean, I'm sorry, but that's pretty much, like, the way things *are*. The way I am."

Now her little smile faded and her shoulders sagged. I did this kind of sigh-scoff-laugh thing. "I mean," I said, "I'm sorry, but what . . . ?" I stopped.

She looked down and wiped at her eye.

"Cubby!" I said. I wanted to reach over and take her face in my hands—a kind of tender-masculine gesture that turned me on when I did it—but instead I gripped her arm and stroked it. I felt resolute and hopeless.

I had stopped because, once again, I wasn't so sure of myself. Was I really what I said I was? Did it really have the power to break me and Liz up? Yeah, there'd been Nate (and God, Liz could never find out; we were technically broken up when it happened, I'd said we were, anyway, but if she knew she'd be insanely pissed, like I broke up with her so I could do it, which

I didn't). I was still trying to grasp that I was this thing that some *other* people were, but me? Why me? And how? Suddenly, with Cubs in front of me wiping away tears, I didn't know. All the questions I'd asked myself the past two weeks—plus, btw, all of the past however many *years!*—flooded in. Had I been experimenting? Was I bisexual? Did I really really *really* like sex with a guy? Enough to give up . . . everything? Was the whole sexuality thing a choice, like some people said, and I was about to choose wrong and let go of the perfect thing, the only girl who'd ever love me?

After a second of wondering that, suddenly, for a second, it all cleared away, and in a plain, almost boring way, stirring and disappointing, too, I knew. Being with Nate was awkward and secretive, but it was real. It was grown-up, even though we did it on the floor. It was honest, there in his parents' living room: how I longed to heal his bruises, how I wanted to have him inside me. Not *that* way, though yeah, maybe someday, but to consume him and meld with him. Have his soul. There *was* a choice—I guess there always is— and one path would be easy on the outside and excruciating on the inside, and the other path would be hard and confusing and maybe lonely all around—at least for now and maybe for a while, maybe a long while. But the hard, confusing, lonely path was mine. It was James Howard Wallace's path.

"Cubs," I said, "I'm sorry, but I explained. The best I could. In, I swear, the only language I had." Wallaçonian. Would I ever speak anything else? "But we're, you know, you and me . . ." Now I was the one suddenly wiping my eyes. "We're not going, like, *back*, you know?" I took a big gulp of air. In the gym, the band was getting into "Life in the Fast Lane," which you totally can't dance to. "It wouldn't be right," I said, and I immediately felt like an idiot.

178

She looked up. "Like the rest of this is 'right'?" she said. Her mouth stretched out and her face crumpled. "You always understood me before!" she wailed softly. "You understood every word I ever said, and now you don't, and I don't know why."

She gasped and her body shook, but she tried to keep it all quiet because someone might hear. I stepped up and just enveloped her. "Oh, Cubs!" I said. I knew she was thinking of her dad, too.

"But I could go to you, and you would understand. On the worst, shittiest day, the weirdest, stupidest thing, the thing my mom wouldn't get, the stuff no guidance counselor would get, I could tell you, and you'd listen, and you'd hear, and you'd understand! I want to know why you won't listen now!" She pulled back from my chest and looked me in the eye. "Why won't you understand that *I love you?*"

That hit me so hard, right in the chest. Of course, she'd said it before, including when we had sex. How come I hadn't heard it then? I mean, really heard it, like this. And I'd said it to her. And meant it, as much as I possibly could. Was "being gay" a real reason to reject what I had just felt? To break a precious thing like this? Couldn't I outgrow childish stuff like staring at guys on the beach? Couldn't I do it for Cubs?

But then I saw myself, almost face to face, and it was the weirdest thing. I didn't know everything about who I really was right then, but I knew I would know more, soon, and I knew what it would be. Even though I didn't know it yet. I knew what I would know.

Liz turned her head and nuzzled her face into my chest. I wanted to respond, but I couldn't. Not fully. I patted her on the back. The insane thought crossed my mind that, if she knew about Nate, then the argument and the uncertainty would be over. I looked down at her, resting in the center of my chest, and I knew it would be the totally wrong thing to do. Now or ever. But if the encounter with Nate was so honest and real and who I really was, why did it have to be this eternal secret?

"You're right, Cubs," I whispered, patting her back. "None of it's right. Or, it is. It's *true*. It is *true*. It's just not fair. And that hurts. I get it. It shouldn't happen. But it is happening. I'm in this body. I know. And there's nothing anyone can do. But I swear I didn't know, before. Or maybe I had some idea, but I just couldn't imagine. . . .

"I was just a different person then. Two people. Jim One and Jim Two. One had the other one locked in a trunk or something, and he could never acknowledge it. And the one in the trunk thought he'd never, ever get out. It hurt. Physically! But I promise you, Cubs, I never, ever made this decision to go mess you up with it. I love you, too. And then life came along and turned me into, well, what I am."

"But you said. . . ." And she repeated something that sounded like something I probably did say, in her bedroom at Christmas or in one of our mumbled conversations since, but that I definitely didn't mean the way she heard it. About the only answer I could come up with was another, "I didn't know!" Pretty soon she was saying, "You said," over and over, and I was saying, "I didn't know," over and over, both of us trying to keep our voices down and checking up and down the hall every now and then when we couldn't bear looking at each other.

Eventually she said, "We should go back," and I agreed real fast, like there was a rule about when you had to go back. What if we hadn't gone back, though? What if we hadn't gone back to the shiny, droopy snowflakes? What if we'd said good-bye right there? What if we'd walked out in the night, me holding her? See, that excited me, too. But it would never excite me—be a part of me—like the other thing. Wanting

Nate like I did. Wanting guys. All guys. Masculinity pulled me like the moon pulling the ocean. That pull was who I was. Liz was really, really great, she turned me on, in a way, but part of what made her great was that I got to be normal with her. Except I wasn't normal.

Anyway, we went back. We even danced to another three songs. I held her during "The Long Run," and I tried not to think about Nate and failed (a little deliberately) and felt so guilty. Imagine being a girl and knowing a guy wants what another guy's got, wants a penis and all the rest of it, instead of what you have.

After that we drove over to Dennis with some other kids for fried clams. And all I could think, staring at my greasy Cape Cod placemat with ropes all around it and a lighthouse, compass, and sailboat was, how the hell were we going to say good night? I should take her home, but then what? But Alisha offered before I said anything. She said it suddenly and too loud, and she couldn't help glancing at me when she said it. She had to know. I was kind of relieved by that. Liz had said the words aloud to someone.

In the parking lot, we said this stalwart good-bye in front of Alisha. We kissed on the cheeks; then Liz gave me another peck on the lips and ducked into Alisha's car. I drove home alone. I felt like I had nothing, and I'd have to wait forever for the next thing. I was finally someone, but I was alone. I was finally alone, but I was someone. Some *one*. No more Jim One and Jim Two. Just one now.

One who might never again hear "I love you" the way I had heard it that night.

After that, it was day after day of emptiness and strangeness. I'd have one funny or exciting thing I had to tell someone, and without thinking I'd think of her. I'd go to her. Then stop. What was the point? But I'd go crazy because there was no one else to tell this thing to, no one who'd get it but her. But if I told her this thing, I'd be wondering if she was wondering why I was still telling her stuff, or I'd be wondering if she was wondering if me coming to her meant I wanted her back and wasn't gay anymore.

It hurt. Imagine if you were a gull and you had an egg inside that you couldn't get out. You just flew around and around with this egg until it was reabsorbed or whatever. Then a new egg would start. You'd want to get it out, too, but you couldn't, so you'd wait for it to go away, too. Then another and another.

Did she feel the same way—wishing she could tell me stuff only I would understand? Stopping herself every time because of what I might say or not say? Did she have things she wished she could tell her dad? She must. Like, how she lost her friend Jim because he liked guys? She could never, ever sit for one more afternoon in an Adirondack chair by the bay with the sun going down and tell him about losing her friend and have him hold her. Shouldn't I make it better for her? Couldn't I? The most awful thing is when there's nothing you can do. When you just have to wait out the awful, unfair thing, hour after hour, day after day.

Oh, and by the way, what I eventually learned from going online: if a bird has an egg like that and can't lay it, pretty quickly the bird just dies.

I didn't look at Liz's Facebook page. At the same time I dared myself to look. Of course it would say "Single" by now. I didn't *want* it to say "In a Relationship." Of course not! Still, I wouldn't look. Then one day I just did. Three, two, one. Yep. "Single."

I stared at it, letter by letter: "Single."

I was relieved and sad. I went through her photos. She'd kept a few pics of us together, clowning, but she'd deleted most anything romantic. And she'd taken down most of the ones of me alone—the serious, thoughtful ones she'd said were sexy. That really threw me. I wished she'd just taken everything down. Then I could be the angry lover. Instead, I existed, but only as harmless Jim making faces in his paper ice cream hat, her virginal friend off in some sunshiny land.

All winter I saw Mr. Baxter go down to his books each morning, by the lonely, gray cove, under a lonely, gray sky. At night, as the first stars came out and the wind sang in the pines, he'd come home to read and listen to music. We waved, and sometimes on weekends I went down to say hi.

We made coffee and chatted. He apologized that he had no work for me. Business was slow, but he said there would certainly be work in the summer, and he lent me books from his "LGBTQ" section. I read them late at night or early in the morning and stored them under a floorboard in my closet. One March Sunday was rainy and slow, so we watched a DVD, *White Frog*, about a young guy who finds out his brother is gay after he dies. He also let me borrow his classical CDs, and he pointed out composers who were gay, like Benjamin Britten (my favorite) and Tchaikovsky.

I'd read about bookstores closing. I worried that, if Bay View failed, Pat would leave. Who would I talk to then? I'd told him about Liz and the Winter Informal, but I didn't elaborate. Maybe I didn't want to hear so much about him and Saralynn. Maybe I thought he wouldn't like that I sometimes still got uncomfortable or uncertain about being gay. I think he understood. We just sat side by side and watched movies and then made coffee and took them apart. It filled my heart just to have a man to do that with. A man like me. It was better than any sex, almost.

I wondered if he knew everything that was going on
with Nate. I didn't think it was my place to tell anything; he knew Nate better. Nate emailed me about the
IDF. He had registered online. You had to choose between noncombat and combat service; he said he
chose combat. My stomach sank. He had to tell them
why he wanted to enlist, and he had to "describe his
relationship to Israel." I wished he would show me
what he wrote, but I guessed I couldn't go there with
him. He did tell me the application "made him think,"
and that he "felt stronger" answering those questions,
that he was "becoming a soldier already." I asked,
what about being gay in the Israeli army?

Typical of Nate, he wrote back: "Gay men and
women serve openly in the IDF, including special
units." Straight from the website. I checked. I liked
that I thought of something as "typical Nate." I was
also pissed that the army would treat him better than
his own dad.

One night in March the smell of the marsh entered
my room. Daylight savings came, and Nate was home
on vacation. I asked if we could get together. He said
he was coming to visit Pat. All winter I had imagined
being in bed with Nate, going slower, doing more, or
just lying there naked saying, "Hey, Yehonatan," and
"Yeah, Yirmeyahu?" and me reaching over and finger-
ing his nipple, pimply from the cold. But as it worked
out, I would see him only for a few minutes when he
came to visit my neighbor. (They'd already been talking a while when Pat called me down.) I felt like a
woman brushed off by the devil-may-care army guy.
Nate and I did have a few minutes alone afterward, in
the driveway. He didn't say a lot, but he stood close.
He stared at me very seriously and then suddenly
smiled a little. He did hug me at the end, quickly, not
saying anything about how this could be the last time
we saw each other, at least for a while.

184

The next evening I was sitting with Pat in Bay View, talking about the Nate visit. I had confessed my attraction to Nate and said we had hung out together; I was discreet about what we'd done at Christmas, but I think he got the idea. I also told him that Nate had explained to me his role in the Benleigh incident. I had thought all this would make Nate and me closer, but I said to Pat that Nate basically seemed as reticent as ever.

"He's probably scared," Pat said.

"Scared of his dad, you mean?" I said.

"Oh, dear. Awful," Pat said. "I looked online to see what you could do legally—besides call the cops—but he never would, and it's not my place. It's complicated because they are my friends. But that's not what I meant by 'scared.'"

"Then . . . scared of *me*? Because I 'persecuted' him in seventh grade?"

"Scared of your *desire*. I doubt he has much experience in that arena."

But he'd had me. We'd been naked together. I'd touched his bruises. That made me feel responsible for him. I felt bad that I couldn't quite say the same about Liz. Not anymore. The really weird thing, though, was discussing all this two steps from my parents' front door. I was this new person, and they didn't know. So that really made me the same as ever. Plus, they also didn't know that, with college acceptance letters coming soon, I was thinking of picking my safety school.

"Your life hasn't been easy," Pat said, "but when *you* have sex, you know you'll go on being a fairly stable version of you. Nate probably thinks it will destroy him. He's less afraid of being a soldier than he is of being a lover. I mean, the family owns three cars, and yet he drives that ridiculous Hummer. *Hummer*. Even the *name!*"

I had come to like Pat's humor. It felt good to laugh at it, even to answer it with humor of my own. I felt more like a man, more like myself, when I talked that way with him.

"I asked him, 'Are we off to invade Beirut?' He doesn't laugh like you, but he lets me say it. Just the fact that he would talk to you. He sees something special in you."

"Has he said anything to you? About me?"

"Oh, no. He wouldn't. I can just tell, here and there. And I know you. If I were Nate, I'd be happy to know you, too. Well, I am happy to know you."

"And I, you," I said, still disappointed that he didn't have intel about Nate's exact opinions of me.

"Now, speaking of conversations about you—"

"Uh-oh!"

"Just checking in about college plans. No pressure. I was too forceful before, I know."

"No! I mean, you could be right."

"You have to make the decision on your own. It's part of life. I've watched hundreds of young people make hundreds of decisions. I had my opinions and was not always right. If I heard that someone regretted a decision, I said, 'How can we work with this? How can we see your decision as part of who you were and learn from it and grow?'

"Maybe I shouldn't insist you go to Boston. I've pointed out a few things *about* Boston, versus the Wild West. But you are your own person. I would be remiss, though, if I didn't challenge that person. It's been remarkable, how you opened up to Nate Flederbaum. You made a friend out of someone who doesn't trust easily."

That felt good to me. And frustrating, because Nate would probably never tell me.

As I left Bay View, Pat said, "Wait! I always meant to get a picture of you. For the store's Facebook page. Would you mind?" He already had his phone out.

I shrugged. Before I knew it, he had taken me leaning against the counter, next to a stack of books; then it was over, I said so long, and I walked up to the house.

The stink of the marsh came on the southwest wind, the mud and peat softening, water melting, racing sticklebacks to the sea. Far out an egret stood, S-curved neck, one leg up. I thought of Nate. Not sex with him, but the two of us cross-legged on the floor, naked in the chilly air, our bare knees touching, the hairs on my arm grazing the hairs on his. He clicked, "Ask God," and I said, "I'm not going to get struck by lightning, am I?" He smiled, his eyes big and blue, his look intense but shy. The Low Anthem singing, "Once you've known love you don't know how to find love." My arm around him. Waiting. His around me. Us breathing together. Every part of me and every part of him good and right. I felt myself growing limbs, reaching for him.

But he'd gone away. And I was going away. College! Jeez! Pat could say it was my call, but I couldn't forget his argument for Boston. I drew in the marsh smell again. I had grown up on this—fish running in spring, heat rising from the bicycle path all summer, brilliant fall colors, kitchen lights left on in winter. I had visited the Berkshires last fall, when the hills blazed red. The sharp night air smelled of wood smoke. The stars came out, and you felt like you were right up in them, like here, being out on someone's boat. As for Boston, who was I to mingle with kids from Harvard and MIT? I'd see them on the T or at cafés (T = Boston subway), but would they speak to me? They'd be discussing top-secret projects or planning summers in Europe.

Why would some MIT genius even look at me? Math geniuses were never gay anyway.

That night I went online and looked at the gay center at the college in the Berkshires. They tried to make it sound exciting, but you could see it was just one room. And for the whole spring, their only events were a "Diversity Dance" and a talk by a gay writer. Needless to say, the college in Boston had more, including links to every gay thing at Harvard, Tufts, BU, and so on. Did I want to "be gay" like that, running to every dance and discussion? They had a picture of a guy with a bullhorn, his face painted in rainbow colors and people with signs protesting "lack of gender equality." That wasn't me, but I wished it was. I wished I could know the rainbow-faced boy. They also put on a drag show to benefit a trans kid who was in jail. I didn't want to put on drag or makeup, but I did want the freedom those guys had. I also wanted brick dorms and autumn nights with wood smoke. What was wrong with liking what you liked? But weren't you supposed to explore other parts of yourself? The part that might run long distance? The part that might sing or paint your face? After you ran a race, or won a race, or sang, or got made up, who would you be? Could you go back if you wanted?

I closed my browser and opened my Exercise folder. Maybe neither place would accept me.

Through my window came the raspy screech of a barn owl—like the nozzle of an espresso machine going off.

Nate.

Gone.

Liz.

Gone.

Downstairs our TV murmured.

I went to the Bay View page on Facebook. There I was, by that stack of books. Pat had written, "Everyone—this is Jim, the fine young fellow who has been such a help here the past few months. Look for him again this summer!" I stared and stared. I wasn't sure what I thought of myself-in-the-picture. Maybe I thought I looked like someone that someone else just might like. Who might be a little bit upright after all.

I stood and went to the window. From the marsh I could hear the crickets and the frogs singing. I looked down. The lights in Bay View had gone out.

CHAPTER 17

TERRA NOVA

"JIM??" MOM RAN toward me, holding up an envelope. "Look what came in the ma-a-ail!" In the corner I
saw the seal of the college in the Berkshires. My heart
sank. I could have looked online for the answer, but I
didn't want to know. "Open it, open it!" She was
standing closer to me than she had in a long time. I
mean, it's weird having to duck your mom's breasts.

I was in. Mom let out a yell and hugged me. It
seemed strange, until I reminded myself that I hadn't
said a word about what I was thinking. I'd let them
talk on and on about this school, and I talked about
it, too. *Oh, what the heck*, I thought, as she hugged. *I'll
just go. It probably doesn't matter.* She had her phone
out and was calling Dad in Falmouth. Aunt Lillian had
had a rough spring but we told people she was "hanging in there." Dad congratulated me, and I said,
"Thanks, yeah, great news, huh?" and we hung up.
"Well," Mom said, "no reason not to call and accept
right now!" I couldn't stop myself from balking. "Oh,"
she said cheerfully. "You'd like some privacy. You can
call from your room."

I could promise to call from my room and not do it,
but the idea of lying again weighed me down. So I took

a deep breath and, trying to make it sound upbeat and casual, I said, "I think I'm not going to call quite yet."

Mom paused. Her eyes went left-right, and she wrung her hands. "I don't see why not," she said. "We decided this. At least, I *thought* we did." She straightened her spine and gazed down her nose, which was weird because I'm taller than she is. "We *all* liked it. It's a wonderful school. We *thought* it was *perfect* for you!"

"I'd just like to get all the letters," I said, my voice pleading a little.

Her eyes got hard and she pointed a finger. "Well, maybe you're not aware," she said, "what happens if you miss their deadline—"

"Mom," I said, "tell me one time I ever turned in anything late. Tell me!"

"Well, we're not just talking about any—"

"I just think it's a better idea to get them all."

She took a deep breath. "Well," she said, "it's your life. Do what you want!" She marched off. Suddenly she turned around and came back, finger pointing. "You might think how your father and I are paying for this, so if that date goes by—"

"If I let that date go by," I said, "I shouldn't be in college. I should be digging ditches." That was Mom's shorthand for failure, as in, "So-and-So will end up digging ditches." When I said it she marched off again. I couldn't believe I'd won. At least this round. I stood in the empty foyer and counted the days till I'd leave home.

I was upstairs when Dad got home, but I could hear them talking. He called me down.

It was Mom who spoke. She wanted to know my "thinking." She was using her I'm-trying-to-be-calm-and-reasonable voice. She said, "No one's going to get upset. We just want to know your *thinking*." What she meant, as usual, was she wanted a chance to repeat *her* thinking.

I said the bit about wanting all four letters. Then I took a slow, deep breath, and I thought of Pat and how they'd react if they knew that my "thinking" was partly his. Referring to the college in the Berkshires I said, "I'm not sure that it's my absolute first choice." So of course I had to say what my first choice might be. I mentioned the school in Boston. Mom's mouth fell open.

"What . . . ? That is your *safety* school, young man!" she gasped. She threw up her arms and looked at Dad, bewildered. He just raised an eyebrow. "Why," she wailed, "would anyone *choose* to go to their *safety* school?"

I said, "I'm not definitely going there; I just need to stop and think a minute." I started comparing the Berkshires and Boston. When I used the phrase "urban environment," Dad frowned. He said, "You've spoken to Pat Baxter about this, I take it."

I remembered how Pat had told Dad I should go back to choir, and Dad hadn't told me. "What do you know about Pat?" I said.

"We damn well know he got thrown out of Benleigh for molesting a student!" Mom snapped. Dad held up his hand to try to slow things down.

"That is not true!" I said. "I know the kid who ratted, I know him personally, and he lied. He told me. And they knew it was a lie. Benleigh. Pat left anyway because he wanted to start the bookstore. He loved that barn. That guy lied; he told me so himself. He lives here, in South Sicassett." Mom was thrown, which happened about once a decade, so I kept going.

"But once someone says that, what do you do? Especially if it's that old bag, Viola Budd! 'Oh, he's'—I dunno—'*gay* or whatever, so he must have done it,' right?"

Mom panicked. Sex was her least favorite subject. In the silence I imagined them wondering, *Why would he be so exercised about Pat if he wasn't the same way?* I had to change course. "He was the college guidance guy at Benleigh," I said. "That was his *profession.*" Another Mom word. Not, "What's his job?" but "What's his *profession?*" Funny, because she didn't exactly have one. She was a receptionist.

Dad held up a hand and said, "Now, that is true. Pat was in college guidance." He didn't say any more about Pat, though. He did think waiting for the other colleges was not a terrible idea. Mom slumped back in her chair and scowled. My heart thudded away, because I'd brought up Pat being gay. I heard it echoing. Dad expounded on the wisdom of waiting, carefully, like he was wrapping a bomb. "No one's going to miss any deadlines," he said. Mom pouted. "Well," she said, to no one in particular, "all I know is, I heard nothing for months but one clear first choice, and now I guess we're going to blow that all away and just flush our money down the toilet!" She snatched her dish towel up from the coffee table and went to the kitchen. Dad cleared his throat and reached for his *Cape Codder.*

Two more acceptances came Monday, including the safety school in Boston, and the last one Wednesday. I sent Pat an email saying all four schools had accepted me. He replied, "Let me know if you want to talk." I thanked him and said I'd stop by the store the next day.

But that night at the dinner table, Mom said something I would never have imagined. "You know," she said, in her aggressively cheerful way, "you could visit one or two of those schools again." She glanced at Dad and then away.

Okay . . .

So, we decided I knew enough about the Berkshires, and the two schools I haven't talked about were not so different (plus, one hadn't offered me enough money, so it was out of the running). It was just Boston I couldn't decide about. Why was Mom suddenly being reasonable? Did she think, if I saw grimy, boring downtown Boston, I'd come to my senses and choose the picturesque Berkshires? Whatever the reason, we decided Dad and I would go look again. We would drive up the following Tuesday.

Well, maybe you can guess what happened next. Monday, April 15, 2013, at three in the afternoon—the Boston Marathon bombing. Pressure-cooker bomb went off right near the finish line and killed three people and, like, blew the legs off some runners. It was awful. I was hanging outside school, and suddenly people were saying, "Oh, my God!" and checking their phones. A girl whose uncle was in the marathon was crying; no one knew who'd been injured and who hadn't. They had the city in lockdown and that night was the manhunt and finally the video of them taking Dzhokhar Tsarnaev, one of the bomb guys, out of a boat in a back yard in Watertown. On TV I saw the guys in riot gear, and I thought of Nate in the army. My parents watched the TV nonstop.

The thing that kept me awake at night wasn't the blood. It was those people running twenty-six whole miles, getting ready their whole lives, then at the last second, with the finish line right there and their families watching, . . . Thinking about that made me nuts.

Anyway, I figured Boston was out now. It was too complicated to visit, and Mom would say it was too dangerous to go to school there. I'd resign myself to the Berkshires. Maybe I was stupid to ever have thought anything else.

But on Friday, Dad said that by the next week "all should be clear," and it was true. The news was obsessed with Tsarnaev, but Boston had to keep going. The following Monday we set out early. We stopped at the Dunkin' on Cove Road in Wellfleet, then on to Provincetown to catch the ferry across the bay. We left the car below and went topside.

On the upper deck, in the misty light with the salt spray in our faces, we stood at the railing and watched gulls floating next to us, then lifting off. Dad said, "You remember a pal of mine named Doug Hyland?"

I did. They were in ROTC together, back in the day. Time for a nostalgic Dad Story.

"Well, Doug's brother, Fred, as it happens, works in college guidance at a private school in Connecticut. A school like Benleigh."

This would be interesting. Dad used "as it happens" when something big was coming. He cleared his throat. "And it seems Fred, Fred Hyland, knows Pat Baxter."

My stomach flip-flopped. Dad must have info on Pat that was worse than anything so far. Did they catch him with a hard drive full of sex videos? If they did, though, there was nothing about it online. I'd Googled Pat's name and "Benleigh" and found just an old pro-file for an alumni magazine. I felt guilty for having looked.

"Apparently," Dad said, gazing into the mist, "Pat is not your ordinary college guidance counselor. He is actually somewhat legendary in those circles."

As in "Ten Most Wanted"?

He looked up at a gull, floating alongside, preparing to take flight. "It seems Pat was one of the reasons you sent your child to Benleigh. So he'd get them into a good college. Fred said Benleigh is hurting now. He thinks they begged Pat to stay. I asked why he left. Fred didn't know."

"But," I said carefully. "What about . . . what Mom said?"

"Well, I don't know anything about that," Dad said. "So, since I had Fred on the line, I asked him about your two choices. He didn't see much difference, academically. He said college is ninety percent what you make of it, anyway. And then. . . ." Dad watched another gull lift off. I waited. "He said, 'You live next door to the Svengali of college admissions. Ask him!'"

"So did you?" I said, a bit impatiently.

"Let's see what you think," Dad said, "after you've looked at this place today."

Water splashed against the side of the ferry as we rose and fell. "Dad," I said. "Did Pat talk to you a while ago about me taking choir again this year?"

He pretended not to hear, so I asked again.

"How should I know?" he said.

So I said it differently: "Dad, Pat *did* talk to you about choir. I know he did." Dad rubbed his hands together and stared off.

He was not going to say anything, so I did. "It looks like we could have had Pat's advice all along, maybe." I kicked myself for the "maybe." But you can't come out and accuse an adult of anything, because they'll pull out some extenuating circumstance that you suspect is crap made up on the spot, but they'll get all offended and how-*dare*-you, and you'll have to back down. "If," I said, "we hadn't been so, like, 'Ooooh, look out for the *gay guy*! What could the *gay guy* know?'"

Dad flinched. He looked down at the water. His jaw was working. Maybe I'd said enough. I had him dead to rights, and that scared me a little. I stared at his hands, weathered, his ring almost, like, fused to his skin. Dug in. Some things were forever, and that was nice. That's what I would be leaving.

The towers of Boston appeared from the mist, one minute far off in a distant world, the next minute clear and looming over us. The engine cut, and we bumped

against the tires bolted to the Fish Pier. Gulls rose and
fell and circled. As we drove the car off, the ramp
clanged. We parked up by South Station, got falafel at
the Clover Truck on Atlantic Avenue, and took it inside to eat. To get Dad in a better mood I asked him to
tell stories about him growing up in Boston; I knew
he'd like that. Then we caught the T over to the college.

I'd seen the school before, but I hadn't paid that
much attention, because it was my safety school. It
was big, with a lot of kids, but some of the dorms and
classrooms looked cramped and grubby, for sure,
compared to the Berkshires. The street outside the
freshman dorm was narrow and all potholed, and kids
were coming and going everywhere, dressed every
which way from preppy to grunge to thrift shop. Inside, dim elevators lurched open and banged shut,
and chicken-wired glass was covered with bits of old
tape and posters for shows and rallies and parties,
many at Harvard, Tufts, MIT, or clubs or parks or
theaters that were just part of Boston life.

Back outside we passed the library with graffiti on
the steps. In some places you couldn't tell what was
school and what wasn't. There'd be two blocks of college, then a loading dock, then the physics building
(#incrediblyugly), then a Starbucks or a Subway, then
admissions. My other choices had all looked like English estates. Here, buildings had been stuck wherever
they fit. Even the new all-wood-and-glass arts center
was jammed at a funny angle, like it was fighting for
space with chunky old brick bunkers and dormitory
towers. The quad had litter and the leaves on the trees
were splotchy and eaten away. *This isn't me*, I thought.
Stars and crickets and wood smoke are me. Dad looked
around and said, "I imagine you'd learn to navigate it,
in time. After all, you can sail. And you'd have the
whole city."

He asked if I wanted another tour of the campus. I said no. We'd been up in the freshman tower before, and the tour guides were just going to say the good stuff—like how great the "social opportunities" were. I didn't want social opportunities. I just wanted to survive and maybe make a friend here or there who was kind of like me.

"So let's get outta here," he said, with a little smile and a raised eyebrow.

And we were out of the shadows, leaving the towers and grimy brick façades behind and heading for the T. Dad didn't say any more about the school. It didn't seem like he was going to try talking me into or out of anything. We got on the Green Line and rode it to the Fenway stop. Coming up we took Park Drive to Clemente Field, then went into the fields and woods of the Fens themselves. The wind was strong and nippy; the heads of the tall grasses tossed, like they did at home, and dried leaves blew up in loops. Blossoms were out on the trees. Kids my age sat on the grass, sketching, studying, sunbathing, and playing guitars and hacky-sack and Kan Jam. We passed fountains and rose bushes and entered a part of the Fens that was wilder, the paths less definite. The most beautiful sights were off the paths anyway—a heron with its neck like a question mark; a tree so twisted it looked like it was dancing, all by itself, forever. Sometimes you couldn't see a path that would get you close to what you loved; you had to dive randomly into the bushes where maybe you weren't supposed to go. It was weird that we came to Boston to decide my future and ended up bushwhacking. Or I did. Dad stood on a path and watched and got smaller as I clambered desperately toward that dancing tree.

After the Fens we walked up Mass Ave. under an arch of trees, past statues of soldiers and social reformers, past the old Hotel Vendôme and brick mansions with bay windows and pale-green copper trim, up to the Public Garden with its new tulips and weeping willows and George Washington on a horse. Okay, so Boston had nature, too, and places to get away to, maybe a little like the Berkshires. Behind the willows, the buildings rose, standing guard. Swan boats full of tourists glided on the ponds. I remembered, when I was little, Dad brought me to ride the Swan Boats and took me to the top of the Prudential building, "the Pru," where I paid a dime and looked out over all six New England states.

The sun was "over the yardarm" as we cut across Boston Common to the T at Park Street. We rode to the Charles stop.

On a side street we found a place with those cream cheese brownie things and cappuccinos. Gold lettering on the window cast shadows on the wall. Dad spooned foam from his cappuccino and reminisced about Aunt Lillian. I wondered when we were going to talk college.

Aunt Lillian was my grandpa's twin, but they grew up separately. Their mother died, and their dad had trouble keeping jobs. He sent Aunt Lillian to live with some cousins. They wanted kids but never had any. Once they got her, though, they were mean to her. Dad said she had never had children of her own because of how badly she was treated; she was afraid she'd treat her kids the same way. I'd always thought Aunt Lillian was happy—putting out toys for me and letting me lick the beaters when she made frosting. And all that time she was mad at her cousins and maybe sorry not to have kids. I guess I was her kid, in a way. "You knew that, right?" Dad said.

"Sorry?" I said.

"That the house wasn't hers. On Skunk Tail Road. It was her father's. My granddad. She took care of him till he died, and then she lived there until she went to Sea View."

Wow. So when we went there, we weren't going to Aunt Lillian's at all. It was like some place where she was held—by the guy who hadn't wanted her. "So whose toys were they?" I asked. "That she gave me, when I was little? If she had no kids?"

"Mine. She bought them for when I came over. I remember her telling you."

"Yeah, yeah," I said. "I remember now." Though I didn't; not at all.

Dad sipped his capp and stared at the wall. The shadows had slipped away; the wall was dark. The girl who served us came by and turned on a light. "There!" she said. "Isn't that better?"

Finally I said, "So, if maybe I do go to school here"— damn! There was that "maybe" again!—"you guys *will*, um, pay for it?"

He made a face and said nothing. In other words, we weren't going to acknowledge that Mom had flown off the handle and said something crazy. Instead, we talked for a while about "opportunities" and "the school environment." Dad didn't say where he thought I should go. I wished he would. I wished *someone* would tell me what to do—if what I was told could be the thing I, in fact, wanted to do! But I didn't know exactly what that was. Could someone tell me that, too? I guessed not.

In the dusk we walked the cobblestone streets with little brick buildings and ivy, fancy iron fences and window boxes with flowers. It was like Dickens, only clean. The windows glowed yellowy-orange. Inside I saw brass clocks and paintings and forsythia in Chinese vases. On Louisburg Square some doorways had lamps with gas flames. And I smelled wood smoke.

Maybe I was supposed to come here, not because it would be better or I saw a heron or smelled wood smoke, but because Dad had done this for me. Maybe he had been telling me all afternoon that stuff like dancing trees and wood smoke *did* matter. It was good to want them, and I might find them in places I wouldn't think. Maybe he put the whole trip together because he wanted me to see I could have everything I wanted. In the grimy towers, in the Fens, in the streets of Beacon Hill I saw that I could have what I liked and more than I liked and still be myself. Then I did something I hadn't done in a long time. As we walked, I put my arm around his waist. And he put his arm around me. I hadn't planned it, but I turned and stopped us both, and I hugged him and dug my face hard into his shirt and said, "Dad, I love you!" Suddenly I started to cry. I don't mean I sniffled. I mean I freaking *wept.* We were right on the street, but he didn't try to stop me. He just held tighter, and I moaned like a moose. I sort of figured, if I can be gay, I can weep and moan in the middle of a city street. Finally I straightened up, and through all the tears and snot and stuff I said, "I'm sorry if I disappointed you, Dad! I'm sorry!"

I saw tears in his eyes, too. He smiled a little and said lightly, "How would you *ever* disappoint me, Jim?" He paused and then said, "Just by liking that boy who worked for Pat Baxter?"

I stared at him, with mucus running down over my lips.

"You'd only disappoint me, son," he said, "if you went on being unhappy over something you can't control."

"But, wait." I wiped my nose. "How did you *know* that? Did Pat say—?"

Dad shook his head. "Pat didn't say a word. I'm just a good observer," he said, clapping me on the shoulder.

"Observer of what?" I demanded.

"Oh, this and that."

"This and that *what*, though?"

201

"Oh, for instance that time at Christmas. You paced up and down. Forgot your gloves. Your scarf. You were gone almost four hours, and you came back looking"— and then his voice broke just a little, the closest I ever saw or heard my dad come to crying—"looking kind of *relieved.*" He straightened up and looked off at nothing in particular. He nodded. He managed to get out the word "relieved" one more time, softly. I guessed I was supposed to pull myself together now.

"Does Mom know?" I said.

He paused before saying, "I wouldn't be surprised." But he didn't offer to help tell her. This was going to be *mucho* tricky—Mom with her moods and drama.

"Okay," I said, "but seriously, what else? It couldn't have been forgetting gloves or a look I had."

He wouldn't say anything more than that there were "things here and there." He wouldn't say what they were or when he first suspected anything. "Like, back in middle school?" I asked, and he quickly said, "Oh, no, nothing like that!" So, what was the "that" that I was "nothing like"? I'd never really told them Liz and I had broken up, just that we were "seeing less" of each other. Did that tip him off? "No, not especially." I gave up. This was how our family handled things in the communications department. When you finally brought up something big, you put it right away again, as quickly as possible.

We resumed walking. I put my arm back around him and squeezed, and he put his around me a little while. It was nice, but weird. We hadn't done this since I was a kid, and not that much then. He probably felt a lot of stuff over me being gay or what have you. Maybe relief, like I felt. I also thought that maybe love with another guy should be like this, like being a dad, but more.

We walked down to Copley Square to make one last stop. I was a little scared to see and feel what was left from the bombing. As we came up out of the T, though, it was more like what the bombing had *added*. As we came around Trinity Church, people were everywhere, and piled on the ground were American flags and teddy bears and candles and Red Sox caps and tons of running shoes and "We love you, Boston!" and "Boston Strong" written on the pavement. People strolled and stopped and stared. They cried and pointed. Dad and I stood awkwardly and looked hard at teddy bears because now we didn't want to look at or touch each other.

I guess overall I don't like memorials. I know I'm supposed to feel something big, and I think I'm a bad person if I don't. The marathon bombing was awful, but I didn't know anyone affected, and the flowers and teddy bears were just too much. What could I do about it? Well, I did think of one thing. It was kind of crazy.

I'd been thinking about the teacher who kept asking me to run cross-country, and how I regretted saying no to him. But now suddenly, surrounded by all those memorials, I thought, *I'll run the Boston Marathon!* I could practice over the summer and maybe get back what I had lost. I'd sort of known people who had run it. They weren't super athletes, just regular people who practiced a lot. I could practice, too, and maybe somehow make up for what happened to the people who practiced and hoped so much that year and then . . . I didn't tell Dad, but I decided right there that, yeah, I would run in the Boston Marathon! And—

Whoa! Maybe the point of the Aunt Lillian story was: she made a big decision—not to have kids. She was afraid she'd be like the adults who brought her up. She'd been extreme and regretted it. Dad wanted my decisions to be based on a balanced view of things. So I could come to Boston; I could run the marathon and maybe even love someone! I wouldn't be stuck with the way things always were.

Shadows now fell across the square. We had missed the last ferry back to Provincetown, so we drove down Route 1 to the Pilgrims' Highway, then over the Sagamore Bridge and down the Cape to home.

Out of the whole day, it seemed like college had been the least important thing. I thought I knew and loved my dad in a way I hadn't before, and I saw how he might know and love me. And I was going to run a marathon! I did have to say one thing, though. "Dad?" He kept his eyes on the stripes on Route 6. "I think you already know this by now, but all that talking about 'Mr. Baxssster' you used to do?" His expression didn't change, but I knew I had his attention. "Not cool," I said. "Definitely not cool."

He cleared his throat. He made a funny tilt of his head and a raised eyebrow that together said something like, "All right, if that's the way you want it." I turned away and stared at the scrubby pines passing us by.

When we got home, Mom didn't say much about college, either. She enthused over the Fens and Beacon Hill. She thought "Like Dickens, only clean" was cute. We had brought her a cream-cheese brownie, and she gushed over that, too. I went upstairs to dump my stuff and decompress. I looked out at the marsh and thought of wrought iron and Chinese vases on Beacon Hill. Copley Square had got me all stoked, but now I thought again that I might get buried in Boston. Or ignored. I had to talk to Pat.

When I heard Dad call "Jim," solemn and softer than usual, I realized how quiet things had gotten downstairs. I went to my door and called, "What?" No sound. "What?" I said again. Silence. Oh, no! He'd told Mom I was gay. And maybe he himself wasn't so okay with it, and now they were going to say no to Boston for college. Or maybe after he'd seen all those memorials, they'd decided it was too dangerous. I came downstairs all ready to say, "That's ridiculous!"

Dad stood at the bottom of the stairs with his phone still in his hand. "What?" I said, for the third time, really annoyed now.

"I wanted to let you know," he said quietly, "Aunt Lillian passed away. Just now."

I don't remember coming the rest of the way down the stairs. I just remember hugging him like I was the father, and he was suddenly the son.

CHAPTER 18

THE PAIN OF WINNING

RAIN ROARED ACROSS the barn roof. A customer left, and Pat and I pulled our chairs up by the stove. He set a pot of water on top.

"So," I said, "I read you're not supposed to tell your family you're gay if there's another crisis going on. But they don't say what to do if your dad gets it, then his aunt dies, and your mom still doesn't know."

"An uncommon variation!" Pat said. He took out the strainer. "I might wait. But this is your thing, not your dad's. You can tell her yourself."

"Plus," I said, "I've got to make my college decision, and it's kind of related to that." I explained how I felt about Boston. I said I'd be "uncomfortable." Pat said, "Who says you have to be comfortable all the time?" He scooped coffee into the strainer. This was my favorite way he made coffee, because he put in condensed milk.

"At Benleigh I told kids, 'Go where you will be a little uncomfortable. A place that makes you stretch. Don't pick college or a job or anything based on who you are now. Think who you *want to be*. Curiously, that is what Nathanael is doing. I'm not crazy about this army business, but he did choose based on something out in front of him." Rain rattled on the windows. Did Pat know that Nate felt he *had* to go, that he needed the IDF to replace his parents, especially his dad? Pat went for the condensed milk.

The night before, I had gone by myself to the spring choir concert at school—another thing I could have been part of. Choir or cross-country might not have changed anything, but I worried that, in rejecting it all, I had rejected some noble part of me. Sure, I could sign up for music or sports in college, but I thought, had I *joined* those things at fifteen, one special moment would have been mine. I would have acquired beauty, and that moment was gone. Eighteen seemed so old.

Pat poured a dollop of condensed milk for each of us, then poured hot water through the strainer. He handed me my mug. I took it gingerly. The coffee swirled and then was still.

"Where did you go to school again?" I said.

He mentioned the college in Pennsylvania. "I wanted to be in 'the theater.'" He said it dramatically. "But I didn't look at universities with professional programs. I was terrified of exposing my soul. Or they would see I had *no* soul, because I was 'defective.' So, no Carnegie-Mellon, no Juilliard. I came from a prep school family, so I went to a little place in the country that looked just like where I came from—bricks 'n ivy—with just had a few plain ol' acting classes, no great expectations. I could be in Neil Simon and *The Fantasticks* and not bare my soul.

"After that, well, actors go to New York or L.A., right? I couldn't do it. My folks knew people at Benleigh, it made sense, so I went and interviewed. The second I drove onto that campus I felt, well, so *comfortable*. Safe. Protected. I knew the ropes. It didn't feel oppressive yet, because I wasn't out. I hadn't thought it through. So I took the job.

207

"After I started living in a dorm, with all those young men in some state of undress twenty-four/seven, I had to get away. I started sneaking off to Boston on weekends. To 'clear my head.' I'd walk. And I'd look. If anyone looked back, I looked away and sped up. Get a safe distance away and then look back. Be terrified if they were still there and crushed if they were gone. Or I'd stand *across* from places and watch who went in but not go in myself." We each took sips of coffee.

"The next year—" He suddenly leaned forward. "Look, Jim," he said. "The last time I told you about my . . ." He cleared his throat. ". . . about my marriage, I didn't quite tell every detail. I thought maybe it didn't matter. Really, I was afraid you wouldn't quite understand. I find you very sympathetic. I do. Very accepting. But some things, unless you've been there. . . ." He sat back and slumped. "Or maybe I just didn't want you to think badly of me."

"I wouldn't," I said. "Honest." Still, I was scared of what he would reveal. I was afraid that whatever happened to him would happen to me. Or, in fact, that I might think badly of him and would never be able to think better.

"Well," he said softly, "whatever happens, I think I have to tell you." He coughed, took a deep breath, paused, and then began.

"My second year they hired Saralynn. We'd see each other. The faculty lounge or across the quad. She was very sweet, and we found we were quite sympatico. We began to seek each other out, I guess. I was, what, relieved? Now I wasn't sneaking off anymore. I stayed home weekends. Went to movies with her. Library duty together. I told myself this was better. More right. More *me*. This was who I'd been waiting to be. Now I was allowed. There was a God; I could do this! Sometimes I wanted to sneak off again. One more time. Not the looking. Just the freedom! For one day. The *freedom!* But we were better friends by then. Sara and I. More than friends. And I couldn't. *That,* out there, versus *this?* Well, no contest. And then we, you know. . . ."

My heart was thumping. I wished he'd hurry up. Then I paused and looked around at the store, and I realized this wasn't happening to me. I was, maybe, probably, pretty much "out." I had no idea what to do next, but whatever happened, I guessed I'd never have to do this.

"She was writing a novel. That captivated me. I thought it was brave and creative. And studious and hopeless and it made her so free. Made us free. Her writing that book validated so much for me. She said none of 'them' would ever want it. Big publishers. Critics. I said there'd be people who'd appreciate her. I told her I appreciated her. I kissed her and said, 'You can write just for us—the ones who appreciate you.' I read it, of course. Finally. I wanted this to work, and I liked it. I was the one who said, 'Screw everyone, let's start our own publishing company!' Cozy and safe, like the Benleigh quad. Cocoon within a cocoon. She loved the idea. I loved the idea. And the idea made us love each other more.

"And so, you're up late, discussing edits and the cover, hopping up and making drawings, and it's, 'Isn't this great? I wish we could always do this.' And then it's, 'Well, we can, if we . . . get married!' And she said yes. Very quickly, like she'd thought about it. And then getting married and the book and the next book all mix together."

"But the book, the first one, was about, um, your relationship, right?"

He frowned. When he spoke, his voice was sharp and precise. "It was about some unfulfilled part of her. Some indecision. I didn't see, at the time. Or, if I did, I

didn't relate it to me. I had my doubts, way underneath, but it never occurred to me she did. She
seemed happy, and so we seemed happy. I seemed
happy. I could live with it.

"Anyway, we put it out, the book. We had a party,
did some readings, gave away more copies than we
sold, and after that?" He looked down into his coffee.
"I hadn't thought about after that.

"After that, she was pregnant. And wanting the next
book! So this was who I was now. What I did. I wished
she'd never stop writing, because so long as there was
another book, we were fine. Risa was born. I adored
Risa. I had been scared, but after she was born, it was
fine. She was a little miracle. But she cried. It was the
two of us and four walls and her *crying*, all the time.
The doctors suggested this or that or said it would
stop, but it didn't. It filled the house." He looked
pained, as if she was right there, still crying. "Meanwhile, I was teaching, and we were doing the new
cover design. But it wasn't like before. We were short
with each other.

"And then, finally, and this is what I didn't tell you,
one day, I planned a trip to Boston. *By myself.*" He
shook his head and smiled sadly. "With a box of
books. The new ones. To sell, supposedly." He looked
down. "But this time around, I didn't believe. As
much. In the book, or in. . . . Well, a couple of stores
took one or two, on consignment. But I was a failure. I
couldn't sell them. And the box was so *heavy*. I hated
myself. I couldn't take them home. So I threw them in
a dumpster. It was awful, throwing out what she had
worked so hard on. Pitching it behind. . . ." He shook
his head again and ran his hand over his face. "Then I
went off and, well, I stared. At some fellows. Just
walked, basically. Walked and stared. I'd made it an
overnight trip. I'd made up some complicated reason
to tell her. So I had a room. An empty room where I

could do anything, and I had nothing to do. Shouldn't I at least find out what it was like, once, so I could go home and be a good husband and father, knowing that *that* was the right thing?

"Eventually some guy looked back. And this time, I didn't look away. It felt okay. Like a relief. Talking to him. Walking, just us two, up Commonwealth Ave. Innocent, kind of. He was married, too. He came to my room. For 'tea.' Ha! We didn't do any more than guys in Benleigh dorms did when they were bored on Saturday nights. I didn't even. . . . Because, with the germs and all. . . .

"After he left, I swore I would never, *ever* do that again. It was settled.

"I told Sara I'd sold the books. I gave her cash. She didn't care about the money, though. She wanted to tell her story—*to* someone. To have someone hear and know. Someone going through a dumpster. Huh!

"And still Risa cried. So I 'dashed down' to Providence. To sell more books and 'meet a college friend.' This time I *gave* them away, left some in a café, just *left* them, like babies on doorsteps." He stopped halfway, like saying that had hurt. "And then I went and did what I had really come for." He sighed and his voice dropped. "I'd already met a guy, online. A Brown professor. His wife was away at a conference. Beautiful house. Antiques. Maps.

"We had a big argument about New Haven. Sara didn't see why I couldn't take day trips. But the guy this time could only see me late. She said, 'New Haven doesn't have that many bookstores.' Then she smiled and said, 'Pat, what do you *do* on these trips?' Was she onto me? At that point, I almost . . . I didn't think I could keep on. More than any reaction she'd have or our families would have, what horrified me was the thought of being thirty-five or forty and still saying, 'I didn't do anything in BostonHartfordProvidenceNew-

Haven. I sold books. That's it!' Her work would be in dumpsters all over New England!" His breathing seemed labored, and he looked so sad. I felt like he still thought, *Poor Sara!* While I thought, *Poor Pat!*

"Finally, I 'fessed up. The guy in New Haven didn't show up, by the way. She was repulsed. She could barely comprehend. I had to say it a hundred different ways, but she was so, *so* hurt. Naturally! I swore right off that I'd done . . ." He coughed and cleared his throat. ". . . done nothing unsafe. She didn't believe I couldn't have it. The virus, you know. So I had to get more specific. I told her I'd never even *kissed*. . . . But just saying the word, even in the process of denying it, was as bad to her as if I'd done it. She still thought I had to have—you know. I kept trying to explain. She wouldn't even let me touch her. Or Risa. I couldn't touch Risa. She slammed the bedroom door with the two of them on the inside, and she packed. Right that night. Went to a hotel. We divorced; I lost the apartment and went back to a dorm with the jocks. I got tested so I could hold Risa. At the end of the year she resigned and that's when the whole California thing happened. Risa stopped crying in California.

"I thought I still loved Sara. We were supposed to be a family. I thought of fighting for custody—claiming the Big Sur commune thing was bad for a kid—but my family didn't have the money. My parents thought these things didn't happen to people like us. When they did, we caved, then we stewed over it. And I was afraid that, if I didn't cooperate, she'd tell the Benleigh people about me. So she got custody.

"Meanwhile, though, one little beacon of hope: I had been an associate in college guidance, in addition to teaching, and now they put me in charge. The top guy was going to dry out!

"It kept me busy, but I was *painfully* lonely." He rubbed the center of his chest around and around.

"One weekend I got in the car and drove. Next thing I was at Dartmouth. Next weekend, Brown and Yale. *Researching.* I made it my mission to find out everything about every college in New England and New York. I talked to admissions people and strolled campuses. I would be the magician who would do for Benleigh kids what I thought no one had done for me: start them on a great future.

"I also wanted to go back in time. Start over as an unspoiled lad walking Benefit Street in Providence."

It was funny. Even as a high school senior, I still understood about going back to being unspoiled.

"I thought I'd find myself on those trips," he sighed, "or become someone else. I talked. Introduced myself. Asked about kids' experiences." He squinted out a window, over the marsh. "'If you were starting over, if you knew what you know now, would you come here again?' Most said yes.

"At Benleigh I could not touch my young men physically, but I could touch their lives. I loved thinking who they might become because of me."

Suddenly I saw Pat not as some know-it-all authority figure, but the way he was back then, a guy in his twenties alone and scared, yearning. I thought I could feel the ache in my own chest of having a child taken away. "Do you see her now?" I asked. "Risa?"

"Occasionally. At first, I thought I didn't deserve to. She went to high school out there. She's your age. Off to college next year." Before I could open my mouth he said, "The Sorbonne. Of course, she said her French wasn't good enough."

"And you told her the way to make it better was to go."

He grinned and said, "Seriously, I didn't give an *inch!* Sara's more laissez-faire. I shouldn't criticize, though. She raised Risa by herself, mostly—she remarried about three years ago—and she did very well.

I get hold of my daughter, and I have to fix everything in one phone call!" He sighed. "Sara. Never bargained for what I brought her. I never meant to destroy anything. Each time I thought, *This will satisfy me.* But emotions either matter, or they don't."

A middle-aged couple had entered wearing Lands' End–L. L. Bean kind of stuff, and were browsing the shelves. I lowered my voice. "So, somewhere in all that, like, your parents found out about . . . ?"

He folded his arms. "My mother said I was just 'blue' about Sara. Dad said I shouldn't 'go thinking' I was abnormal because of what happened. I did *not* tell them I'd, you know, done things. It would suggest I'd done them during the marriage, and Sara had already sworn to her parents that I hadn't and made me swear to go along." He threw up his hands. "I was twenty-five, 1994, people still thought AIDS was a death sentence. So I agreed." His hands settled in his lap again. "I'm happy for you, Jim. You've already had it happen—the relationship, being torn—it's behind you. I don't mean you don't still have uncertainties and regrets, but you didn't do any permanent damage. It feels to you like you did, right now. You confused and disappointed someone. Hurt her. Yes. But I mucked someone up completely. Of course I also have Risa. Occasionally. I created a life; I destroyed a life. She's so lovely."

His gaze went all over the place like me as a kid at the top of the Pru, sweeping the binoculars across whole states, not knowing what I was looking at or what I was supposed to be looking *for.*

"Well," I said, motioning with my head toward my parents' house, "I still haven't told *her.*"

"All right," he said. "What about *her?*"

"I, well, I love her," I said. "I do. We're just different. I'm not what she was hoping for."

"Mmmm, don't be so sure."

214

"I know. Parents love you and say they only want you to be happy, you don't have to be anything special, you be yourself." I shrugged.

"And you think—"

"They have expectations. Of course they do."

"And how does your being gay go against their expectations?"

What? Wasn't it obvious? "It goes against *everybody's* expectations!" I said. "Sons are supposed to be strong. Fix stuff. Do stuff. Be sturdy, hardy, whatever. Admirable and capable."

"And how are you not those things? Strong, hardy, admirable. How does preferring men to women sexually take away from that?"

"Well—"

"Doesn't it enhance them? Look at the huge decision you made. The strength it took. The abyss you're willing to stand over. The schoolwork you do and the work you do here. Very capable."

"Let me put it this way," I said, raising my voice. "You're just never the hero. A gay guy is nobody's hero!" He frowned and folded his arms. "Except to other gay guys," I added. "Like, you know, how you are to me."

"And you to me," he said gently.

I blushed. The animal in my chest wriggled like a puppy being petted. "Or," I added, "unless you're Barney Frank." For years I'd sort of kept an eye on him, our famously out representative.

"And what makes Barney Barney?" Pat asked. I fumbled around about forcefulness and toughness, but Pat stopped me. "Barney Frank is Barney Frank," he said, "primarily because he is *out*. Everything else follows from that."

While I took that in, Pat said, "As for your parents, it seems you don't want to disappoint two people you think are disappointed already. They know you broke up with Liz."

"They didn't ask about it."

"You didn't tell them about it."

"Which is what they wanted."

"What do *you* want? You have to want something. Other than comfort."

I did a huge, dramatic face palm. I hoped it was funny and would also make him back off. But he didn't laugh, and he didn't say anything reassuring. Finally I said, "You have plenty of silence and comfort here!" Wasn't the bookstore another Benleigh? For me, too.

"We're not talking about me," he said, a bit severely. "And while I regard us as friends, as close friends, you do not know everything about what I do or do not have."

"Um, right. Sorry," I said.

"No harm done."

"Can I go now? Am I under arrest, Officer?"

"Go any time you like!" For several seconds we stared at each other. "It's always your choice."

I stayed seated. "Well, I don't want to go," I said, a little more irritated. "I guess I just don't want to discuss this stuff anymore."

"Also your choice." His eyes twinkled.

"You make it sound bad that I've simply had enough of a conversation!" Wait. What had become of building fires and brewing coffee and Bay View being a safe sanctuary?

"I *make* it sound?" He shook his head. "There's no way that I am making anything sound."

"I want to scream right now," I said. I felt a headache coming on.

"It's the toughest lesson of all, isn't it?" he said. "Choosing."

I stood and said, "Look, I really do have to go."

"All right." He didn't say it suggestively, like, "Your choice, but a braver guy would stay." He really said it like he believed me and it was fine.

"I really do," I said.

He stood, too. "Fine. Be sure to keep me apprised." He spoke as warmly and genuinely as he ever had. I saw his smile and his firm stance, hands on his hips, and I saw he was not going away. I could choose whatever I wanted, and he would not go away. That voice—which I would have to describe as loving just then—would not go away. The fire and the coffee would not go away. I would just not be able to stay by that fire. I'd come and sit, and when it was time to go, I would take some coals to build my own fire somewhere else. My friend, who loved me and whom I loved, had his fire, and I had mine.

It was kind of an amazing, scary moment— standing, realizing, waiting a moment to go. I would never see Mr. Baxter or the store the same way again. It had happened before: thinking the first day how he was really a salesman; then seeing *Hunk*; hearing about Larry, about Sara and the men in other cities. And he knew I had bullied Nate and lied to Liz and my parents. And yet, when I opened the door to leave Bay View that afternoon, his smile was even warmer and more appreciative than the night he opened the door to his house and said, "Hello again. Why don't *I* invite *you* in?"

And so before I went, I blushed two or three or six shades of red and mumbled, "By the way, you're my hero more than ever now."

He kept the same stance and turned a couple of shades of red himself and said, "Thank you. The same here."

Strolling up to the house I thought, *Why do I have to do any of it?* Why did I have to go to college? Couldn't I

take a year off and work at Nuts 'n Beans? Live at
home with my maps and shells and sunrises and sunsets? It wouldn't be so bad. And no one said I had to
tell my parents every detail of my personal life. There
were families where stuff like this was "understood."
No one went around confessing or talking about it all
the time.

No. I had been here too long already. And there was
stuff for me to do in Boston, including the marathon. I
wasn't crazy about those high-rises, and I didn't think
I'd mingle with geniuses from MIT. I would feel more
like myself out in the Berkshires. But I was tired of
feeling like myself. By the time I got to the Berkshires,
I would be totally bored with it.

Coming up to our house I felt heavy in my hips and
between my legs, like ballast, weighing a ship down,
but balancing it so it survives wind and storms. Pat
Baxter, my friend, had left his wife with a crying baby
to go do stuff with guys in hotels. He'd thrown her
books away and lied to her. And I loved him. I suddenly loved him so, so much. I didn't know what to do
or think. Not loved him like wanting to make love to
him. But yeah, sort of. I couldn't quite imagine sex
with him, but I wanted somehow to encompass him. I
felt that weight again, low in my body, like I'd grown a
keel. Oh, plus I had to tell my parents about Boston.
That thought almost blew the boat over! Plus, there
was other stuff to tell, eventually.

I announced my decision over dinner that night. My
parents weren't leaping over the moon, but they did
their best to act positive. They hoped I would be
happy. They emphasized that one could always transfer. That made me nuts. Like, my choice couldn't
really be okay unless there was an escape hatch, and
they were already planning on me using it. After dessert I went online to the various college sites to give
my acceptance and my rejections. My heart pounded

away as I clicked. A voice kept asking, "Are you sure? Are you sure?" And I just kept clicking. Finally, everything was settled. I emailed Pat.

"Congratulations!" was all he said. I was taken aback. Wasn't he going to tell me I did the right thing? Did he think I already knew? Or was my decision not completely made? Would I keep deciding more and more and going deeper and deeper into life?

I went to sleep thinking of Liz—how we were and what happened, how part of me still longed for her, and how I'd once thought that by now, in spring, we'd be making love all the time.

Early the next morning I got up and went running for the first time.

I stopped, gasping for air, after less than a mile.

A marathon, by definition, is 26 miles, 385 yards.

It's harder to measure the distance between being straight and being gay. Between who you thought your parents wanted you to be and thought you were, and who you really are. And whatever the distance between those things, there's no way to say how fast you should run it. No signs telling you you're halfway or in the home stretch. You can even cross the finish line and find out there's more to run, or a piece to go back and run again. And it might be hard to tell who the winners are.

So you just start.

I think races make more sense than life.

CHAPTER 19

FLY BY YOUR WISDOM

WE HAD THE funeral for Aunt Lillian. Dad stood up and went through a whole bunch of history and memories, very heartfelt, a lot of which I never knew. I felt deprived. He wasn't that heartfelt about stuff around home. Was this something you did only when people died? Should I have listened better to his stories? I couldn't even remember exactly what he'd said about Aunt Lillian in that café in Boston. Now I was leaving home.

I waited a few days, then decided to try the Big Announcement at the dinner table, so we'd all have props handy and stuff to do. I used the college thing as a lead-in. "I thought," I began, "I should tell you more about why I picked Boston for college." Mom was buttering bread, and at this point her buttering became very detailed and dramatic and even aggressive. "Dad and I talked a little bit about this," I told her. But Dad went on with his soup and tried not to seem startled. "I didn't think," I went on, "that I'd exactly *fit in* out there in the Berkshires." They kept buttering, slurping, whatever, and looking away from me.

"I thought it would be constricting, because I'm probably not like most of those kids." Then I added,

"Socially." I practically heard a prayer go through Mom's head: "Please don't say it!"

"Socially," I continued, "the Berkshires will be the same as Sicassett: the same guys going after the same girls, the same girls going after the same guys. But I, um, feel differently. As Dad sort of, I dunno, spotted about me." He didn't look up. "I am a guy who kind of goes for guys." I kicked myself for saying "kind of." I felt around for the next sentence. Suddenly Mom looked up and said with mock annoyance, "Well, you know what I don't understand?"

"What?" I said, relieved that at last someone else was going to help out and do some talking.

"I just do not understand why it's such a big deal! I mean, it's 2013, it's nobody's business, anyway, why can't we just leave it at that? Honestly!"

Oh. Okay. I hadn't counted on that. I looked to Dad. "So we're not going to discuss it?" I said.

He frowned like he was thinking of something important to say, but he didn't speak. I guessed everything in that house had to have Mom's permission, even our "thinking." Maybe Dad took me to Boston so we could think without Mom. And he had thought something nice. Now he couldn't say, "Son, we love you no matter what," because she had said it was stupid to talk about this stuff. But he loved her. I knew he did. And they loved me. But all that love wasn't helping us talk. If there was going to be a conversation, it was up to me. So I started in again.

I linked how I was (I didn't use the word "gay" a lot yet) to my choice to go to college in a city. Mom interrupted and said it was *fine* that I was going to Boston. Like Dad, she mentioned "opportunities" and "experience." Dad piped up now: "Exactly. Yes, indeed." And, Mom said, I could always transfer! Then suddenly she was clearing the table, then they were washing dishes, then the counters were wiped dry and the lights were out, except for the buzzing fluorescent tube over the stove. In the den the TV went on, and once our TV is on, nothing is discussed. It sort of set me free and made me lonely, wishing for them to say what they'd never say and be a way that they never would be. I went up to bed early, wondering if I'd actually said anything! In order to know that what I felt was real, I flipped back and forth through the Exercise folder several times.

Over the next few days I ran some tests. If Mom said a guy was handsome, like a movie star or base-ball player, I'd agree. She'd get all quiet. As for Dad, even though supposedly he understood, I thought maybe he was a little disappointed. I was the only son he'd ever have, and while it was okay with him that I "liked the boy who worked for Pat Baxter," I'd never be sterling, like he probably dreamed of. There'd never be any trophies around. (I could run in the marathon, but I'd never win it, although that's not supposed to matter.) I watched him around the house, somber and preoccupied, his face hanging just a little. Maybe he had had lots of ideas over the years. I think Dad had this alternate reality, where stuff was basically okay, even me in love with a guy. It just wasn't said, be-cause Mom took center stage announcing how far it was to Falmouth and what the chance of snow was and how to give someone a pill and what subjects a young man could bring up at the dinner table. So that's how we lived in "The Mom Show."

"They probably don't know what to think," Pat said. It was August. We sat out on his deck. The cove was still and glassy, the bay out of sight. I had just come from running. I was up to four miles, four times a week, plus two and a half miles one other time. That was the regimen recommended by a running site I found. I didn't exactly "like" running while I was doing it, but I didn't want to stop. Now I was collapsed all sweaty in an Adirondack chair. Pat made some sangria. The pieces of orange and lemon were like jewels in the setting sun.

"You came out to them on the heels of your decision to go to Boston."

"They think I chose Boston so I could, like, binge?"

"No no. You just showed some assertiveness. And the influence of your 'invert' neighbor!" I rolled my eyes. My parents did at least concede that Pat was the Admissions Guy, and Dad had stopped the "Mr. Baxssster" thing. "Parents get jealous. Who kidnapped their little one? What will I turn you into?"

"I just told them I'd fit better socially in Boston."

"Maybe they're thinking of AIDS. The whole thing must feel like a plot hatched behind their backs. Maybe they think someone should have seen something or said something. About college or your sexuality. Or they might be remembering things they said that seem insensitive now."

With a flash of white a male eider took flight over the marsh, its "woo-woo" fading on the breeze. On the Cape time flows all around you. Birds migrate, leaves turn, stores selling flip-flops and beach plum jelly close, cottages empty, creeks freeze. Guys who come from someplace better, whose money and muscles make our little Cape better, leave. They'll come back Memorial Day, taller, more confident, or they won't. They'll have fellowships in New York or Zurich or someplace. But there'll be new guys, and next summer will be *their* summer. No summer was mine. No one said, "Here is all the world, for you." Until Pat. I realized that's what he did. And I had begun to understand what it was to love someone.

"I emailed Nate," I said. "Apparently he's really going to Israel."

"Oh, yes!" Pat said. "Got his ticket!" He smiled re-signedly. We might never see Nate again. He'd spent the summer in some advanced science program at Brandeis up in Waltham. He'd been back once. We'd walked at Namskaket Beach, and we'd hugged. He'd kissed my cheek. It was nice, but somehow he'd moved on. He'd talked a lot about the army. "Another round?"

Pat poured us more sangria, holding the fruit back with a wooden spoon. I wasn't really drunk, but it was about the closest I'd come. I wanted to feel it a little more.

A path of orange-gold light stretched to the horizon. More eiders flew up and away. I rose, light-headed. Pat took my arm to steady me. I stared down at his hand. Then I reached for it and missed and sort of kept reaching and I lost my balance and there was broken glass and wine and fruit splattered all over the deck, and I was saying, "I'm sorry! I'm sorry!" and he said, "No, no, not your fault," and his hand was dripping blood! He went for the door.

I followed him inside. I felt alone all of a sudden, the beautiful, grown-up drinks spilled, the deck left empty, the light going. I didn't know if I was supposed to be in here. He rushed to the bathroom without looking back, and I followed. I wanted to help, espe-cially because this was my fault, but—the two of us, so close? I hung back in the doorway. He ran cold wa-ter over his bloody hand. With the other hand he opened the medicine cabinet. I sort of leaned in, my head off-balance. His hand was right there. I took it and looked at the cut. I felt a little stirring, if you know what I mean. He looked at me. Then he let me lower his hand to the water, and he winced.

The blood swirled down the drain. He took down a box of big, square Band-Aids. The actual cut turned out not to be that bad—jagged, on the web of skin between the thumb and forefinger. He sent me for an old towel from a closet in the hall. I felt strange, digging through his towels like we were two guys housekeeping. Suddenly I wanted that. Someone to take care of. And breathe with, like Nate.

I came back with a towel. "Well!" he said, taking it, "this is an adventure, isn't it?"

I tried to apologize, but he shook his head and said it was probably his fault. I realized how protective he was of me. He'd dismissed my bullying Nate as kids' shenanigans. Once, when I'd charged someone wrong for a book, he said the way he'd marked it was confusing and added, "I'm not in this for the money anyway." He knew I felt bad about stuff I'd done, and he didn't want me to. By not letting me feel bad about the past or present, maybe he was prepping me for the future. Suddenly I had to be close to him, though I couldn't get much closer physically than I already was. He clutched at the towel and passed me the Band-Aids. I unwrapped one while he held that hand—that broad, handsome hand—out to me, palm up, and blood ran twisting into his palm. He dabbed it again.

Fitting a Band-Aid onto that skin-web is not easy, but I did it. I still held his hand in both of mine. I looked up and met his eyes, and I said, "Are you all right?" He smiled and then with his other hand stroked my hair and the outer edge of my ear. Then he brought me close and embraced me. "You . . ." he began. "If I had a son . . ." And then in a soft, dry voice, as though he was going to cry, he said, "I would want him, excuse me, to be good and strong, like you." I thought he would let go, but he hung on. His hands went up and down my back, like he was feeling me, not in a sexual way, but just, like, making sure he remembered me. It would be a while. I felt his hands moving up and down me. I guessed there was even more to his life than I had imagined. I didn't know if I should do the same to him, so I just hugged and left it at that.

Then he broke the embrace and tousled my hair. "Why don't we go back outside?" he said, with a sad smile, his lips pressed together. He gathered bits of wrapping from the Band-Aid and dropped them in the wicker basket. He washed the blood away and shut the medicine cabinet. As it swung shut, for a second I saw the two of us side-by-side. I would get married, I thought. I would find someone, or someone would find me. That someone would get how I wanted to take care of him.

Pat took me by the shoulders and turned me around. I had to go. The assertiveness was sexy, though. Suddenly, in the bathroom doorway, I stopped and stiffened my body. He pushed. I got stiffer, and he stopped. I looked back at him. "It's okay what you did," I said. He tilted his head and raised an eyebrow. "Leaving," I said, "and . . . with the books. And the guys. It's, um, it's all okay." I began to tear up. He was nodding. He mouthed "Thank you," then very quickly kissed the back of my neck and pushed me out the door.

Once outside again we went down to the gate. I still felt him behind me. His power and his decisiveness. His hand. Even bloody, it was in charge. I looked over toward the barn. "So," I said, "you dreamed of the barn."

"Beg pardon?"

I stopped. "All that time. As a kid. You dreamed of that barn."

He lit up. "I did," he said. "We summered in Wellfleet. Long days. Walking the beach at sunset, knowing I had a whole other day tomorrow and the day after that. Like I'd never have to go home and be picked on and feel hopeless." He shook his head. We faced the barn. "The day we left, I tried not to cry. We drove the back roads to prolong it, stopped at little inlets and coves, bakeries and ice cream places. And of course, bookshops. We came down 65 and took Goody Barron because my mother loved the name. And I waited for the barn.

"I saw the cupola over the trees, and I pretended this was all my own special country." He swept his arm in a semicircle that took in the marsh, the barn, and his house. "A land where I was a prince and could come any time I wanted. I even named it!" He chuckled. "Get this: 'Baxteraña'! Ha! And, I will have you know that that was with an *n* with a tilde!" He clapped his hands with one loud report and laughed.

And there we were, in the middle of my own Wallaçonia, and I didn't know how to tell him. I couldn't say, "Hey, me, too: Wallaçonia!" Because Wallaçonia was always more than a game. I still didn't know completely what it was. So it still needed protecting.

Chapter 20

Over and Gone

THINKING ABOUT WHAT Pat said, I told Mom and Dad, "I'll be right on the other side of the bay. I won't be seduced by the big city. Gonna be chained to my desk!" Well, baloney. I was going to go out and explore. I was definitely going to have more sex!

I had tried that summer but wasn't too successful. You'd think, Cape Cod in summer, full of guys, right? Well, it's too full. Ninety percent are gorgeous but straight and don't even look at you. Some of them might do something if you posed and swaggered like them, but they wouldn't hug or kiss or hang around. The gay guys I saw were a mixture of not out, halfway out, snooty, not my type, or already had boyfriends. I just wanted to ask some guy his favorite book and treat him to ice cream. And breathe with him. I just didn't seem to find anyone with that vibe. For one thing, I was busy, working at Bay View and at this boat-rental place in North Eastham. But I did try with a couple of guys, both tourists, just in their hotel rooms. It was hot, doing what we did. It made me feel more confident and real. But we didn't bother to stop long enough to breathe together. We were all leaving on Labor Day.

Mostly I concentrated on my running, on the bike path down the shore to Brewster. I saw guys walking there, real slow with suggestive eyes, but I had a goal every day, and I wouldn't let it go, even if one of them stared at me, which was not that often.

My parents didn't ask why I was running or what my goal was or anything. The weight loss was noticeable, though. Mom said, "Don't lose too much, now! You should go to the Internet and see if they have precautions about all that running." She even sent me a link to a "Height and Weight Chart for Boys" and one to a *Runner's World* article, "What's Your Ideal Weight?" I deleted both, and she never asked again.

Pat noticed, too. He remembered the teacher who had wanted me to run cross-country, and so he understood. I didn't tell him about the marathon, though. I didn't tell anyone. Then I'd really have to do it.

I tried talking to Mom again about the gay thing. I brought it up when she was washing dishes. I stood in the kitchen doorway and said, "So, when we were talking about college before, I told you something about myself, about liking guys more than girls?" Suddenly Mom, in a voice I can only describe as *aggressively merry*, said, "You know what? I still don't understand whose business it is but yours! All these people sticking their nose in other people's business and then posting it on the Internet. That's what I have to say about that!"

After that, I didn't know how to bring it up again. I guessed one day I'd introduce them to a guy. Mom would be aggressively merry, and Dad would shake the dude's hand, and we'd all go on. That's what we always did. We were polite. Or said we were.

Soon I had to leave and maybe not completely return. I was nervous. I had all sorts of ideas about parties and fun things I'd do and sexy guys I'd meet and running through the Fens at dawn, but I also kept reassuring myself that I had X-number of days left there on Wrestling Cove—X-number more sunsets and sunrises, X-number more visits with Pat.

But the moment came, the one you think is just a little further off. For just a second you smell autumn on the marsh. Suddenly the light changes at dusk. I saw it while coming out of Bay View one evening. Pat now trusted me to do the reconciliation at the end of the day. He seemed to be away more than usual. I was locking up, and I saw the light, different. I looked up at Pat's house. Dark. I climbed the hill. As I stopped and looked at his house again in that golden-pink, summer-is-over light, I felt as though he had left. Not that he wouldn't be back tonight or tomorrow. Certainly not that he wasn't my friend. He always would be. I just felt that, in some sense, he had *left*.

A little before Labor Day, Liz texted. She wanted to see me before I left. I texted, "Sure, come over." Except for liking some of my stuff on Facebook, she hadn't been in touch in weeks. I'd seen her at the superette in Chatham with this guy Gary from choir, and I ducked down an aisle. I knew she had to go on and live her life, but seeing her with another guy made me remember what we had had together and what I had been then. There was no longer Jim One and Jim Two, but there was an Old Jim and Newer Jim, and when I saw Liz with Gary I suddenly missed Old Jim, with his shells and maps and longings and hopes, all worried and conscientious. New Jim had hopes, too, but none of them had come true yet, and he worried when or even *if* they would. New Jim was a baby raccoon, kind of naked and shivering and wondering if he should be more like Gary and if so, how?

The day was hazy. She swung into our driveway fast, throwing some gravel, and hopped out of the car.

She was pretty dolled up, more than when we dated. Like me, maybe she was trying to be different now. She had pale pink lipstick and her hair was shorter and a little wavy. We hugged and were very smiley and animated, because my parents could be watching. For a while all she could say was, "Wow, look at you!" A lot of people did that. I didn't know what to do with it. No one had ever given me or my body that kind of attention. Was Liz still interested in me that way? The thought made me interested in her again. For a second I had this crazy idea that she was there to get back together. But being with Nate, thinking about Nate and other guys—even just the summer quickies—felt so much more intense and clear and right. As Liz and I suddenly fell silent, it came back to me again that, for me, being grown-up, being a man, had come to mean being gay. And saying I was gay.

I suggested a walk on the marsh. Away from parental eyes. Liz changed her shoes, and we were off into the breeze. "Going to a party?" I said. I had to ask twice. I finally got it out of her that the party was at Gary's. She didn't say anything else about it.

We hopped across creeks, leaping from one tussock to the next, unsure how far we were going. The air had that salty, gassy stink we love on the Cape. Flowers were out all around us—red coast blite and fleabane, pink and purple. The spartina was going to seed. Birds darted, and now and then greenhead flies buzzed us.

I asked her about college. She wasn't going to that school near Albany anymore. She was going down to DC. I said, "Congratulations," and she said, "Mm-hm." After a few more leaps, she mentioned that Gary was going to school nearby. She said she was "seeing" him, and she guessed they might be serious. She sounded hesitant, and I didn't pursue the subject. Suddenly she looked at me, but didn't slow down. "Do you have someone?" she asked. I shook my head. I said I wasn't interested in "the guys around here." She blushed and looked frowny and annoyed. So, I should suppress the little detail that, like, anyone I'd be interested in from now on would be male? I decided just to go on. I said I'd had a couple of "summer lovers," but that I thought I might have better luck with guys in Boston.

She stopped on a broad, firm tussock. She frowned and said, "Wait. What?"

I felt guilty. After all that time we'd spent together, of course I should have said something.

"But that was your *safety school!*" she said, waving a greenhead away. "I mean, I'm sorry, but—"

I got annoyed. I balanced on a muddy rock and ticked off on my fingers all the things that weren't "safe" about Boston: the huge mix of people from all over, the choices I'd have to make, the social expectations, plus navigating the gay life. I deliberately said "gay life," and I said it again and didn't care what she did—if she was going to talk about my "safety school."

Still, after I enumerated the challenges, she said, "Oh, I hadn't thought of it like that."

Maybe I'd sounded harsh. Did I really believe Boston was the right choice and that there'd be *so* many great challenges? I wanted to apologize, but I wondered, why?

We went farther out. The shore receded; it was us and the hazy sky joining the hazy cove. For a while we didn't say anything, just swatted at greenheads. After a while she said, "You know, it's funny. I thought, even, that we might, you know, that we might get married. One day."

"Wow!" I said. "So this is serious!"

"Wait. What is?"

"You and Gary."

"Gary? No. No." She paused and said, "I meant us! You and me."

"You thought—"

She shrugged and said, quickly and tensely, "I just thought maybe we might eventually get married! Natural? Right? At the time." She looked out to the cove. "Just a thought." She sighed. "Once upon a time." The afternoon was still. A little haze obscured the boats at anchor. She bit her lip. A breeze came up, and the surface of the water went ripply. A mast swayed a bit.

"I thought so, too," I said. I felt a tear in the corner of my eye. I'd thought that so recently, and now it seemed crazy.

"We were friends," she said. She wasn't as animated now as when she stepped out of the car.

"Still are," I said.

She shook her head. "Nah. There was no one like you, Wallace."

"Hey," I said, trying to sound lighthearted, "there's no one like you, either."

She smiled, like she thought she had to, and folded her arms. "I mean—" She heaved a big sigh. I thought she would cry. "Most guys," she said, "I don't understand a *word they say!*" I smiled, and Liz herself even broke down and laughed a little at that. "No. But, I mean," she said, "my brother can put together a sentence of, like, six words. Six English words, all of which I know the meaning of. And the grammar's fine. E. B. White would love it. And I have *no idea* what he's talking about." Her shoulders slumped. "I have no idea what planet he's on. I have no idea what's *important* to him. When he was eight, I did. I knew. I understood perfectly. Now?" She folded her arms. "Plus, he's rude to Mom. I can't stand it.

"But you were the *opposite!* Other guys, I didn't understand no matter how much they said. I understood you *before* you said anything. And you understood me." She tossed it off lightly so she wouldn't cry. "You just had to come down the hall with that look. No one

233

understood like you." After another pause she added, "I felt safe with you. I felt the world was safe again."

So was I a good stand-in for her dad? I guessed I had tried to be. But I ended up hurting her. Leaving her, like he did. I'd felt something for her, and I had been just so relieved. I thought *she* was taking care of *me*. I thought what I felt was love. But if you took what I felt for her and subtracted the huge relief over a worry-free life ahead, what was left?

Through all that I had an underground river. I thought if I put my foot in, the current would grab me and pull me under. Finally I did put my foot in, and the current did pull. I was no longer safe. So was I *dangerous* now? That was sort of a cool idea, but it hurt, too. "Dangerous." Damaging. To Liz, to my family.

The breeze came up, and the water went dark with ripples. Masts tipped back and forth like metronomes. Liz was looking out to sea. In a soft, high voice she asked, "Did you ever wish that, like, there could be some, I don't know, administrative screw-up, and we'd all have to stay in school, here, just one more semester? Just till Christmas. Till New Year's. And then we could go on."

I was relieved and disappointed that she didn't want to talk about us anymore. I said no. I was anxious about the future, I liked the safety of Sicasset and our house, but I was tired of waiting around, not knowing stuff. Not knowing more about myself. I had to go. I stared at the masts. You could smell fall, a whiff here and there. I shook my head and said, "I can't *imagine* another semester of high school!" She blushed and cut her eyes away. "Sorry," I offered.

Her voice a bit hard, she said, "It was just a thought."

I looked down. At my feet were clumps of glasswort, still green, except the tip of one stem was red. A few weeks and the whole marsh would blaze. Then just to the right, in the grass, something moved. A nose. A raccoon! He turned and waddled off. Funny, because even in summer you don't usually see them in daylight.

Suddenly she said, "Can I ask . . . ?"

"Sure," I said.

"As a friend . . . ?"

"Sure."

"When we were together, what were you, like, *thinking*?"

"What was I—?"

"Thinking. About me. Us. *It.*"

I squirmed. Like, was it her business? This whole thing wasn't about what I was *thinking* at any one minute or another. I answered anyway. "I *thought*," I said, "that you were beautiful, and I liked you and then I loved you. I even thought, yeah, we might get married, eventually. If I could get rid of certain other things I *thought*. Like that there was something deep-down wrong with me, some travesty no one understood"—she sort of recoiled at the word *travesty*—"but if I tried hard enough, I could fix it. Or it would fix itself. Meanwhile I couldn't stop looking at certain guys at school or the beach or wherever. I thought I just envied them, and when I grew up more I'd be like them and stop envying—"

Liz made a face and took a deep breath.

"Hey, you asked!" I said. "And I'm telling you just the tip of the iceberg. This was the inside of my head, every day! I wondered how this *thing* could have happened to me. Answer? It didn't. It couldn't have. Thinking about guys was a bad habit with a perfectly good explanation. Liz, my parents are normal." I pointed to the shore. "In that house, you cannot conceive of anything other than what's normal and expected. They don't yell, they don't spank, they don't ground me. Discipline in that house is all about how *normal* everything is. So I had to be normal, but in here and in here"—pointing to my head and my chest—"I kept failing. I loved you, Liz. I didn't plot against you. The other thing was just bigger than either of us."

"I didn't say you 'plotted' anything!" Her chin trembled.

"Aw, Cubs," I said and reached for her. She stiffened. I thought then that I was Old Jim again, wanting to reassure everyone. New Jim seemed so selfish by comparison, wanting sex and blowing a hundred bucks on electric-blue running shoes (okay, they were awesome) and actually having the temerity to say he was going to run in a marathon. I felt guilty going for all that without permission, and yet I was afraid I wouldn't get it.

"Liz, I didn't ask to feel how I felt. You watch *Will and Grace*, you think, oh, some people are gay, and they're like *this*, and everybody else isn't, and they're like *that*. When I was six, we were over at Boat Meadow Landing. Sunset. There was this blond boy, a year older than me. I couldn't stop staring at him, wanting to be him. Just staring, heart pounding. For a couple of minutes he was everything. I wanted to know his name, what he liked to do, his favorite TV show, everything. He was one of about a hundred, by the way. A lot of them I remember to this day. Not their names, obviously. Ninety-nine times out of a hundred I didn't know. But I remember exactly where we were, how they were standing, how ugly and stupid I thought I looked by comparison, and they were angels. How alone I felt. How I wanted them all for my very own. So strong and simple and scary and strange for a six-year-old. Or nine or twelve or whatever. Like I saw a secret room and couldn't tell anyone. But what was the secret? Why did I think about that boy's legs and his hair? Why did I think about him in church? He was the son my parents really wanted. That's what they were praying for! I had to try to be like him. I tried. I thought I could do it. But the wanting and the weakness didn't go away. I tried to be good at sports, but I wasn't. I was weak and mean. If anyone ever did say anything nice about me, I wished they wouldn't. I'd think, 'If only they knew.'"

"Oh, Jeez, Wallace." She took my hand. "No!"

"Now," I said, "I don't know what's going to happen. But it feels better. I still think I'm a disappointment. To them." I nodded toward shore. "But loving you was all part of it."

"Wait. Loving me was part of disappointing—?"

"No! Just part of feeling everything. I thank you, Cubs. I knew I could love someone because I loved you, and you loved me. It wasn't easy, because I kept thinking I didn't deserve it. But it wasn't wasted, you know? It's over, but it's still a great thing that happened."

She didn't look like she was listening. She chewed her lip, and her eyes went back and forth. The breeze had picked up. It tugged my hair. The heads of the spartina tossed back and forth and scattered seeds, and then I heard it in the pines.

"Have you?" she asked. "Ever? With a guy?"

"Liz!" I said. "That's what I meant about 'summer lovers.'"

"So," she said. "These guys—'summer lovers'—were your first . . . ?"

"Why?" I said. "It's not really your business who my first was."

Her shoulders fell and she said, "Oh, God!"

"Liz, it was after we broke up—my first—if that's what you want to know!"

"So you were, like, *waiting* to—?"

"No! It was a *while* after." An excusable lie, I thought. "It was unexpected. Liz, my life is not some machine programmed to mess up yours! It's not like it's *Star Wars* and I'm putting a target lock on your happiness!"

"I hate *Star Wars*."

"I know. Sorry."

"Are you still with him?"

"No."

"Oh, right. 'Summer lovers.'"

"But still friends, I guess."

She narrowed her eyes. "Was it him? In the bookstore?" She pointed to shore. "The blond?"

"The 'weirdo.' Yeah."

"Oh, Jeez!"

"Elizabeth, you keep asking. You keep hoping for answers I'm not gonna give."

"He was *right there* in front of us? And you were—?"

"And I was aware of his good looks. Is all I was. I knew him before, in middle school. I had no idea Pat knew him, too. It was a total surprise. I was just, like, marveling at how he looked. Until you came in." She rolled her eyes. "Then I marveled at you. Liz, I'm sorry."

"For what? Just for looking at some—?"

"For not figuring out stuff in a logical order and not knowing all I know now."

"You don't have to—"

"I'm not apologizing. I'm just sorry it happened *to you*. It's unfair. I regret it."

"Maybe there's something wrong with *me*," she said, sighing and rolling her eyes.

"No! If I could have made it different, Cubs—" I stopped and asked myself, *Could I have?* I still didn't know. "But you shouldn't go around thinking you did something wrong. You did everything right."

"Apparently not."

238

"Every! Thing!" I took her in a bear hug and kissed her cheek hard. "You loved!" I said, and I let her go. "You're beautiful and smart and hilarious, and you loved! And I loved, too. And I could have done stuff differently. I just didn't know what I knew." I felt a tear again. "I was ignorant and afraid. And I made you feel unsafe. And lousy. That's what I'm sorry about."

"I know you are," she said.

"And *I* know it doesn't help much."

"A little." She tried to smile. "I should get going," she sighed. "Party's at four. Chatham. Cockle Cove Beach." She didn't move.

"What?" I said.

"Just, you know, knowing what you were thinking." She shrugged.

"But what do you *mean*, Liz?"

"While you were *inside* me!" she hissed.

"I thought about *you*," I said.

"Did you have to, you know, think about guys in order to—?"

"No, Liz," I said. "I thought about you. I was with you. We were together."

She nodded. I looked down and saw the tide was coming in. Tiny snails were climbing the reeds. "Good," she said, and again, "Good." She turned to shore. "Hey. So. I've gotta go. I'm sure you've gotta do whatever." Suddenly she leapt a little brook and then stopped and stood. I leapt after her. After a while, she leapt to another tussock and waited there another while. I kept following. She didn't look back or ask for a hand. Eventually we got back to solid ground, each on our own.

We climbed up to her car. The Yahtzee and Bananagrams and long walks and movies and making fun of teachers and listening to each other's problems were all over. Or could we be horrifically mistaken? No. I was what I was, we had reached a natural impasse, maybe beyond the power of friendship to solve. We were both hurt, and we applied apologies and explanations and silences to our cuts. Our relationship was still frustrating to look back on, but I think now we both felt a little better. One kind of love goes, the kind where you penetrate. Can you still have the kind where you support and care and want the best for the person, but don't go certain places and feel certain things? I think people say, "We'll still be friends" because they can't handle the idea that there might be nothing. Like when you die. You have to believe there's something beyond.

We hugged, and kept saying, "Email me," "I'll text you," "We'll Skype," almost like nothing had happened. I liked who I was now, hugging Liz. "Cubs, wherever I am," I said, "I'll still take care of you." As skeptical as I was, that came out a hundred percent sincere. She said, "I know you will," as she turned away, but I don't think she quite got it.

After her car door closed, I wished a whole bunch of things. I wished I'd listened better and asked her more questions. I wished I'd reassured her better. It was just so hard to hear how I'd disappointed her. But I couldn't run after her now. I had to leave it alone— maybe for quite a while—and live with disappointing someone one more time. In all of my uncertainty and feeling bad, though, one thing I didn't wish was to be Old Jim again. In spite of the problems I'd caused and the mistakes I'd made, for a few fleeting seconds that afternoon I felt at home in my skinny body. I thought, At least the guy making mistakes is really me now. He was the guy I wanted to be. He just had to get better at this being-himself thing.

After Liz's car disappeared I turned back to the cove. The wind was up. A whole fleet of metronomes swung, and a huge, beautiful dark cloud rose over them.

A few days later we packed the car, did the last load of laundry, and I went to say good-bye to Pat. He was the whole reason I was going where I was going. If I was going to have a special adventure or be a special person, it would be because he was concerned, because, one night last winter, he saw a kid who needed some help knowing what to do, and he gave it. Like Liz said: Pat didn't just make me feel safe and encouraged. Because Pat was in it, the world felt safe. I could do anything in it now that I wanted to.

I heaved open the door and stepped in from the brightness. It took a second for my eyes to adjust. I realized I was looking at a stranger behind the counter. He raised a hand and greeted me. I raised my own hand, but hesitated to reply; after Nate, I was afraid of who else might come back to me courtesy of Bay View!

It turned out the guy's name was Dennis. From the way Pat asked him to check the computer—a soft word or two and a quick gesture—you knew something was going on. Plus, Dennis sometimes acted happier than you'd expect ("I would *love* to do that!") or more flustered ("Oh, you didn't tell me that!"), like he was trying to please Pat and fretted when he didn't.

So this was where Pat had been. This was why it felt as though he had left.

I was introduced as "the *slender, fit* young man who saved the business last Christmas!" It was one of those awkward things adults say, but I liked it. Dennis smiled and his eyes sparkled, and he said, "I've heard a lot about you," and that made me want to cry a little, because Dennis saying it somehow made it definite that this was the end. For now. I would come back to Bay View, for sure, but I'd never again be that kid who "saved the business" so long ago.

Dennis asked if I was going to run the marathon. I hemmed and hawed, but I realized, people were going to ask that now, a lot. I had to have an answer. "Pretty much probably maybe," I said.

"That's a 'yes'!" Pat called, and Dennis laughed.

"Sorbonne!" I said. I looked at Dennis and he smirked and said, "I know!"

Pat came back out from behind the counter, and we hugged. Again, he was *feeling* me. Who I was underneath my skin. It was over too soon. My body had much more to tell him. He shook my hand a long time, clasped between both of his. They felt so warm and loving. I guessed I had to get used to this kind of touch. As I told Liz, once upon a time, if people were nice to me, I'd think "If they only knew." Now Pat knew. A few people knew now. A bunch more would at school.

He reached up stroked my hair, like how Dad or a coach might muss it up, if I'd ever had a coach. I guess he was my coach, sort of. "Get in there, Jim! Go win one for Bay View!" I decided I would.

After that it was him saying, "Thanks for everything," and me saying, "Thank *you*" and everyone saying, "See you at Thanksgiving," and I was back out in the sun. I didn't look back. I felt Bay View becoming smaller behind me as I walked away.

We hiked up to the house slowly. Mom sat on the living room couch with her sewing kit and a pile of my socks and underwear. I'd already packed them, so she'd taken them out of my suitcase. "What are you doing?" I asked.

"Just sewing in name tapes!" she said, cheerily. "I don't trust the iron-on kind, and who wants magic marker all over your underwear?"

I looked at her and didn't say anything. Yeah, I loved her. And yeah, tomorrow couldn't come fast enough.

CHAPTER 21

BOSTON'S RIVER IS CHILLY AND WIDE

BOSTON BOSTON BOSTON Boston Boston.

Boston strong Boston noisy Boston confusing Boston in a rush.

Boston exciting Boston unpredictable Boston challenging, Boston up-and-down in elevators, running through six lanes of traffic, trying not to let people see me looking at a map, searching for windowless rooms where classes had been moved, flyers on crowded bulletin boards, emails filling my inbox, all of us packed on the T on Saturday night going someplace that somebody's friend said would be awesome.

Running was hard. In the chopped-up city, I had no idea where to go. There were stoplights everywhere. I'd look at the crowds and think, *There are so many people who can do more than I can. Why bother?* But I couldn't stop. I'd hate myself. (Like, even more than I already did. No, no. Joke!!) I forced myself to go out and figure out some kind of path. I found extra time in my schedule (easy; I'd do anything to get away from the idiots on my corridor). I forced myself to run farther. The third day, coming back to the dorm, I ran into this guy, six feet plus, dark, curly hair and dark

243

eyes and a big, wide, beautiful smile. He saw the running outfit, came right over to me, and asked what races I'd run and what my training schedule was, and when I told him, he wanted to rearrange it. I must have looked annoyed. This girl I knew, Cristina, was passing and said, "Don't mind Manoel. He does that to everyone. But he's run the marathon, so he's probably right. Oh. Jim, Manoel, Manoel, Jim." She pointed at my feet. "Awesome shoes, by the way."

Manoel ran his long fingers through his epic curly hair, and he nodded. "Good enough for what you're probably doing now," he said.

I looked Manoel up and down. And up and down and up and down. I mean, there was a lot to look at. He was stunning. His calves were perfect. His veins stood out. I felt hopeless. You had to look like that to run the marathon? Okay, I never would.

But Manoel kept on talking, and it was obvious he thought I would. He didn't think I was a lightweight for running only five or six miles. He talked like I was a real runner, no different from him, just less experienced. "You running the marathon?" he said, and I said, "I guess, yeah." "So that's Patriot's Day," he said, "giving you seven and a half months. Hm. We'll have to look at the qualifications. Have you done a half?"— meaning a half marathon—"No, you haven't. Maybe we're talking 2015." He took out his phone and searched. His hands were huge and his fingers long and beautifully proportioned. I stood next to him, feeling small, and I looked at the phone.

Looking at the qualifying info, we decided I couldn't do the marathon till 2015. I had to run one full marathon before, and there were cutoff dates and qualifying times and other stuff that made me just want to quit. Manoel took my hand, hard, like in a brother handshake, and held our two hands up between our chests. "Jim, people do this!" he said "You will, too!"

That hand was strong and warm and enveloping. His lips were full and perfectly shaped, and those eyes just bore into me. It wasn't long, though, before he referred to "my girlfriend—ex-girlfriend, really." Well, I had an ex-girlfriend, too, but it turned out Manoel had had a bunch of girlfriends, including a current one he wasn't "too serious about, but we'll see." I also learned pretty quickly that he hugged and touched and put his arm around everyone's shoulder and gripped everyone's hand, male or female. Still, when he did any of those things to me, my heart thumpety-thumped, and I'd imagine his long, beautifully muscled arms around me, those full lips pressed to mine and his tongue and mine working away. Then he'd move on to someone else.

But he always came back to me about running. He'd come hang out in my room in running shorts and a shirt with the arms and collar torn out. You could just see the hair on his chest, and you could sure see it under his arms. He extended his beautifully shaped bare legs and feet. Sometimes he'd put them apart and touch himself just quickly.

He said I should do a 5K right away (there was an Oktoberfest run in Cambridge in a month), and there was some famous 7.6K run in Connecticut, on Thanksgiving Day. I liked that I'd miss Thanksgiving at home, but my parents couldn't argue, and it would make them take the running thing seriously. Then I'd do a half marathon—there were some on the Cape, including Harwich and Falmouth—and then we were side-by-side, knees almost touching, so close I could feel his heat, doing my schedule on Google Calendar, right up to April 19, 2015. You kind of fall in love with a guy who does that for you, especially when he grins and gives you a love tap or puts his bare arm around your shoulder for a second.

Oh, did I mention we went running together, too?

Manoel's legs flexed beautifully when he ran—long, elegant, tan, with just a little hair, muscles well defined and all working together. I ran behind him so I could look. Plus it felt wrong for me to be out ahead of him.

I ran way shorter distances than he did and ended sooner, so we never showered together. Our dorm was really old and still had gang showers, and what I wanted more than anything in the world was to be completely alone and completely naked with Manoel, the water running over us and us just talking about running. But it kept not happening.

There are blogs and Yahoo threads and whole websites about getting a "straight bro" to do stuff with you. I tried not to think about doing any of that stuff with Manoel. Seducing someone is a lot of work. You have to say and do all kinds of awkward, creepy crap that wouldn't be me. Besides, I didn't want any weirdness between Manoel and me. He was going to get me to run the Boston Marathon. I was not going to suddenly do shots with him, and then start a game of poker and then say, "It's hot in here, let's play *strip* poker!" I'd done exactly one shot in my life, and I'd played maybe three games of poker. But I did wish we could just be alone and naked and talk.

I began to get something from being around Manoel, though. I decided that, however much a straight guy is your friend and wants to help you, however much he might be willing to "do something" under whatever circumstances, basically straight guys live in their own world. They run pretty much everything, and they're not going to let any of it go.

It was hard for me to keep thinking this sober, critical stuff, because Manoel's smile and his belief in me never failed. I'd swear that after my first 5K I'd go my own way; then I'd pass him talking to some guys and he'd turn away from them and say to me, "Three o'clock, we run, right?" He'd smile so broadly, like he really wanted to run with me. And I loved him again. But only so much. Some days I made sure that I would have to run at a different time. But then he'd come around to my room and ask how it went. I couldn't ask him why he did that. I knew the answer. He liked me. And I couldn't quite handle that.

I also had a lot of trouble handling the humongous hug he gave me when I crossed the finish line at the Oktoberfest in Cambridge. (I was 78th out of 202.) He made a big deal of it, clicking pictures and putting them on Instagram and making sure our friends stayed for the post-race party on Hampshire Street. I might have quit after that. I might have decided, *Well, I managed to run five kilometers more than I ever thought I could. Why do I have to bother running 26 miles?* But I liked seeing Manoel happy. I liked Manoel hooting and hollering and hugging me and saying, "Marathon twenty-fifteen!" I was trying not to be in love with Manoel, and I was doing pretty okay at that, but I did want to see his reaction on April 19, 2015. I had to keep running because I had to see him celebrate it.

Manoel went away for fall break. I was glad. I needed my own break—from his beauty and his closeness and his belief in me. I stayed in Boston deliberately. I was hoping to meet someone. Not a superstar like Manoel. Just my old dream of someone to breathe with. My roommate, Doug, would also be away, along with more than half the dorm. I could go explore and hook up, maybe. I'd seen gay ads online but didn't know what to do with them. I'd sit in a café on Boylston Street and suddenly the cutest, sweetest, most Manoel-like guy ever (but more easygoing and modest) would ask if he could sit at my table, and he'd be a little shy and confused, too, and we'd talk about how crazy those ads were, and suddenly we'd fall silent, then start to speak at once, stop, laugh, then one of us would finally tell the other how handsome he was and we'd laugh and blush and wasn't that how it went?

But instead, with the school emptied out and time on my hands, I had less of an idea than usual where to go and what to do. I had my running. I ran through the Fens under cloudy skies. The tall grass reminded me of the Cape. The marsh was blazing red by now. One fall when I was eight my dad and I actually saw a puffin out there. For a long time I said that was the best day of my life.

I wondered what was Pat doing right then. I knew from Facebook and some emails we traded that Dennis was still in the picture. I hoped he stayed. I ran on, and when I was done, I couldn't think what to do next. I didn't actually want to sit in that café on Boylston Street, because I was afraid I wouldn't meet that guy, and then what would I do? There was something about the big city I just didn't get. No, more like something about *life* I didn't get. It was all right there; maybe I just wasn't equipped, mentally. Was the breeze in the Fens asking, *"What ever will you do, little boy?"*

At the dorm I hung with some friends who had stayed. We decided on a movie in Cambridge that night. Going out like that I'd see gay guys, but no one I thought I could have a conversation with. There were geeky types who *seemed* gay, but they only talked about the government or the economy. Other guys were totally out, with earrings and dyed hair and tats, but if you said two serious words they'd brush you off, even if you were agreeing with them. If they LOVED a certain movie, and you LOVED it, too, they'd be like, "Well, I really didn't LOVE it. I just think Tilda Swinton is a goddess."

I couldn't mix these groups. If I had a campy friend, I couldn't introduce him to Doug, even if Doug was an "ally" or whatever. And the femmy friend would roll his eyes about Doug, and the way he carried his lacrosse stick everywhere, twisting it back and forth, cradling the ball. Or if it was me, Doug and Manoel, the two of them would talk "guy" stuff, and if I brought the femmy friend he'd be all over Manoel. Manoel liked attention from gay guys, but every few sentences he'd mention one of the girlfriends. I'd done it, too—saying "my girlfriend" without the "ex." It made me long for the big, simple emotion I had felt with Nate. But he had his problems, too. Like being in Israel, for one.

Nate and I emailed occasionally. I called him "Yehonatan" and got him to call me "Yirmeyahu," and then it was "Yeho" and "Yirm." I thought the IDF would be all hush-hush, and he wouldn't tell me anything, but he actually became quite the correspondent. He even sent these kind of hot pictures of him in uniform, even one with his shirt off and a tan. After a lot of debate, I made a comment how I'd like to take the pants off, too, and he said, "I'd like that."

He often said where his unit was and what they were doing. The place names gave me goose bumps: Haifa, Golan Heights, Sea of Galilee. He said he was excited to get up every morning, that he was being "tested," and he talked about "defending this ancient place," which he called "Eretz Yisrael." I Wikipedia-ed that; it just means "Land of Israel."

There were other American Jews there, too, "defending American and Israeli values side-by-side." I felt how stoked he was (he didn't mention there being other gays), and I understood that he was doing something that mattered hugely to him. It was part of a grand scheme, not like a marathon, which I kept thinking was selfish. He walked where Moses and

Abraham walked—two guys who didn't play a huge role in my life, but still. He said he would happily die there. I hoped he wouldn't, but I didn't argue with him.

I also didn't talk politics with him. Doug had a friend, Fakhera, from Palestine. She went to Tufts, and the stuff she said about the Middle East was totally opposite from what Nate said. I felt stupid and got angry. For example, say "drone strike" to either one of them and suddenly you were the target of one, stuff that was scary and insane, complete with figures about babies dead or maimed. When Nate wrote, "You probably think I'm crazy," I wrote back, "I'm just proud and happy that you're doing what you believe in."

I decided, since I couldn't find the right gay friend at school and had trouble going out and hooking up, I'd put an ad online. But I hated the idea of advertising or competing with other guys, so I put it off and went to a folk concert on Porter Square. Maybe there I'd meet someone.

I didn't, so the next morning I started my ad. I tapped out a few clichés. "Regular guy." Everyone said that. "Fun guy." Was I? I wasn't sure. "Looking for fun." Shallow. "Let's take a long walk together." That was what I wanted, but it sounded uncool.

I had a secret idea that was even less cool. I imagined an ad with the subject line, "Breathe with me," and that would be all. No body. The more I tried to think of beginnings like, "Normal guy interested in . . ." the more I liked just, "Breathe with me."

Now, would I answer that ad? No. I'd think the guy was too intense. So I forgot about it, break ended, classes started, I ran with Manoel, and I did some actual schoolwork.

I decided I was annoyed—at myself, at the gay guys or possibly gay guys at school, at the whole scene. Finally I thought, *You won't pay attention to me, boys of Boston? Take this!* I went to "men seeking men" and posted an ad with subject line "Breathe with me" and nothing else.

As I expected, no one answered.

The whole thing embarrassed me so much that I deleted it and went back to revising, "Regular guy interested in . . ."

Then I thought, why not check out ads that were already there? Duh! I hadn't done it before because a guy who posts (with the exception of myself) gets tons of messages, so I'd have competition. But I couldn't resist looking, and I'm here to tell you: there are a lot of six-packs standing around in a lot of bathrooms out there! (And a lot of toilets with the seats up.) So I was going to add "runner" to my own ad and get Manoel to take a picture of me in my running shorts.

Suddenly, browsing through, I saw that "Breathe with me" was still there. But I'd deleted it! Maybe I'd clicked wrong, and I'd be stuck with that stupid ad for weeks! No. Wait. It *wasn't* the same. This one said, "Breathe with me????" I clicked it. It said, "Saw advert with this title a few days ago. Thought it was the most brilliant mistake or the most brilliant of an idea forever. I wanted to respond but I got the cold foot and now it's gone. Please, who is the author of 'Breathe with me'?"

I felt invaded. I thought about all kinds of security stuff. Could this guy find me? Was I worried because the English wasn't perfect? Except it was, in a way. It was sincere. I pictured a guy in a pressed shirt. Who else would answer "Breathe with me"? You'd have to be as big a dork as the dork who wrote it!

I answered back, but with no picture and no name. It looked stupid, though, just my height and weight and age. "Jim" is a common name, so I gave it, and I had to chat a little bit, so I said I was glad he liked my subject line because I hadn't been able to think of anything else.

What came back, six hours later (not that I counted or anything) was: "Hi Jim! This is Khalid here, 22yo MIT grad student. Breathe with me, haha! You are very smart! Would you like to meet up sometime?"

I spent the next half hour pacing, sitting down, then getting up again. Doug came in, and I asked him to read it. He just whistled. Like I said, he was officially okay with the gay thing, until you tried to have a specific conversation. In this case, he said I should call Fakhera.

She was outside a café in Davis Square. "Why do you call me, Jim?" she asked. "Every time someone has an issue with any person comes from between Greece to Kazakhstan, they check me if he is all right. How do I know? Go meet him!"

I told Doug what she said. "Meet in public," Doug said, and then, hearing how prejudiced that sounded, he said, "like with anyone."

"Like with anyone gay?" I said. "Or with anyone Muslim?"

"Like with anyone!" he said, suddenly pretending he was *really* interested in his email. I guessed he might be right.

Khalid and I exchanged more emails and texts— including pictures. He said my picture was "sweet" and said, "You look like a good soul, Jim." His picture was pretty sweet, too. He had some scruff and a big smile, too wide for his face but even more adorable because of that, and he had dark eyes, almost black. Best of all, he didn't look like he was trying to impress. His pictures looked like he was just being himself.

Khalid had been born in Pakistan, but he was a "Canadian national" with a student visa. (He assured me it was an "F" visa.) Ultimately, he wanted to be recruited by an American tech company. He came off a bit snooty. He said I probably wouldn't understand his area of math. I figured he was right, but I said, "Try me!" and he said, "Alright, I will Haha!" ("So long as he doesn't say 'LOL,'" said Doug. "Then you have to dump him.") He was right; I didn't understand. He apologized about five times, said he shouldn't have said anything and it totally didn't matter, because he could tell I was smart anyway.

"Your apology was sweet," I typed back. "It made me want to kiss you." He sent back a picture of himself hiding a big grin behind his hand.

I thought, *Can this really be happening?* I had never actually *attracted* anyone. Nate, maybe, in some way that was not about me. And Liz, but she just found me safe. There'd been this kid in middle school who stared at me at lunch, and I sort of knew and sort of didn't know why. Now, Khalid saying "sweet" and sending cute pictures was a jolt. Khalid, period, was a jolt. Has he been with lots of guys? Would he be disappointed that I was inexperienced? Thank God I'd lost enough weight to gain a quarter-inch on my dick! Seriously, I actually thought that.

The night before I went to meet him for the first time, I lay awake. Twenty-two and a genius and about to work for a high-tech company. The "graduate student" part that kept sticking in my brain. What about that?

Pat.

Driving to all those colleges—he was meeting guys! He was scoping out the schools, but I bet he was also picking up grad students! Hitting on profs would be weird; he spoke to them professionally. And undergrads are kids, even if they're not minors. But grad students—they were Pat's age at the time, and he had wanted to be with guys for so long.

This weirded me out at first, but it also made Pat more real. At Benleigh he couldn't pat a kid on the back. He couldn't hold his daughter. So what he did was a good idea. I hoped he had fun. I wondered what he'd think of Khalid. I thought he'd say, "Go for it!"

I had a hard time concentrating on homework the next afternoon. All the expectations Khalid would have. Would he bail? We had confirmed. Should I text him again?

It got dark. I lingered in the shower, then finally got dressed.

Now, I know you've probably already looked ahead to see how our date went. And you found out it's not there. Originally there was going to be a date scene, and it was pretty funny.

But then I remembered something that came to me that fall, in the shower, after running with Manoel. Because Manoel ran longer, I was alone in the shower. I stood there wishing I had that tall, strong, beautiful man next to me. And then out of nowhere a voice said, "You do have a tall, strong, beautiful man. You have you." I felt this tingle all over. I looked down at my legs, which had gone from not running to running six or seven miles. I looked at my penis. The water felt good on me. I *was* tall. I *was* strong. I was beautiful. I wasn't Manoel. But I was Jim. I didn't need another, better guy next to me. I cried a little then, because it meant saying good-bye to Manoel. And to a whole kind of dream.

So, now that I'm tall and strong and beautiful, I've decided I didn't write 81,993 words leading up to how I found a special guy named Khalid. He's important, but the real reason I wrote 81,993 words was to tell you how I found a special guy named Jim. *I* am your date this evening, and that'll have to be good enough for you.

Now I was almost ready. I checked my phone to make sure Khalid was still in. He was.

There was also an email from Nate. He was shipping out in the morning; he couldn't say where. I felt an ache in my chest. I was shipping out, too, and I would not see Nate again. Not the Nate I knew, not the Nate I was struggling to remember, even then. All the technology in the world wouldn't help.

He said:

Since I may not come back, I should tell you this now.

I understand why you persecuted me. Back then, you had to protect that part of you that actually makes you a good friend now. Back then you thought it made you weak. You did what you did to survive. Here, everyone feels that way all the time on every side, and it's terrible. Where we are going tomorrow might be dangerous. I could die there. If that happened, you would be the only person I ever had sex with. It would be a good memory. You were kind and you really wanted me. I think about it sometimes. It would be okay if that was the only sex I ever had, and if you were the only person who remembered me that way. I pray that everything goes all right. See you soon.

Your friend, Nate.

And then, "P.S. See below." So I scrolled down. There was, with no further explanation from Nate, a long paragraph that began, "My dear, dear Nathaniel." It was time-stamped the day before.

First she said how brave he was, how much she admired and loved him, and how important it was to defend Eretz Yisrael. Her parents, and most of their relatives, had died in the Holocaust, which she called the "Shoah." And then she said:

Nathaniel, my heart has been very, very heavy. Some days I do not know how to get up and get through the

255

day. We never really discussed why you went to Eretz Yisrael, but I know, and it is a terrible, terrible thing. I cannot bear the thought that I played a part in it. I bore you, Nathaniel, and I named you, "G-d has given," because I saw G-d in your little face. You were beautifully made, and as you grew, I only saw more beauty in you. But there was something else, something I thought was not supposed to be there. Could it be true? How? Perhaps G-d was testing us. I am ashamed what I thought: If only it would go away, that way he talks, that way he holds his hand. They picked on you at school. I told you to fight back. I told you to stop whining, because I didn't want it to be true, and because I didn't want your father to hear. I told you not to bother him. And then it happened—what he did—in my own house. I was sick. I didn't know where to turn. I know I should never, ever have allowed it, but how? How can I justify myself to you? And now you are gone.

Nathaniel, I ask G-d every day to forgive me, and now I ask you to forgive me. There you are, my beautiful one, given by G-d, standing in the desert in a uniform. As great a thing as it is to defend Eretz Yisrael, I pray that someday soon you will take that uniform off, forever, and be free.

I adore you, my beautiful beautiful one, and I pray for your safety and for your forgiveness. Write me as soon as you can.

B'shalom, Mamele

Wow. Coming from the woman who threw me out of the dry cleaner's in So-Sick. I guessed now I couldn't blame her. To tell the truth, I kind of wanted to put my arms around her, a little. I wasn't sure how much to react, though. Nate had given me no idea what to think. So I just typed back:

Nate –

Thanks for what you said. I felt the same about you. And thanks for sharing your mom's letter. I admire what you're doing and I love your bravery, but I agree: I want to see you take the uniform off, too. I'll be thinking of you.

Love, Jim.

It was so neat to sign an email to a guy with "Love," even though at this point we were probably mostly friends. Maybe the fact that we were just friends now made the "Love" even neater. I had my first gay friend my age. And whatever we told each other or imagined about each other, we also knew the body naked underneath.

Before I went to the T, I did one more thing. I called my mom. She sounded surprised to hear from me. More like startled. I took a deep breath.

"I wanted to call you," I said, "because, um, I have a date tonight."

"Oh?" she said.

"I'm nervous," I said. "He's older than I am. And from MIT. I mean, he's *smart!*"

"Well!" she said.

I wanted to say, "You remember I'm eighteen years old and gay, right?" Instead I plowed on: "I met him online." Then I stopped. I couldn't think of anything else to say except the Pakistani-Canadian thing, which I didn't think she was ready for. Or maybe I wasn't ready for it.

"Well, have fun," she said.

"I'm sorry," I said. "Is this a bad time?"

"No, no."

"I'll call you tomorrow and let you know how it went."

"All right," she said, in kind of a high, sighing voice.

And we hung up. I was sad. I guess I'd already shipped out, weeks or even months ago. Maybe you just keep shipping out and out and out, and you never come back.

Once I was out in the night air, I felt better. I swiped my CharlieCard at the turnstile and ran downstairs. Saturday night in Boston was cranking up, kids crowding the T, talking, singing, carrying balloons and paper bags with cans in them, standing their bikes up in the cars, wearing glitter on their faces. The Alewife train swooped in and I crowded on with all the people with all their dreams.

I rode past the Charles Street/Mass General stop, where Dad took me to walk narrow streets and smell wood smoke, and we crossed the Longfellow Bridge, over the Charles River. Harvard shone inverted in the water. Soon, just as Pat and Khalid had both told me, there it was: Kendall/MIT.

I wished I'd called Pat. It had crossed my mind, but he was probably with Dennis. When I saw him again, the ducks would be gone and the marsh frozen. Christmas lights would hang from the widows' walks— those lookouts atop old houses where wives went to see their husbands return from sea—and people would call Bay View Books for maps and books for loved ones. We would sit by the stove, and I would tell Pat the thing I did not tell him when we said good-bye. I would tell him I appreciated him and what he did, and that I loved him, in the most complete way I have loved anyone. I hoped when I said it, Dennis would hear. Dennis knows what he's found, I'm sure, but it would be neat for him to hear it from someone else. I hope I can say it right. If I do, I know Pat will say the same thing back.

The train came to a halt. Heart thumping, I hopped off. The station walls were covered with stories of great MIT geniuses. I looked away from them and took the stairs two at a time. Behind me the train receded, bound for Harvard and Alewife, and for just a second, this weird tubular-bell sound came from somewhere. I don't know what it was, but it sort of lifted me up. Like it came from inside, and only I could hear. I thought maybe things would be okay. Maybe more than okay. Maybe beautiful.

I strode up Broadway and crossed Reardon Square, heading for the place Khalid had suggested, checking the blue dot on my Maps app as I got closer and wondering, *What if he doesn't like me? What if he wants something I don't?*

I saw the restaurant, a little way off. I looked down at my map.

That blue dot was funny. It had a little triangle pointer on it that was supposed to show the direction I was going. But mostly the pointer went around and around, clueless where to go. Then sometimes I'd go a whole block, but the dot would be stuck. Then it would run to catch up, its little triangle nose swerving this way and that, like a baby raccoon, in spring, climbing out of its nest, raising its nose and drawing in the world, really taking it in, for the first time, before setting out to seek new lands.

ACKNOWLEDGEMENTS

My undying thanks to the peerlessly steady and supportive Louis Flint Ceci at Beautiful Dreamer Press for rolling the dice on a novel with a made-up name with a cedilla and lots of salt marshes.

Don Weise and Rogério Pinto were devoted early readers and editors, and my old friend and co-star, Jane Lincoln Taylor, took the greatest care with final edits.

Though Cape Cod was once my stomping ground, I needed a refresher course, which I got from David Alan Gates's thorough and lucid *Seasons of the Salt Marsh*.

The exterior of the book owes a great debt to a San Franciscan, the photographer Dot, and a North Carolinian, Ann McMan, who held off Hurricane Matthew with one hand and created a great cover with the other.

Thanks to Bill Konigsberg and Jim Provenzano for their kind words, and thanks as always to Eva Mueller for making the author look his best.

ABOUT THE AUTHOR

DAVID PRATT is the author of the novels *Bob the Book* (Lambda Literary Award winner) and *Looking After Joey*. Selections from his short fiction are collected in *My Movie*. David has performed his work for the stage in various venues around New York City. He lives in Michigan.

CPSIA information can be obtained
at www.ICGtesting.com
Printed in the USA
LVOW11s0226150517
534422LV00001B/8/P

9 780998 126203